FAITH, CHRIST OR PETER:

Matthew 16:18 In Sixteenth Century Roman Catholic Exegesis

John E. Bigane, III

WITHDRAWN

University Press of America

To all dissatisfied readers of the Bible whose dis-
satisfaction causes them to dream dreams, to see
visions, and thereby to come to the very heart of
the text.

ACKNOWLEDGEMENTS

My interest in Protestant and Roman Catholic views of Matthew 16:18 began in 1973 with "The Story of Church History" seminar at Marquette University. For providing a way into the diversity of late medieval and sixteenth century exegesis and for holding up a high standard of critical scholarship I am deeply indebted to my Doktor-Vater, Professor Kenneth G. Hagen. I also profited from the insights of Professors Keith Egan and Matthew Lamb into medieval exegesis, as well as from the interest of Professor Joseph Lienhard and the John La Farge House hospitality of Professor Robert Wild.

Thanks are also due to Marquette University for several years of financial assistance, to John Downey for constant encouragement and criticism, to Susan Bigane Sheehy for indefatigable typing, and above all to my wife Catherine for too many good times to mention here.

v

TABLE OF CONTENTS

. . . .

x

INTRODUCTION

"Give us this day our daily text!" Well may that be the cry of scholar and believer alike, for if there is one constant in the history of the Christian churches and groups it is that Christianity's sacred writings have never lacked readers and interpreters. The significance of this phenomenon has been expressed more formally in Gerhard Ebeling's insistence that one should study the development of the Christian churches in terms of the history of biblical exegesis.[1] The history of Matthew 16:18 is especially deserving of study, particularly in one of the forms that it was known in the sixteenth century: "Et ego dico tibi, quia tu es Petrus, et super hanc petram aedificabo ecclesiam meam, et portae inferi non praevalebunt adversus eam."[2] It is one of those passages that occasioned violent disagreements between "the Roman church and the Protestant ones."[3]

Explanation of Terms

This study will restrict itself to an investigation of who and/or what is the "petra" of Matthew 16:18. Such investigation is merited in light of two factors. First, "petra" was a highly controverted term during part of the sixteenth century; it was the occasion not only of long (and short) commentaries but also of treatises on papal primacy (e.g., those by John Fisher, Tommaso de Vio, and Roberto Bellarmino),[4] and of long sections of church histories such as Caesar Baronius' Annales ecclesiastici. Secondly, the question of the "petra" remains significant and even disputed in our own day.[5] Ecumenical discussion might also profit in recovering and uncovering the history of this particular verse (this is one lacuna of

1

recent Lutheran-Roman Catholic dialogues).[6]
Finally, the examination of "petra" in Mt. 16:18
may reveal that biblical commentaries are just as
"occasional" and contextual as supposedly more
polemical writings and yet at the same time have
the advantage of at times transcending the strict
confessional lines adopted by treatises say on
papal power.[7]

Secondly, what is meant by "sixteenth
century" in the title? For the purposes of this
study let "sixteenth century" equal the period
between 1516 and 1605. In terms of commentaries
on Matthew Erasmus' Novum instrumentum of 1516
begins a new era for sure, since it was the first
such commentary published in the sixteenth century
and because it marks a definite turning point in
the history of exegesis with its combination of
textual criticism and scholarly commentary and
concern for "modern" questions (for example,
Erasmus challenges the traditional view that there
ever was a Hebrew original underlying Greek
Matthew). The ad quem of 1605 suggests itself for
several reasons. First, that date marks the death
of Theodore Beza, a man similar to Erasmus in
several respects (both published five editions of
the New Testament) and whose work (1556-1598)
moved exegetical matters significant steps forward.
A second reason for this date is that in the
1590's and the early 1600's many more geographical
places and schools involve themselves in published
commentaries on Matthew. Catholic commentaries
are first published in Herborn (1594), Madrid
(1592), Burgos (1598), Pont-à-Mousson (1596), and
Commeliana (1599). Some significant Jesuit
exegetes only begin to publish commentaries on
Matthew around 1600: Juan Maldonado (1596-1597),
Sebastian Barradas (1599, 1604-1611), Manuel de Sa
(1596, 1598).

The concern throughout is with Roman
Catholic commentaries. The restriction to Roman
Catholic ones was motivated by two concerns:
first, there should be a certain amount of control

2

over the study; the Protestant explosion of biblical commentaries is material enough for a separate
work. Secondly, until quite recently, Roman
Catholics tended to suppose that their past and
traditions were monolithic. It is one concern of
this study to see if this is actually the case
with commenting on Mt. 16:18 in the sixteenth
century or if there was much more diversity than
one otherwise might think. One word here on what
is meant by "Roman Catholic." He/she is a Roman
Catholic who considers himself a Roman Catholic,
associating with that church in fellowship and
cult. To apply other criteria is both to second-
guess the individual under consideration and to
apply certain standards which are unbending and
static.[8] This principle enables one to see the
sixteenth century as it saw itself, or better
to see individuals as they saw themselves, instead of how we or later ages might prefer to see
them. Thus, by this standard Erasmus must be seen
as a self-conscious Roman Catholic throughout his
life and not as a latent Protestant.

Finally, the title of this investigation
mentions "exegesis." The use of this term is
meant to give a certain control over our topic
given the number of different literary forms in
which this verse is discussed. The particular
literary form that grounds exegesis is the Biblical commentary and this term too needs some elab-
oration. By "commentary" here is intended a
scholarly investigation of the text qua text.
This necessarily excludes from consideration those
investigations of the text inasmuch as it is not
only text, but also gospel reading (homilia,
postilla and sermo)[9] or proof text (tractatus); we
also omit from consideration those attempts to
synthesize the various gospels into a coherent
whole (harmonia, historia and concordia). Now
investigations of the text qua text were known by
many different names in the sixteenth century and
the titles investigated in this study will reflect
this pluralism of names for the same genre:
Commentarius, Annotatio, Scholion, Expositio,

Explicatio, Lectura, Praeparatio, Interpretatio, Ennaratio, Animadversio, Nota, Notatio, Paraphrastica elucidatio, Phrasis, Lucabratio, Syllabus, Paraphrasis; commentaries on other New Testament books are also known as Explanatio, Digesta, Glossa and Collatio.

"Status quaestionis"

For over fifty years the need for a history of the exegesis of Mt. 16:16-19 has been recognized. Kurt Guggisberg, before outlining a brief history of this passage in the patristic period, called for the need for someone to write such a history in its entirety.[10] Guggisberg mentions only the exegesis of Luther and Calvin, although he does allude to the Berne Disputation of 1528 where the Catholic side did quite successfully provide a defense for the singularity of the person of Peter with reference to Mt. 16:18-19.[11] Twenty-five years later (1960) Oscar Cullmann in his significant study of Peter noted that:

> We lack a detailed history of the way in which our section [Mt. 16:17-19] has been interpreted throughout the centuries, from the ancient Church Fathers down to our own day. Such a work would be of the greatest value not only for exegetes but also for the historians of doctrine and of the Church. Apart from a study of the most ancient period, however, there is lacking a complete and connected presentation of interpretations of the saying.[12]

Cullmann's student, Joseph A. Burgess, covered the period 1781-1965;[13] Burgess notes that "No one has ever written a history of the interpretation of Mt. 16:17-19 during the Reformation and the period following the Reformation."[14] Another of Cullmann's students, Karlfried Fröhlich, produced a brilliant study on the earlier history of the passage: Formen der Auslegung von Mt. 16, 13-18 im lateinischen Mittelalter (Tübingen: Präzis, 1963).

This is not to say, however, that Roman Catholic handling of Mt. 16:18 was unknown before 1935 and 1960 respectively. Joseph Turmel in dealing with the question of Peter's primacy of jurisdiction discusses Roman Catholic use of the passage, and although he omits altogether commentaries on the passage, he does contribute these insights: 1) the beginning of "the fight over the fathers" with reference to Mt. 16:18-19 was the Leipzig debate between Luther and Eck in 1519;[15] 2) Eck's De primatu Petri of 1520 served as a fertile resource for any commentator looking for patristic references to Peter as the rock;[16] Pigges' Hierarchiae ecclesiasticae assertio of 1538 proved to be another such source and contributed the first discussion of the important philological key to "Petrus" and "petram."[17]

Pontien Polman simply indicates that this Matthaean text was employed by Catholics to show that Jesus had constituted Peter as the chief of the apostles.[18]

Yves Congar advances the claim (which will be partly challenged by this study) that Roman Catholic interpretation, in order to oppose the Reformation understanding of Mt. 16:16-18, has laid aside the interpretations of the fathers and of "the ancients."[19]

Several studies have emerged since 1960 which are comparable in scope to this present study. Léopold Willaert briefly discusses a few Protestant positions on Mt. 16:18 (Luther, de Dominis, de Launoy), simply mentions that theologians (again Luther and Eck) and exegetes (none mentioned by name) appealed to patristic authorities in discussing Mt. 16:18, and praises certain Roman Catholics (Eck, Cajetan, Pigges, and Bellarmino) for actually doing exegesis of Mt. 16:18 rather than simply citing authorities.[20]

5

Bernard L. Ramm's catchy title ("The Exegesis of Mt. 16, 13-20 in the Patristic and Reformation Period") promises much but delivers significantly little (that is, six pages on the exegetica of Luther and Calvin); no mention is made of Roman Catholic exegesis except to contrast Luther's approach with the supposed monolithic Roman Catholic exegesis of his day: "he approaches the petrine passage in an evangelical and Christological spirit in contrast to the authoritarian, ecclesiastical and sacramental spirit of the Roman Catholic interpretation of his day" (this last judgment will be challenged by the present study).[21]

There also exists a body of literature on individual exegetes and their understanding of Mt. 16:18. Roland Bainton briefly records that Erasmus in his Paraphrases interprets "petra" with reference to Peter's profession of faith and not in terms of Peter himself.[22] C.A.L. Jarrott briefly discusses the treatment of the Mt. 16:18 passage, among others, in Erasmus' five editions of his Novum Testamentum; she reports that Erasmus' mind was made up (petra=fides) by 1516 and that "the later editions merely add more examples from the Fathers and other theologians to fill out his argument."[23] James D. Tracy argues that the Basel "Erasmians" probably deserve part of the credit for the appearances in the notes to passages like the argument that Peter was not first among the apostles, or that "thou art a rock" referred to Peter's faith and not to Peter himself; Tracy sees all this as reflecting the growing emphasis on Christian libertas in Erasmus' writings.[24]

Alexandre Ganoczy brilliantly examines John Major's exegesis of Mt. 16:13-19 and 18:15-19 in his two commentaries on Matthew (1518, 1529).[25] This study will build on and go beyond Ganoczy's insights into Major's sources. It will also advance a possible reason for the change in Major's estimate of "petra"; Ganoczy argues that

6

the movement from "petra" as Christ to "petra" as
both Christ and Peter reflects an anti-Lutheran
context and does not reflect the deepest conviction of Major.[26] Ganoczy also indicates that
there is a need for a synthetic grasp of Major's
theology and for more analysis of the presuppositions of his exegesis.[27]

Guy Bedouelle sees Augustine's exegesis as
inspiring Lefèvre d'Etaples' own interpretation of
"petra" in terms of Christ and also argues for a
certain identity between Lefèvre's position and
that of Guillaume Briçonnet, bishop of Meaux.[28]

I. M. Vosté recognized that Tommaso de
Vio's exegesis of Mt. 16:18 is not restricted to
Vio's actual commentary but also takes up a major
part of Vio's De divina institutione pontificatus.[29] Angelus Walz indicated that Vio treated
this passage under four general questions in the
De divina institutione but does not go into an
extended discussion of Vio's remarks about this
passage.[30]

Richard Heinrichs briefly discusses the
commentaries of Mathias Bredenbach on Psalms and
Matthew.[31] Heinrichs emphasizes Bredenbach's
linguistic ability to work with Hebraic and
rabbinic texts firsthand.[32] Heinrichs points out
that such philological expertise is evident in
Brendenbach's discussion of "Tu es Petrus . . ."
in his De dissidiis and in his commentary on
Matthew where he appeals to Jerome and to the
rabbi-grammarian Elias the Levite as support for
his connecting up of "Petrus" and "petra."[33]
Finally Heinrichs noted Bredenbach's apologetic
concern not only in interpreting Mt. 16:18 but in
writing all of his commentaries.[34]

José Nieto has classified Juan de Valdés,
whom this study will consider as a Catholic, as a
"Nicodemite," and a "heretic by the standards of
the Catholic Church both in Spain and Italy."[35]
As evidence for this claim Nieto mentions that

7

Valdés' views greatly limited papal authority, that his exegesis of Mt. 16:17-19 says nothing about papal claims, and that he rejected the medieval interpretation favorable to papal claims, of these verses.[36]

There exists neither book nor articles concerned with commenting on Mt. 16:18 in the following commentaries: Anton Broickwy, Jean d'Arbres, Isidoro Chiari, Frans Titelmans, François Vatable, Nicolas Zegers, Johannes Wild (Ferus), Sisto da Siena, René Benoist, Cornelius Jansen, Benito Montano Arias, the Rhemes New Testament of 1582, Manuel de Sa, Juan de Maldonado, and Sebastian Barradas.

Method

The "Bibliography" to this study will list approximately eighty commentaries on Matthew written by Roman Catholics in the sixteenth century. The study itself will examine the commentaries of twenty of these exegetes. My primary concern will be to allow these exegetes to speak for themselves. Thus, the four main chapters are attempts to typify their answers to this question: who/what is the "petra" of Mt. 16:18? Four distinct answers will emerge: petra=fides, petra=Christus, petra=Petrus, and petra=varia.

These positions in turn will be examined in terms of the patristic and medieval sources that the sixteenth century commentators employed: What were these sources and how did the sixteenth century use them? Here we will be especially concerned to see how the main lines of patristic and medieval commenting on the term "petra" were continued or discontinued in the sixteenth century. This concern for the traditions of commenting on "petra" helps to relativize the sixteenth century achievement and simultaneously serves to illustrate what was unique to the sixteenth century commenting itself.

8

Joseph Ludwig,[37] Franz Gillman,[38] and
Karlfried Fröhlich (Formen) have identified four
main lines of patristic and medieval positions.
First, the position petra=Petrus was very much
present in the patristic period first with reference to Peter considered as the individual present
at Caesarea Philippi and later in terms of the
primacy of jurisdiction claimed by the bishops of
Rome. In the middle ages the first patristic
position became subordinate to the positions
petra=fides and petra=Christus and the majority of
medieval exegetes and theologians treated the word
primarily as evidence of the Christological ground-
ing of ecclesiology.[39] Second, the position
petra=fides was secondary to and existed in harmony with the petra=Petrus position in the patristic period. Later the faith of Peter sometimes
was stressed in terms of a faith that lives on in
his successors and sometimes Peter's confession of
faith was separated from Peter himself. Third,
the petra=Christus position, although present in
the patristic period, became dominant in the
middle ages. The writers of this period emphasize
Mt. 16:18's connection with Mt. 7:24-25, I. Cor.
3:11 and Eph. 2:20. Finally, Fröhlich advances
some "spiritual" interpretations of "petra" which
surfaced in the middle ages: the perfection of
virtue, special virtues of Peter, Scripture,
Christ's teaching, the doctrine of the apostles
and the prophets, and the metaphor of firmness.[40]

Another methological concern will be to
attend to the way in which our commentators argue,
that is, what rationes do they give for the positions that they adopt. Here especially we shall
look to see if linquistic and philological tools
are used by the different exegetes.

Where possible, this study will point out
the presuppositions and Begrifflichkeit of the
various exegetes. Less concern will be shown for
the social ethos of the various exegetes, not
because this dimension is unimportant, but because

9

to investigate fully these contexts would be the
subject of another study.

NOTES FOR INTRODUCTION

[1]Gerhard Ebeling, Kirchengeschichte als Geschichte der Auslegung der Heiligen Schrift (Tübingen: J. C. B. Mohr, 1947), p. 22.

[2]This is the common Vulgate rendering in that century.

[3]Joseph Scaliger, ". . . syllabus locorum Novi Testamenti. . .," . . . Novum Iesu Christi D. N. Testamentum . . . (Genevae: Apud P. de la Rouiere, 1620), n. p.

[4]See also the indices to Juan Tomás de Rocaberti's Bibliotheca maxima pontificia . . . 21 vols. (Romae: I. F. Buagnus, 1697-1699), specifically "petra" and "Petrus."

[5]Oscar Cullmann's Petrus: Jünger-Apostel-Märtyrer (Zürich: Zwingli-Verlag, 1960, second edition; ET: Peter, Disciple, Apostle, Martyr: A Historical and Theological Study, trans. F. V. Filson (Philadelphia: Westminster, 1962; second revised and expanded edition) was highly instrumental in providing a via media between Protestant and Catholic exegesis by arguing for an understanding of "petra" in terms of the historical Peter, but not in terms of the bishops of Rome; Max Wilcox' "Peter and the Rock: A Fresh Look at Matthew 16, 17-19," in New Testament Studies 22 (1975), 73-88 argues that behind the Caeserea Philippi narrative was a tradition linking Jesus with the rejected stone of Ps 118:22-23 and that "petra" reflects this tradition.

[6]Papal Primacy and the Universal Church, eds. P.C. Empie and T.A. Murphy, Lutherans and Catholics in Dialogue V (Minneapolis: Augsburg, 1974), an otherwise excellent resource book, lacks any in-depth study of the history of Mt. 16:13-20.

[7]Examination of Mt. 16:16, 17, and 19 will only be tangentially involved in this study in order to give control of the data and since very different problems are sometimes involved in these verses, especially verse nineteen with the thorny question of the keys of the kingdom of heaven and the power of binding and loosing. On this latter point see Herbert Vorgrimler's "Das 'Binden und Lösen' in der Exegese nach dem Tridentinum bis zu Beginn des XX. Jhts.," Zeitschrift für katholische Theologie 85 (1963), pp. 460-477.

[8]We shall see a certain example of this in regard to Juan de Valdés in Chapter One.

[9]Part of the patristic and medieval heritage is the employment of the genre Sermo as actual commentary. Mr. Guy Carter pointed out John Stoudt's "John Staupitz on God's Gracious Love," The Lutheran Quarterly 8 (August, 1956), p. 225 where Stoudt reports that Staupitz "wrote an exposition of the Book of Job in sermonic form . . . ." Carter dates this 1494-1498. Other examples abundantly flow from the patristic period.

[10]Kurt Guggisberg, "Matthaeus 16, 17 und 19 in der Kirchengeschichte," ZKG 54 (1935), p. 276.

[11]Ibid., p. 297.

[12]Cullman, Peter, pp. 164-165.

[13]Joseph A. Burgess, A History of the Exegesis of Matthew 16:17-19 from 1781 to 1965 (Ann Arbor, Michigan: Edwards Brothers, 1976).

[14]Ibid., p. 15.

[15]Joseph Turmel, Histoire de la théologie positive du Concile du Trente au Concile du Vatican (Paris: Beauchesne, 1906; second edition), p. 153.

[16]Ibid., p. 157.

[17]Ibid., p. 173.

[18]Pontien Polman, L'Élément historique dans la controverse religieuse du xvie siècle (Gembloux: Duculot, 1932), p. 153.

[19]Yves Congar, "Du nouveau sur la question de Pierre," La Vie intellectuelle 24,2 (1953), p. 21, n.5.

[20]J. B. Duroselle and E. Jarry, gen. eds., Histoire de l'Église: depuis les origines jusqu'a nos jours, 21 vols. ([Paris]: Bloud and Gay, 1960), vol. 18, part one: Après le Concile de Trente: la Restauration catholique, 1563-1648, by Leopold Willaert, pp. 346-349.

[21]Bernard L. Ramm, "The Exegesis of Mt. 16, 13-20 in the Patristic and Reformation Period," Foundations 5 (1962), p. 212.

[22]Roland H. Bainton, "The Paraphrases of Erasmus," ARG 57 (1966), p. 72.

[23]C.A.L. Jarrott, "Erasmus' Biblical Humanism," Studies in the Renaissance 17 (1970), p. 135.

[24]James D. Tracy, Erasmus: The Growth of a Mind, Travaux d'Humanisme et Renaissance, CXXVI (Geneve: Droz, 1972), p. 145.

[25]Alexandre Ganoczy, "Jean Major, exégète gallican," Recherches de Science religieuse 56 (1968), pp. 457-495.

[26]Ibid., pp. 457, 459.

[27]Ibid., p. 494.

[28]Guy Bedouelle, Lefèvre d'Etaples et l'intelligence des Ecritures, Travaux d'Humanisme et Renaissance, 152 (Genève: Droz, 1976), pp. 212 and 212 n. 1.

[29]I. M. Vosté, "Cardinalis Caietanus S. Scripturae interpres," Angelicum 11 (1934), pp. 495-496.

[30]Angelus Walz, "Von Cajetans Gedanken über Kirche und Papst," in Volk Gottes: Zum Kirchenverständnis der katholischen, evangelischen und anglikanischen Theologie, Festgabe für Josef Höfer, ed. R. Bäumer and H. Dolch (Fribourg-en-Br.: Herder, 1967), p. 344.

[31]Richard Heinrichs, "Der Humanist Mathias Bredenbach als Exeget," Der Katholik 73 (1893), pp. 345-357).

[32]Ibid., p. 356.

[33]Ibid.

[34]Ibid., p. 357.

[35]José C. Nieto, Juan de Valdés and the Origins of the Spanish and Italian Reformation (Genève: Droz, 1970), p. 181.

[36]Ibid., pp. 154-158.

[37]Die Primatworte Mt. 16:18-19 in der altkirchlichen Exegese (Münster: Aschendorf, 1952).

[38]"Zur scholastischen Auslegung von Mt. 16, 18," Archiv für katholische Kirchenrecht 104 (1924), pp. 41-53.

[39]Fröhlich, Formen, pp. 124-125.

[40]Ibid., pp. 160-162.

CHAPTER I

"PETRA" AS FAITH

Ever the systematician, Roberto Bellarmino
toward the end of the sixteenth century listed
four responses to the question "an Petrus sit illa
petra super quam fundatur Ecclesia." Desiderius
Erasmus was located between the "catholicorum
communis" on the one hand and John Calvin and
Martin Luther on the other.[1] Such singular attention by so influential a theologian suggests that
Erasmus' exegesis of Mt. 16:18 merits close
scrutiny. Specifically this study will examine
his remarks on this passage in the <u>Annotationes</u>
affixed to his five editions of the New Testament
(1516, 1519, 1522, 1527, and 1535) and in his
"commentary" on the verse in his paraphrase of
Matthew's gospel. It will also take note of the
comments of those who followed Erasmus' supposedly
"uncommon" interpretation.

<u>Erasmus' "Novum instrumentum" (1516)</u>

First I provide Erasmus' rendering of the
New Testament in parallel columns of Greek and
Latin. Matthew 16:18 is translated as follows:

"At ego quoque tibi dico, quod tu es
Petrus, et super hanc petram aedificabo meam
ecclesiam, et portae inferorum non valebunt adversus illam."[2]

Erasmus adds the following annotation,
beginning with a remark on the Vulgate rendering:

'Quia tu es'. 'ὅτι' 'that', not 'because,' that is, I say that you are Peter.

'Petrus' signifies rock ("saxum") among
the Greeks. 'Pétros,' just like Cephas
in the Syrian tongue and not in the
Hebrew, means solidity. For Jesus
calls him rock ("saxum"), because he is
solid in the confession of faith and
does not vacillate here and there with
the fickleness of common opinion. And
'super istam petram,' that is, on that
solid profession of faith I will build
my church, and if it shall stand firm
in this foundation no one of hell will
be able to be against it. Even though
saint Augustine in his homily on this
passage accommodates these words 'super
hanc petram' to Christ himself, not to
Peter: '"you are," Jesus says, "Peter,
and upon this rock ("petram") which you
have confessed, upon this rock ("petram")
which you have acknowledged, saying 'you
are the Christ the son of the living God,'
I will build my church, that is, upon me
myself the son of the living God, I will
build my church. I will build you upon
me, not me upon you." For men wishing
to be built upon man were saying: "I am
certainly of Paul, but I of Apollos,
truly I of Cephas," who is Peter himself.
And others who were unwilling to be built
upon Peter, but upon the rock used to say
"but I am of Christ."' Therefore I mar-
vel that there are those who twist
("detorqueant") this passage to refer
to the Roman pontiff. Truly there are
those for whom nothing is enough, unless
it be immoderate. And so, some extol
Francis with outlandish praises, coming
close to envy, and they should have explained him rather than to extol him
immeasureably. For to the virgin mother
of God and to Christ it is probably not
possible to ascribe too much. However
here also I wish that all were so in-
flamed with the desire of imitating, as

16

those we see fanatic in exaggerating
praises. However, our interpretation
differs only as far as words are concerned from the Augustinian interpretation which we already have mentioned,
which seems quite forced, to which
nevertheless he preferred to go, rather
than to crash on another rock, namely
that one may place the foundation of
the church on man. . . .[3]

Erasmus philologically relates the meanings of "Petrus" and "pétros." The next passage
is crucial for an understanding of Erasmus' position on "petra." Erasmus, having established the
basic meanings of "Petrus" and "pétros" in terms
of rock goes on to comment how Peter came to be
called "Peter." What is solid about Peter is his
confession of faith, unlike what is superfluous,
trivial and fickle in commonplace opinion. Note
that here Erasmus' concern with the meaning of
"saxum" leads him to stress the connection between
Peter's earlier confession of faith in v. 16 and
the consequent meaning here in v. 18; in the
process no mention is made of Jesus' word of
blessing.[4] Erasmus bridges the gap between the
two verses philologically whereas the commonplace
patristic connection employed the parallelism
between "Tu es Christus" and "Tu es Petrus."[5]

Erasmus goes on in the same breath to
state that upon that rock, which is that solid
"professio fidei," Jesus will build his church. A
clear identity between "petra" and "professio
fidei" is thus posited; Peter's name does not occur, although it is his "professio fidei" that is
being referred to. He goes on to make the fasci-
nating and revealing statement that "if the church
shall stand firm in this foundation no one of hell
will be able (to be) against it."[6] Jesus, according to Erasmus' note, qualifies his promise.
Thus in one sentence we have Erasmus connecting
Peter's "confessio fidei" with his appellation,
and this followed by the "promissio" qualified in

17

that the church is not guaranteed to stand firm in
the foundation of the "confessio fidei." And all
this is significantly different from a tripartite
division of Mt. 16:16-18 containing unconditional
promise found in some medieval commentaries:
Peter's expression or confession of faith in the
incarnation, Jesus' commendation of Peter's faith,
Jesus' unconditional promise to found the church
in truth.[7]

Erasmus then introduces one of Augustine's
positions on the rock (Christ himself) and mentions that it may be found in his homily on Mt.
16:18. There were many printed editions of
Augustine's homilies available by 1516; Erasmus
himself would later edit Augustine's Opera omnia
in ten volumes and see it published by Froben at
Basel during 1528-1529. Augustine, according to
Erasmus' edition, preached at various times five
sermones on the feast of saints Peter and Paul,
but none of these sermones really concern Mt.
16:18, although that verse was included in the
gospel reading of the day.[8] The citation from
Augustine that Erasmus quotes actually occurs in
Augustine's homily on Mt. 14:24-33![9] Augustine
there is concerned with Christ walking on the
waters of the sea and Peter tottering. He refers
to Peter as a type of the one church who often
spoke for all.[10] It is in this context of one
speaking for all that Augustine mentions the
Caesarea Philippi incident; he really is not
preaching an entire sermon on the passage.
Erasmus omits the preceding passage which stresses
that "Petrus" is derived from "petra" and not the
other way around.[11] Erasmus, on the other hand,
is not concerned with Peter as type or figure of
the church but rather as model for all Christians,
including those who would call themselves "Peter."

Erasmus did not here (and in any of the
following editions) mention Augustine's Sermo on
the feast of the Chair of St. Peter. In that
Sermo, Augustine holds a position other than the
one mentioned above, but also different from

18

Erasmus' own position:

> Finally Peter is called a rock on
> behalf of the solidity of devotion of
> the churches, just as the Lord says 'Tu
> es Petrus, et super hanc petram aedificabo
> ecclesiam meam.' For he is called a rock
> because he first will have established
> the foundations of faith among the na-
> tions, and just as an immoveable rock
> he might hold together the structure and
> bulk of the entire Christian work. There-
> fore Peter is called rock for the sake of
> devotion, and the Lord is named rock for
> the sake of virtue. . .[12]

After citing Augustine's position Erasmus
adds a personal remark concerning what might be
called the "negative, twisted sense of scripture."
Perhaps this remark about those who twist Mt.
16:18 was prompted by Augustine's mention of
certain men who did not wish to build themselves
upon the "petra" but rather upon "Petrum"; in that
case Erasmus' personal remark follows quite well
from what preceded it. In any case Erasmus mar-
vels at those (unnamed) who twist Mt. 16:18 to
apply to the Roman pontiff.

Certain groups were anxious to twist Mt.
16:18 to the pope's favor. One of the legacies of
the middle ages was the literature composed by
canon lawyers regarding the authority of the pope.
Among these canon lawyers was a Spanish Franciscan, Alvaro Pelayo (1280-1352) who wrote De
planctu ecclesiae during 1335-1340. This work,
reprinted in 1474 and in 1517, eventually came to
Erasmus' attention. Alvaro allowed for the possibility of taking "petra" in terms of Peter and
his successors, although he argued that the truer
meaning was Christ.[13] But even this concession
would be absolutized by some in the sixteenth
century.

Could Erasmus very well have had in mind
certain exegetes of Mt. 16:18 who interpreted

"petra" in terms of "Petrus" (Roman pontiff)
rather than simply "Petrus" (historical Peter) and
who appropriated all the patristic writers who
identified "petra" with "Petrus" (Jerome, Augustine, and Cyprian) to a Roman understanding of the
rock?[14] The exegesis of Leo I reveals that the
passage was understood in terms of a conferring of
power and the identity between Peter and Roman
bishops.[15] However, it seems that this line of
exegesis was not continued by the exegetes of the
middle ages but was carried over and employed by
canonists and theologians dealing with papal
primacy. That it was carried over is evident not
only in the criticism of Erasmus but also in the
writings of late medieval theologians such as Jan
Hus:

> In the same place the liar [Stephan
> Palecz] even says that Christ going out
> of this world, gave to the church mili-
> tant Peter and his successors as an
> earthly head upon earth continuing all
> the way up to the consummation of time,
> lest his body of the church militant be
> without a head, saying to Peter: 'Tu es
> Petrus et super hanc petram edificabo
> ecclesiam meam,' and saying again: 'Pasce
> oves meas.'[16]

To such a position Hus opposed the "sanctorum . . .
sentenciam," by which he took "petra" in terms of
Christ: this in his eyes was far superior than
understanding "petra" in terms of Peter as head of
the earthly church.[17]

Erasmus' employment of the "negative
sense" is immediately followed by a digression
concerning those who delight in absolutizing
individuals by means of excessive praise. Erasmus
goes on to give a particular example of excessive
praise: those who so extol Francis of Assisi that
their envy moves their praises in the direction of
personal self-aggrandizement rather than devotion
to Francis. In this one sees Mt. 16:18 as the

occasio and not the causa of critical remarks.

In the same breath Erasmus continues his critique of current practice in asserting that although it is "perhaps" impossible to say too much about Mary and Christ he still desires that fanaticism in praising anyone be matched by a desire to imitate the one being praised. There is something unusual about this remark for Erasmus normally radically distinguishes between Mary and Christ.

Erasmus concludes his comment by returning to Augustine's interpretation. Thus he forms an inclusio and further highlights the negative and critical senses mentioned between the references to Augustine. He qualifies remarkably the distance between his interpretation and Augustine's by limiting their disagreement as to the words they respectively use; nevertheless, he feels that to take "petra" in terms of Christ is quite forced, but nevertheless understandable as the lesser of two evils -- the greater of two evils being closely related to the twisted sense that Erasmus outlined earlier.

It is of no use to look to other passages to illuminate further what Erasmus says here regarding "petra." His annotations on other New Testament passages mentioning "petra" either lack comment all together or say nothing significant about Mt. 16:18 (that is, Mt. 7:24-25, 27:51, 60, Mk. 15:46, Lk. 6:48, 8:6, 13, Rom. 9:33, I Pt. 2:8, Rev. 6:15-16); remarkably the comments made by him in 1516 on I Cor. 10:4 say nothing about Christ as rock and contain no cross reference to Mt. 16:18, although in later editions Erasmus does follow Augustine in interpreting the spiritual rock in terms of Christ, "that singular rock whence all those believing derive salvation."[18] The synoptic parallel to Mt. 16:18 (Luke 22:31f) prompts no comment from Erasmus, leaving one to think that perhaps it was not abused in the sixteenth century.

21

Erasmus' "Novum testamentum" (1519)

In preparation for the second edition
Erasmus, writing from Basel in August 1518, pro-
posed, among other changes, to extend some of the
annotations so as to inform the reader as to whose
authority he was following -- this will be seen
very clearly with reference to Mt. 16:18.[19]
Another change was a greatly expanded version of
the 1516 "Methodus" which appeared under the title
"Ratio seu compendium verae theologiae." In this
Erasmus finally clarifies the hermeneutical principle behind his interpretation of "petra." He
does so in the context of recommending the importance of literary criticism.[20] Specifically since
most of Jesus' words are conveyed metaphorically,
Erasmus recommends determining "what persona he
who is speaking takes on, that of the head or of
the members, of the pastor or of the flock."[21]
He then applies this principle to our text:

> . . . when he asks his disciples 'Whom do
> you say that I am?' Jesus acts the role
> of the head. Peter as the voice of and
> in the place of the entire Christian
> populace responds: 'Thou art the Christ,
> the son of the living God.' For there is
> no one in the body of Christ from whom
> that confession ('Thou art the Christ,
> the son of the living God') may not be
> asked. In like manner what is said to
> Peter: 'Thou art Peter, and upon this
> rock I will build my church, and I will
> give you the keys of the kingdom of
> heaven' pertains to the whole body of the
> Christian people.[22]

What is significant here is that what is asked of,
confessed by and promised to Peter is congruent
with all Christian people. On the other hand,
there are other passages (e.g. John 21:15-17) in
which what is said to and of Peter is congruent
with a more restricted group such as bishops.[23]
Erasmus goes on to call for attention regarding

the variety not only of persons but also of times
and things mentioned in Scripture.[24] For those
confused by such variety he recommends dividing
the whole people of Christ into three circles, all
of which have their center in Christ. The three
circles correspond to ecclesial leaders, secular
rulers and common folk. Scripture passages in
turn will have appropriate reference to the
groups.[25]

There is a slight change in the Latin
rendering of Mt. 16:18 made by Erasmus in 1519:
in place of "quoque" he substitutes "vicissim."
This is part of a larger movement further away
from the Vulgate rendering and towards his own
preferences.

There are substantive additions in the
1519 edition regarding the note on Mt. 16:18. He
brings in Jerome as an authority for the philological note on "pétros"/Cephas.[26]

Regarding the negative understanding of
"petra" in terms of the Roman pontiff Erasmus
adds: "whom they uncritically regard as being
above all, even as the restricted focus of the
Christian faith."[27] By 1519 Erasmus definitely
had in mind Sylvestro Prierias, Tommaso de Vio and
perhaps Jakob von Hoogstraeten, all Dominicans.
Writing in October, 1519, to Albert of Brandenberg
Erasmus criticizes both Sylvestro and Tommaso de
Vio for writing immoderately about papal power and
suggests a motive for those who uncritically build
up the pope -- personal profit and increased
power.[28] By April 7, 1519, in a letter dedicated
to Leo X in his Destructio cabalae seu cabalisti-
cae perfidiae Hoogstraeten in a very nuanced way
could connect up excessive papal praise with the
church founded on faith.[29]

Immediately following this remark Erasmus
enlists the name of Origen in support of his
position that the "petra" pertains to all Christians (the flock) rather than one man alone (the

23

pastor).[30]   It is not difficult to understand what
prompted Erasmus' reference to Origen's Homilia in
the edition of 1519, for Erasmus had been using
and profiting from Origen's Homiliae since the
autumn of 1501 and by 1504 Erasmus had worked
through a great deal of Origen's works.[31]
Erasmus is most likely referring to and citing the
Latin edition of Origen's works published in Paris
(1512). "Homilia I" in the third volume of this
collection concerns Peter's confession of faith as
recounted in Mt. 16. A basic principle running
throughout Origen's homily is that what happens in
Christ's time happens in our own.[32]   The elegance
that Erasmus attributes to Origen occurs soon
thereafter:

>   Perhaps if we say what Peter said:
> thou art the Christ, the son of the
> living God, not with flesh and blood
> revealing, but with the heavenly father
> illuminating our mind, we will be Peter
> and we will attain to the same blessing
> just as Peter, on account of our confes-
> sion being similar to his confession.[33]

Erasmus does not stress as Origen does the notion
of the Father revealing truth to and illuminating
man. Further confirmation of the continuity
between Erasmus and Origen may be seen in what
soon follows in Origen's homily. After he distinguishes the confession of Christ according to
flesh and blood and according to revelation, the
latter of which makes us like Peter in faith and
in blessing, Origen writes:

>   Therefore if we, as we have already
> said, with the father revealing to us,
> confess Jesus to be the Christ, the son
> of the living God, we will become Peter,
> and certainly it may be said to us by the
> divine word: 'thou art Peter and upon
> this rock I will build my church' and the
> rest. A rock is indeed everyone who is
> an imitator of Christ, from whom they

24

were drinking, that is those who were
drinking of the spiritual rock following
them. And upon every rock of this kind
is built the church of God. For in each
and every one of the perfect who have in
themselves the combination of words and
deeds and all thoughts which are engaged
in blessedness of this type consists the
church of God. . . But if you suppose
that the universal church is built by God
upon that one man Peter what say you
about James and John . . . and the rest
of the disciples? Indeed it was said to
Peter -- thou art Peter and upon this
rock I will build my church and the gates
of the lower places will not prevail
against it; it also seems that it was
said to all the apostles and to everyone
of the faithful perfect, since all are
Peter and all are rocks and on all
of these is built the church of Christ:
. . .34

Thus Erasmus follows Origen in applying the profession of faith not only to Peter but to all
Christians. They significantly differ in that
Erasmus does not use the related passage in I Cor.
10:4 as Origen does. This illustrates Erasmus'
problem with Augustine's position -- he is unable
to render "petra" in terms of both the profession
of faith and Christ, while Origen can.

Origen's commentary on this pericope is
identical to what we have seen in the 1512 edition; it also contains a Greek passage not translated in the 1512 edition that helps to explain
Erasmus' interpretation of this passage: Origen
affirms that all Christians can become Peter but
also that what the letter of the gospel applies to
Peter the spirit of the gospel indicates that it
may be applied to all that become like Peter.35
And this distinction between letter and spirit
could have influenced Erasmus in his distinction
between the "caput" and "membri" intentioned in a

25

particular passage. Thus we have Erasmus spiritualizing Origen! Erasmus later edited Origen's commentary on Matthew in 1527.

Although Erasmus stresses Origen's support for his own position that "petra" is the "professio fidei" on the part of all Christians, he neglects to mention another way in which Origen interpreted the "petra" of Mt. 16:18. In his homily on Ex. 14:11-12 Origen says "But who is thus blessed, who so throws off the burden of temptations that no thought of ambiguity creeps up on his mind? See what was said by the Lord to the great foundation of the church and very solid rock, upon which Christ founded the church: 'O you of little faith, he says, why have you doubted?'"36

In 1519 Erasmus added another writer, Cyprian, to those previously mentioned in his comments on Mt. 16:18. The mention and discussion of Cyprian occurs immediately after the urging that certain ones be more concerned about imitating than praising the saints:

> Blessed Cyprian in the third letter of the first book, seems to hold that the church is founded upon Peter, saying, but Peter upon whom the church had been founded by the Lord himself. Unless perhaps Cyprian so explains himself that here he takes Peter not for that man, but as a type, as the words of Cyprian which subsequently follow indicate. 'One speaking for all and responding with the voice of the church, says Lord where shall we go. And thus Peter the rock represents the solid faith of the church.'37

Erasmus' attention was called to this passage not because an adversary used Cyprian against Erasmus but because Erasmus had been editing the works of Cyprian (this edition was published at Basel by

26

Froben in February, 1520). The reference is to a
letter of Cyprian written to Cornelius, the concern of which is to urge a united front on the
part of all true bishops against the counter-
claims of Felicissimus' party. The immediate
context for the passage which Erasmus cites is
Cyprian's discussion that while some do desert
Christ and local bishops, others hold fast to
belief in Christ. The reference to Peter as a
rock is incidental and parenthetical; it is in no
way crucial to Cyprian's argument except as a
reminder that true Christians and bishops do not
abandon belief in Christ and allegiance to true
bishops. Rather Peter represents those who hold
on to Christ as the source of eternal life.[38]
Although not mentioning the wider context of
Cyprian's words, Erasmus seems to be on solid
ground in excusing Cyprian for narrowly interpreting Peter inasmuch as elsewhere Cyprian had
described Peter as a type. However, one wonders
why Erasmus did not confront other statements of
Cyprian which either speak of the mother church
founded upon Peter by the word of the Lord, a word
which gives rise to other churches,[39] or emphasize a certain primacy given to Peter, albeit as a
sign of unity for the whole church.[40]

The final addition to the edition of 1519
concerns the phrase as rendered in the Vulgate
edition "non praevalebunt adversus eam." There
was no comment on this in the previous edition but
here Erasmus cites the position of Origen that
"eam" is ambiguous in that "petra" or "ecclesia"
are both likely candidates for the pronoun;
Erasmus adds that the ambiguity matters little as
far as the sense of the passage is concerned.[41]

The 1519 edition contains marginalia not
found in the previous edition, as for example,
"Ecclesia non est fundata super Petrum";[42] unfor-
tunately it is not certain that Erasmus composed
these, although he certainly approved of them for
they also appear in later editions.

27

Between the 1519 edition and the 1522
paraphrase of Matthew's gospel, Erasmus was torn
in different directions. On the one hand, he
became increasingly upset with those who immoderately praised the pope -- Tommaso de Vio, Prierias, Tommaso Todeschi, and Augustin von Alfeld --
unlike others who were more moderate in their
refutations of Luther (Jacobus Latomus, Johann
Driedo).[43] On the other hand, Erasmus was being
tempted by other groups and individuals to throw
his lot in with Luther. Indeed, certain Germans
found his commentary on Mt. 16:18 so appealing
that the entire commentary on chapter sixteen was
translated into German and published in Augsburg
in 1521. Although feeling antipathy towards the
Romanists and sympathy toward the Wittenberg camp,
Erasmus threw his lot in with the "petra":

> It would be very easy for me to join
> Luther as you have urged me, if I should
> see him on the side of the Catholic
> church. Not that I proclaim him to be
> foreign to it, for neither is it my part
> to damn anyone. He stands or falls with
> his Lord. If the affair should come to
> an extreme tumult so that the status of
> the church wavers from side to side, all
> the meanwhile I shall hold on to that
> solid rock ("petra") until, with the
> controversies settling down, it will be
> clear where the church is; and wherever
> there is evangelical peace there Erasmus
> will be.[44]

Erasmus' "Novum testamentum" (1522)

In February, 1522, appeared at Basel the
third edition of Novum testamentum along with
annotations. It contained no changes in the Greek
or Latin rendering of Mt. 16:18; nor were there
any changes in Erasmus' comment. The remarks on
Mt. 16:18 from this edition were later translated
and published in Augsburg, 1522.

28

Erasmus' "Paraphrasis in evangelium Matthei" (1522)

In March of the same year appeared Erasmus' Paraphrasis in evangelium Matthei. For Erasmus a "paraphrasis" was a "commentary" properly speaking.[45]

Erasmus' rendering of our text and its immediate context bears citation:

> Jesus, delighted with this lively as well as solid profession of faith, says: Blessed art thou, Simon son of John. Human feeling did not furnish you that statement, but the heavenly Father by a secret inspiration suggested it to your mind. For no one really knows about the Son except by the prompting of the Father, who alone knows the Son. And I indeed, lest you honor me for nothing with so magnificent a testimony, affirm this: that thou art truly Peter, that is, a solid rock ("lapidem"), not vacillating here and there in the various opinions of the masses, and upon this stone ("saxo") of your profession I will build my church, that is, my home and palace, which community is so set upon an immovable foundation that no powers of the kingdom of hell shall be able to conquer it. Satan will attack you with many machines of war, he will raise up against you a company of impious spirits, but by my protection my building will stand impregnable, so long as that solid profession of faith shall remain. The church is the heavenly kingdom; the world is the kingdom of the devil. From this latter kingdom no one need fear for himself as long as he is Peter, that is like unto you. And I am about to hand on to you the keys of this heavenly kingdom. For it is fitting that he be first in authority who is first in the profession

of faith and charity. . . . But he shall
enter the kingdom of heaven if he pro-
fessed like you what you profess . . .[46]

This Paraphrasis is significant in many
respects. Although it stresses the Origenist
emphasis on the Father inspiring and prompting
Peter to make his profession, earlier Erasmus
stressed not the Father but the human comprehen-
sion of the disciples concerning Jesus' words and
miracles.[47] Secondly, there seems to be more
emphasis here in the Paraphrasis on the person of
Peter himself, most loved by Jesus and destined to
be the chief of the apostolic order[48] and who has
a certain primacy due to his profession of faith
and charity. Although the Erasmian emphasis on
Peter's profession of faith continues--Peter
responds not simply for himself but in the name of
all[49]--it is upon the stone of Peter's profession
that the church is to be built, not upon Peter
himself; as long as that solid profession is made
the church will stand unconquered and undaunted by
Satan's legions; no one need fear the kingdom of
the devil as long as he is like Peter;[50] those who
profess like Peter shall enter the kingdom of
heaven.

These positions remain the same in the
following editions of the Paraphrasis: Tomus
primus paraphraseon . . . in novum Testamentum
. . . published at Basel in 1523, 1524, 1533.

Erasmus' "Novum testamentum" (1527)

The fourth edition of Erasmus' Novum
testamentum was published by Froben at Basel in
March, 1527. It is distinguished by the three
column arrangement of the New Testament text:
Erasmus' Greek version, Erasmus' Latin version,
and the Vulgata editio (Erasmus' Latin version is
in bigger print than the Vulgate!). Compare the
two Latin versions relative to Mt. 16:18:

30

Vulgate: "Et ego dico tibi: quia tu es
                    Petrus; et super
Erasmus: "At ego vicissim tibi dico, quod
                    tu es Petrus, et super

Vulgate: hanc petram aedificabo ecclesiam
                    meam, et portae
Erasmus: hanc petram aedificabo meam eccle-
                    siam, et portae

Vulgate: inferi non praevalebunt adversus
                    eam."
Erasmus: inferorum non valebunt adversus
                    illam."[51]

There are no changes in Erasmus' Greek or Latin
versions of Mt. 16:18 from the previous edition.

        There were significant additions to the
note on Mt. 16:18, all dealing with the patristic
heritage of rock commenting -- Chrysostom, Augustine, and Jerome. Theophylact is also cited.

        Erasmus enlists Theophylact and Chrysostom
as support for the position that "petra" is to be
taken in the sense of professio fidei.[52]

        Erasmus did not have to translate or edit
Theophylact's comments on the gospels for this had
already been done by one of Erasmus' former edi-
torial assistants, Johann Oekolampad: the Ennarationes of Theophylact was published at Basel by
Craitander in March, 1524 (this edition was
reprinted in 1525 and 1527-1528).[53] Theophylact
comments thus on Mt. 16:18:

        The Lord favors Peter, giving him a
    great reward, because he built the church
    upon him. For since Peter had confessed
    Jesus son of God, Jesus said that this
    confession which Peter uttered would be
    the foundation of future believers, just
    as every man should be about to raise up
    the house of faith and should be about to

31

lay this foundation. For even if we put
together innumerable virtues, we, however, may not have the foundation -- a
proper confession, and we build in vain.
Moreover since Jesus said my church, he
showed himself to be the lord of creation: for all realities serve God. . . .
Therefore if we shall have been confirmed
in the confession of Christ, the gates of
hell, that is, sins, will not prevail
against us.[54]

It is remarkable that Erasmus waited so long to
introduce Theophylact (another Greek writer) as an
auctoritas, for Theophylact manifestly supports
the interpretation of petra = confessio and does
not restrict the confessio to Peter alone but
insists as Erasmus does that protection from the
gates of hell depends on our being grounded in
this confessio.

          In the same breath, Erasmus also calls
upon John Chrysostom for support; he has in mind
Chrysostom as mediated through Thomas Aquinas'
Catena aurea. In this work Chrysostom's four-
teenth homily on Matthew is cited: "That is,
[referring to "petra"] on this faith and confession I will build my church. Hence Christ showed
that many were now about to believe what Peter had
confessed, and Christ raises up Peter's conscious-
ness and makes him a very pastor."[55] Erasmus
seems correctly to have evoked Chrysostom's support, for Chrysostom manifestly understands
"petra" in terms of the faith and confession of
many. By 1530 Erasmus was confirmed in appro-
priating Chrysostom because of his editing of
Chrysostom's works. Chrysostom's twenty-sixth
Sermo, which is concerned with the feast of
Pentecost, distinguishes between the man Peter and
the faith upon which Christ built his church; he
also speaks of "petra" in terms of "ecclesia,"
"confessio," and "sermones pietatis," all congruent with Erasmus' position.[56] Secondly,
Chrysostom's fifty-fifth homily on chapter sixteen

32

of Matthew directly speaks of "petra" in terms of "fides" and "confessio" and repeats much of the passage already cited by Erasmus.[57]

The second addition in 1527 involves Augustine's position on "petra" in his Retractiones. These remarks Erasmus appends to Augustine's already cited statement on "petra": "The same in the first book of the Retractions, chapter twenty-one, considered each position -- Christ and Peter, nevertheless he was more inclined with respect to this, that Peter, professing Christ to be son of the living God, represented the church, to which are handed the keys. However, he rendered the reader free to choose which position he preferred."[58] Would that Erasmus had cited more of Augustine here; he could certainly have done this, for two years after this edition Erasmus' ten volume edition of Augustine's works was published at Basel. Augustine there explains that in his "contra epistolam Donati":

> I said in a certain place about the
> apostle Peter that on him as on a rock
> the church was founded; this interpreta-
> tion is also voiced by the mouth of many
> in the verses of the very saintly Ambrose
> where he says about the cock crowing,
> 'With this crowing this rock of the
> church washed away his guilt.' But I
> realize that frequently at a later time
> that I so explained what was said by the
> Lord, 'Tu es Petrus . . .' that 'super
> hanc' be understood as that which Peter
> confessed, saying, 'Tu es Christus. . .,'
> and so Peter called by this rock repre-
> sented the person of the church which is
> built upon this rock, and has received
> the keys of the kingdom of heaven. For
> 'Tu es petra' was not said to him but 'tu
> es Petrus'; moreover the rock was Christ
> whom Simon having confessed just as the
> entire church confesses and he is called
> Peter. However the reader may choose

33

which of these two opinions is more prof-
itable.[59]

Erasmus omits altogether the Ambrosian hymn with
its reference to Peter as rock and de-emphasizes
what Augustine actually said regarding Peter as
"petra" in "Contra epistulam Donati." Erasmus is
mainly concerned with Augustine's modification
that Peter is not the rock but a type of the confessing church.

The final addition in the 1527 edition
concerns Jerome's position on "petra." This
addition was built on to Erasmus' earlier discussion of Cyprian's position: "Similarly can be
excused the places in which Saint Jerome in his
letters seems to say that the church of Christ is
founded upon Peter."[60] Erasmus thus holds that
Jerome like Cyprian uses Peter the rock as a type
of the solid faith of the church. However,
Erasmus does not present his evidence here with
respect to Jerome. There are two places in
Jerome's letters which explicitly refer to Peter
as the rock upon which Christ has built his
church. The first of these letters, addressed to
Damasus, bishop of Rome, was prompted by Jerome's
concerns for the unity of the church, and he
appeals to the Roman see as a symbol of true faith
and unity.[61] In the letter to Marcella, an individual troubled by certain Montanist claims
regarding the sending of the Paraclete, Jerome
recommends Peter's speech in Acts 2:14-18 as
exemplary of the true understanding of Scripture.[62] In neither case is Peter recommended
solely as authority.

Why, though, did Erasmus not mention
Jerome's commentary on Matthew here? His remarks
on the "petra" of Mt. 7:25 support the Erasmian
interpretation.[63] Erasmus also omits mention of
Jerome's interpretation of "petra" in Mt. 16:18:
the rock is pre-eminently Christ; Simon who
believed in the rock-Christ receives the name
derived from "petra," Peter; to Simon, according

34

to the metaphor of rock ("petra"), it is rightly
said "I will build my church upon you."[64]
Perhaps the earlier reference to Augustine prompted
Erasmus not to include reference to Jerome's
position.

Erasmus' "Novum testamentum" (1535)

The fifth edition of Erasmus' Annotationes
was published by the Froben press in Basel in
1535. Erasmus' Greek and Latin texts remained the
same as in the previous edition (although the
Vulgate column drops out altogether).[65] There were
no changes in the commentary, although "amphi-
bologia" was added to the margin; this corresponds
to Erasmus' comment on "Non praevalebunt adversus
eam."[66]

Broickwy's ". . . in quatuor evangelia ennarationum . . ." (1539)

Anton Broickwy (c. 1475-1541)[67] was
originally from Königstein in Germany; it is
interesting to note that Broickwy like Erasmus
grew up in the environs of the Brethren of the
Common Life, for at Königstein there was a foundation of the Brethren.[68] He later became known as
"Noviomagensis" since he occasionally served as
warden of the Franciscan Observants at Nijmegen in
Gelderland, The Netherlands.[69] His reputation
and one of his dominant concerns involved preaching.[70] This is clearly evident when one consults
his Sententias bibliorum, seu, concordantias
breves omnium fere materiarum, quae in sacris
bibliis continentur, non solum divini verbi
concionatoribus, verum etiam studiosis omnibus
summopere utiles, ac necessarias (Paris, 1544 and
1551) and his Postillae, first published at Paris
in 1540. Another characteristic of his work was
the concern for harmonia; he produced a Monotes-
saron breve with reference to the four gospels (first
published at Cologne in 1539). In August 1539 was

published his . . . in quatuor evangelia ennarationum . . . by Quentell in Cologne. It was
reprinted at Cologne in 1550, at Paris in 1543,
1545, 1548, 1550, 1551, 1554, and 1555, and at
Venice in 1548.

Broickwy's comments on Mt. 16:18 fall
within a section which deals with "De interroga-
tione Christi de filio homini."[71] Not only is he
concerned here with Mt. 16 but also with Mk. 8 and
Lk. 9, although he uses Matthew 16 as the base
text. His remarks on Peter's confession of faith
are identical to Erasmus' commentary in his paraphrase of Matthew.[72] Evidence of his independence
from Erasmus may be seen in the way that he cites
Mt. 16:18: he follows the Vulgate "quia" instead
of the Erasmian "quod."

His language and position concerning
"petra" are again taken from Erasmus.[73] Further-
more he reintroduces the Erasmian note found in
the Annotationes but not in his paraphrase of
Matthew: "Satan will throw up many machines of
war against you, but my building will stand unconquered by my help, as long as that solid profession remains."[74] He also repeats the Erasmian
connection between authority, profession of faith
and charity.[75]

Despite this explicit borrowing from
Erasmus there are some important differences.
Broickwy revives a patristic note absent from
Erasmus' work: Jesus rewards the faith of Peter.[76]
Secondly, and most likely because of Broickwy's
tendency to harmonize scripture, he makes exten-
sive use of the collatio technique throughout his
remarks on this passage; especially does he bring
in those passages which in any way speak of a
building: I Tim. 3:15, I Cor. 3:10-11, Rev.
21:14, Eph. 2:19-21, I Pt. 2:4-5, Lk. 22:32 and
Mt. 7:24-25.[77] Thirdly, Broickwy brings in the
reference to Jerome's commentary on Matthew which
uses "petra" of Peter derivatively.[78]

Broickwy, we may say, is Erasmus harmo-
nized! Perhaps this helped him escape ecclesiastical condemnation, an indignity suffered posthumously by Erasmus.

Jean d'Arbres' "Theosophia" (1540)

Jean d'Arbres (?-c.1569)[79] was born at
Laon where he became a canon, and later taught at
the Sorbonne. His intellectual concerns were
broad; aside from his exegetical interests he
produced philosophical works such as Oratio de
laudibus philosophiae and wrote on Aristotle and
Porphyry. By the end of the sixteenth century he
was regarded as "truly Catholic," a writer against
heretics.[80] This reputation was well-deserved for
he battled the Calvinists for control of Paul[81]
and in a letter to Henry II he approved of the
king's practice of burning Calvinists and of
generally putting them out of the way.[82]

D'Arbres produced two exegetical works.
His Commentarii . . . in quatuor domini evangelistas . . . was published in Paris by de Roigny
in 1529 and 1551[83] and his Theosophia was published in two volumes by Simon Colina in Paris in
1540 and 1553.

The Theosophia does not proceed by way of
a continuous exposition of scripture but begins
with a disputed theme and then examines the Biblical and patristic evidence.[84] Our text is
commented on and used as confirmation of the
thesis that "the church was founded on the Rock
and not upon Peter."[85] After citing the relevant
passage in Matthew (using the Vulgate rendering
"quia") he contrasts building the church on unstable Peter with building the church on the firm
rock mentioned in Matthew 7. In support of this
position he turns to appropriate patristic references: Chrysostom, Augustine, Jerome, Cyprian,
Cyril, Origen, Hilary, Ambrose -- Theophylact is
also mentioned. These fathers are cited either in

order to show that they agree with d'Arbres'
position or, where they seem to differ, to explain
the differences in favor of his position. For
example where Chrysostom appears to say that the
church was built upon Peter, he is said to be
speaking tropologically ("per Tropum").[86]
Throughout he seems concerned with the process of
colligere, that is, harmonizing the patristic
opinions by making proper distinctions: "From all
the views of the fathers which seem to conflict
with one another, although they do not, let us
gather them ("colligemus") in a brief epilogue:
simply and most aptly the church is founded on the
rock, and upon Peter in a certain tropological
sense."[87] This distinction, operative also in
Erasmus, is derived from Augustine, and d'Arbres
recognizes this in his discussion of Augustine's
positions on "petra."[88]

D'Arbres' own position is clarified at the
end of his argument, after having synthesized the
patristic evidence. He holds "that the church
depends upon no other foundation than faith; we
say that it has its seat upon faith, hope and
charity, and that it comes forth from this power
on which it must depend, and from the best for-
tified place of faith the helps of an honest life
and good works hang. Because if you take away
faith you upset the church."[89]

Although d'Arbres thus continues the
Erasmian line of interpretation, he stands in
greater continuity with medieval exegesis because
of his ability to hold together various senses of
"petra" due to the influence of Augustine's distinction.

Isidoro Chiari's "Exegetica"

The philological note, characteristic not
only of Erasmus but also of humanist exegetes in
general, is continued in the work of Isidoro
Chiari (c. 1495-1555). Born Taddeo Cucchi in
Chiari in the Brescia region of Italy, he became a

Benedictine monk in 1517. As an abbot, he was in
attendance at the Council of Trent. In 1547 Paul
III made him bishop of Foligno where he served
until he died in 1555 "in the odor of sanctity."[90]

There are two notable concerns of Chiari
that should be mentioned. One was his concern for
the poor. In 1540 he wrote a work entitled De
modo divitiis adhibendo homini Christiane ad
cives Brixianes salutaris oratio. As bishop of
Foligno he reversed a common practice of enriching
relatives and fellow monks by repeatedly using
ecclesiastical properties to support poor people.[91]

Secondly, in 1546 at the fourth session of
the Council of Trent Chiari, speaking for all the
abbots present there, argued that scripture
studies pertain especially to monks and that monks
should not be mired down in contentious and
scholastic lectureships.[92]

In 1541 he edited a two volume Vulgate
version of the New Testament. He renders Mt.
16:18 with the Erasmian "quod": "Et ego dico
tibi, quod tu es Petrus, et super hanc petram
aedificabo ecclesiam meam: et portae inferi non
praevalebunt adversus eam."[93] Chiari's scholion
(for him basically an explanation of a word or
phrase) on "super hanc Petram" is "super hanc
fidei soliditatem."[94] Note that he emphasizes the
philological character of "petra" and does not
refer to the soliditas Petri but rather the
soliditas fidei. This emphasis on the soliditas
fidei continues in his later exegetica.[95]

Bernardino Tomitano's "Espositione letterale. . ." (1547)

Bernardino Tomitano (1517?-1576)[96] translated Erasmus' paraphrase of Matthew into Italian
and published it under his own name: Espositione
letterale del testo di Matthaeo evangelista
. . .[97]

Johannes Wild's "In sacrosanctum Iesu
Christi evangelium secundum Matthaeum
commentariorum libri quatuor . . ." (1559)

Johannes Wild was born in Mainz in 1495.
He entered the Franciscan Observants in 1515.
From 1528 to his death he functioned as a preacher
in Mainz and achieved a reputation of being the
most learned sixteenth century preacher in Ger-
many. He was critical of the excesses of the
Roman curia and was concerned for peace between
Lutherans and Catholics; indeed it was perhaps for
these reasons that he was permitted to remain in
Mainz after the expulsion of the other Franciscans
by the Lutherans in 1552. He died in 1554 in
Mainz.

He is best known for his commentaries on
John and on Matthew. Some held that his remarks
on Mt. 16:18 were altered by Lutheran "heretics"
before they were published.

Wild's treatment of Peter's confession is
very similar to that of Erasmus'. The faith of
Peter is not exclusive, but rather what Peter says
is also the faith of Paul, of the other apostles
and of the whole church.[98] He does not stress
that Peter speaks in the name of all as Erasmus
does. He does agree though that it is Peter's
confession that gives him a certain pre-eminence.[99]

Wild's discussion of "Et ego dico tibi,
quia tu es Petrus, et super hanc Petram aedificabo
Ecclesiam meam" is most interesting. He prefaces
his remarks by pointing out that Satan loves to
use those passages of Scripture and especially
this passage about which there are questions and
seeming conflicts in order to lead men away from
the truth.[100] Specifically this passage should not
be used as an occasion for disputing who is the
greater; he then briefly states his own view of
papal authority: respect and esteem for the power
of Peter which he received from Christ and the
need for Peter's successors to use his power like

40

Peter (otherwise the abuse of this power causes rebellion and chaos).101

He then proceeds to the verse: Peter is called Peter because of his "confessio fidei."102 Regarding the meaning of "petra," he first connects it with strength, firmness and security (this based on its general use in Scripture).103 For this reason Christ did not build his church on any man including Peter, for no one is so firm and constant that he cannot be moved.104 Relying on those Scripture places which speak of Christ as "lapis" or "petra," "petra" is therefore primarily Christ, on whom the whole church is built.105 But he goes on to speak later of the Mt. 16:18 "petra" in terms of faith.106 Later, after an interesting discussion of how we are joined to Christ, he returns to Mt. 16:18 and says that "the rock, on which the church depends . . . is Christ, or better true faith, this which is manifestly drawn from Christ's words."107 Finally he explicates "super hanc petram" in terms of the confessio fidei through which one becomes as a rock.108 As if the connection with Erasmus and Origen were not clear enough, his accompanying remark--whoever is ignorant of this faith does not belong to the church even if he be pope--is further evidence.109

Although we have noticed strong similarities between the exegesis of Erasmus and Wild, one difference should be mentioned. Wild is able to hold together the notion of "petra" as both Christ and faith since he employs the patristic collatio and indeed thinks and writes more like a patristic writer than a sixteenth century one. This is even more significant because he mentions no patristic writer in his exposition of Mt. 16:18!

Benito Arias Montano's "Elucidationes in quatuor evangelia" (1575)

Benito Arias Montano was born in 1527 in Fregenal de la Sierra in Estremadura, Spain.

Later he joined as a cleric the Military Order of
St. James. He attended the Council of Trent in
1562 along with the bishop of Segovia. Together
with André Maes and François Luc de Bruges he
edited the famous Antwerp Polyglot Bible. Because
of this and other works he was recognized among
the finest Orientalists of the sixteenth century.
He died in 1598.

We are in the fortunate position of having
various lists of his library.[110] Among his books
were a 1527 edition of Erasmus' Novum testamentum,
a 1532 edition of Erasmus' paraphrase of the
gospels and Acts of the Apostles, the 1520 edition
of Cyprian's works edited by Erasmus, and the attacks on Erasmus by Edward Lee and Alberto Pio.
He also possessed Chiari's Vulgate Bible published
in 1542.

His Elucidationes in quatuor evangelia
resembles the Bibles of the later fifteenth century in that the Latin text comprises most of the
page with the elucidatio in small print in the
right margin. In his note on "Tu es Petrus" Arias
stresses Peter's testimony ("testimonium") about
Christ not as a prophet but as the son of the
living God as the foundation of the firmness of
Christ's church; since Simon first uttered this
testimony he is called Peter, first of all those
who testify ("testati sunt") that Christ is the
son of God.[111] The Antwerp censors affirmed that
this work was consistent with Catholic faith; the
bishop of Antwerp judged that it could be read
usefully by all.[112]

Another reason for grouping Arias here
is that in his earlier theological book he
describes "petra" as the notitia Christi which
those who are divinely inspired (a designation
including Simon Peter) have and upon which the
church is built.[113]

Juan de Valdés' "El Evangelio segun San Mateo . . ."

Since there is uncertainty regarding the date of Juan de Valdés' commentary on Matthew and because of some doubt regarding his Roman Catholicity, he is considered last in this chapter.

Born around 1500 in Cuenca, Spain, he later studied at the University of Alcalá de Henares (1527-1529) where he came under the influence of the Erasmian Francisco de Vergara.[114] He later left Spain because his Dialogo de doctrina christiana was under suspicion of heterodox tendencies by the Spanish inquisition. He eventually came to settle in Naples where a prominent group centered on him; this group included Bernardino Ochino, Peter Martyr Vermigli, and Peter Carneschi.

His religious allegiance has been called into question. Most recently he has been classified as a "Nicodemite, fully conscious of his break with the Roman Church and de facto a heretic by the standards of the Catholic Church both in Spain and Italy."[115] The same author alleges the following evidence for this conclusion: 1) the testimony of two of his disciples suggests that Valdés held justification ex fide sola and greatly limited papal authority; 2) the Roman inquisition after Trent thought him heretical regarding justification and the certitude of grace; 3) his exegesis of Mt. 16:17-19 says nothing about papal claims and rejects the medieval interpretation, favorable to papal claims, of these verses; 4) some of his letters are very anti-papal.[116]

On the other hand, one should note that neither did he leave the Roman church nor strive to found a new one. Secondly, he died without ever being condemned by church authorities and supposedly according to his own testimony he died in the same faith in which he had lived.[117] Thirdly, the argumentum e silentio regarding his

43

exegesis of Mt. 16:17-19 is sufficiently ambiguous to permit the rejection of this sort of approach as a criterion for his orthodoxy or lack thereof. Finally, the medieval interpretation is much more favorable to Valdés' position than generally thought; it does not interpret "petra" in terms of the Roman pontiff.

Valdés' commentary was seen as being concerned with "the literal sense."[118] Valdés has an interesting hermeneutic for approaching Mt. 16:13-19. He says a true understanding of the text lies beyond human affection, human opinion, and "all discourse of human prudence."[119] A similar tone is expressed at the end of his remarks on Mt. 16:13-19: "This is what I presently understand in these words, which are of such importance that, although it appears that I remain satisfied with this understanding, still I seek to attain another, a better one; and thus I ask of God that he may give it to me either through himself or through the medium of someone, his servant . . ."[120] This un-Erasmian approach appropriates the process described in the text and applies it to the interpreter interpreting.

A similar note is sounded in Valdés' insistence that Peter's faith was, and ours should be, by "revelation and inspiration" and not by "flesh and blood." Peter's confession of faith is the "piedra" and Christ will build his church upon St. Peter's confession, even though this confession is not limited to Peter.[121] Valdés' final word (as of now) on Mt. 16:18 is "In such a way it is that I understand that the Christian church is founded upon belief in Christ according to that which St. Peter here confesses."[122] These statements could very well have come from Origen or Erasmus. Valdés, however, differs from Erasmus in that he places much more emphasis on Christ, rather than on our own believing, as guaranteeing the protection of the church from evil.

44

Conclusion

The period 1516 (Erasmus) to 1575 (Arias) manifests ample evidence that a clear tradition of interpreting the "petra" of Mt. 16:18 in terms of faith ("fides"), the profession of faith ("professio fidei"), the solidity of faith ("soliditas fidei"), or testimony ("testimonium") existed within the bounds of Roman Catholicism. This interpretation was an inclusive rather than an exclusive one, that is, "fides" was taken with reference to the faith of the entire church and not of Peter alone; to paraphrase Erasmus, every Christian can utter Peter's confession of faith and thus what is said to Peter on account of this confession may be attributed to any Christian. On a broader scope some exegetes understanding "petra" in terms of faith also entertained other possibilities, for example Christ as the rock (Wild).

Although the petra=fides interpretation was a secondary strain in the patristic period and existed in harmony with the interpretation petra=Petrus, the sixteenth century writers mentioned in this chapter emphasized those passages stemming from the patristic period which supported their position; Origen and Chrysostom were especially relied upon. Only one medieval writer (Theophylact) was mentioned, although it was in this period that the notion of a confession of faith separate from the person of Peter arose. The writers we have seen in this chapter carry on this autonomous faith position.

NOTES FOR CHAPTER ONE

[1]Roberto Bellarmino, . . . opera omnia, ed.
J. Giuliano, vol. 1: Disputationum de controversiis christianae adversus hujus temporis
haereticos, tomus primus (Neapoli: Giuliano,
1856; originally published in 1586), c. 10, p.
331[a].

[2]Desiderius Erasmus, Novum instrumentum omne,
diligenter ab Erasmo Roterodamo recognitum et
emendatum . . . una cum Annotationibus . . .
(Basileae: Frobenius, 1516), p. 38; hereafter
cited as Novum instrumentum.

[3]Novum instrumentum (1516), p. 272: "Quia tu
es. 'ὅτι', quod, non quia id dico te esse Petrum.
Petrus autem graecis saxum significat. 'pétros',
quemadmodum et Cephas Syro sermone, non hebraico
soliditatem sonat. Saxum enim illum appellat,
quod solidus sit in confessione fidei, et non
vulgarium opinionum levitate huc et illuc vacillet, et super istam petram, hic est solidam istam
fidei professionem extruam ecclesiam meam, in quo
fundamento si constiterit, nec inferi quicquam
adversus illam poterunt. Etiam si divus Augustinus in homilia huius loci, haec verba super hanc
petram ipsi accomodat Christo, non Petro. Tu es
inquit Petrus, et super hanc petram quam confessus
es, super hanc petram quam cognovisti, dicens, Tu
es Christus filius dei viui, aedificabo ecclesiam
meam, id est super meipsum filium dei viui, aedificabo ecclesiam meam. Super me aedificabo te,
non me super te. Nam volentes homines aedificari
super homines dicebant. Ego quidem sum Pauli, ego
autem Apollo, ego vero Cephae, ipse est Petrus.
Et alii qui nolebant aedificare super petrum, sed
super petram. Ego autem sum Christi. Proinde
miror esse, qui locum hunc detorqueant ad Romanum
pontificem. Verum sunt, quibus nihil satis est,
nisi quod sit immodicum. Ita quidam ad invidiam
usque Franciscum, prodigiosis efferunt laudibus,
quem exprimere magis oportebat, quam in immensum

attollere. Nam deiparae virgini et Christo fortasse non potest asscribi nimium, quamquam hic quoque optarim omnes sic ad imitandi studium inflammatos, quam quosdam videmus sedulo in exaggerandis laudibus. Caetrum nostra interpretatio verbis dumtaxat diffidet ab Augustiniana, quam ideo induximus, quod illius videretur coactior, ad quam tamen maluit deflectere, quam in alterum incurrere scopulum, videlicet ut in homine poneret ecclesiae fundamentum." See the "Appendix" for Erasmus' annotation on Mt. 16:18 as found in the five different editions of his Novum testamentum.

[4]A very different connection is found earlier (1513 or 1514) in "Dialogus, Iulius exclusus e coelis," in Erasmi opuscula: a Supplement to the Opera Omnia, ed. W. K. Ferguson (The Hague: Nijhoff, 1933), p. 119, lines 1071-1074 where Peter says to Julius II: "Primum omnium si mihi das Christum optimum esse verumque principem Ecclesiae, ipse mihi claves regni dedit, ipse pascendas oves commisit, ipse meam fidem suo praeconio approbavit:. . ."

[5]Fröhlich, Formen, p. 3.

[6]Italics my own.

[7]This explanation is a synthesis of the examples of John of La Rochelle and Peter of Scala in their commentaries on Matthew (Paris nat. lat. 625, t. 124^{Vb} and 15596, f. 193^{Vb}) as cited by Fröhlich, Formen, p. 5, note 8: "expressio fidei incarnationis - commendatio huius fidei vel credentis - promissio fundandi ecclesiam in fide evangelicae veritatis. . . divini incarnationis plena confessio - confessionis commendatio - divini muneris promissio. . ."

[8]It is interesting to note that Mt. 16:18 was not included among the passages used by Roman Catholics for Sunday readings or for the feasts of confessor-popes in the sixteenth century. How-

ever, this text was used as part of the gospel
reading for the feasts of Peter's chair and of
saints Peter and Paul: Anton Broickwy, Concordantiae breviores omnium ferme materiarum ex
sacris bibliorum libris. . . (Parisiis: Ioannes
de Roigny, 1551), [Hh v, Hhv[r], Hh vii]; Sebastian
Barradas [1542-1615], [Opera] . . . 1742, vol. I,
d2[v], and Anton de Ghislandis, Opus Aureum super
evangeliis ([Lugduni,] 1532), [fo. ccclx].

[9]Augustine, . . . Operum, ed. Desiderius
Erasmus, vol. X (Basileae: ex off. Frobeniana,
1529), sermo XIII, d.2.

[10]Ibid., d.: "Evangelium quod recentissime
recitatum est de domino Christo, qui super aquam
maris ambulavit, et de apostolo Petro qui ambulans
timendo titibavi, et diffidendo mersus, confitendo
rursus emersit, admonet nos intelligere mare
praesens seculum esse, Petrum vero apostolum
ecclesiae unicae typum. Ipse enim Petrus in
apostolorum ordine primus, in Christi amore
promptissimus, saepe unus respondit pro omnibus."

[11]Ibid., d. 2: "Quia enim Christus petra,
Petrus populus Christianus. Petra enim principale
nomen est, ideo Petrus a petra, non petra a Petro,
quomodo non a Christiano Christus, sed a Christo
Christianus vocatur."

[12]Ibid., "De sanctis," Sermo XVI, f. 852:
"Denique pro soliditate devotionis ecclesiarum
petra dicitur, sicut ait dominus, Tu es Petrus, et
super hanc petram aedificabo ecclesiam meam.
Petra enim dicitur, eo quod primus nationibus
fidei fundamenta posuerit, et tanquam saxum immobile totius operis Christiani compagem malemque
contineat. Petra ergo pro devotione Petrus dicitur, et petra pro virtute dominus nuncupatur,
. . ."

[13]Alvaro Pelayo, [De planctu ecclesiae] ([Ulm:
Zainer], 1474), I, a. 55, no page: "Potest autem
intelligere uno modo hanc petram super te et
successores tuos, vel super hanc petram, id est

super hanc quem confessus es, quia petra erat
Christus . . . et aec [the latter] est verior
expositio et sensus. . . ."

14Fröhlich, Formen, passim.

15Ibid., pp. 113-115.

16Jan Hus, Magistri Iohannis Hus opera omnia,
Vol. XXII: Magistri Iohannis Hus Polemica, ed.
J. Ersil (Prague: Academia H.E. in aedibus Academiae Scientiarum Bohemoslovacae, 1966), p. 241:
"Fabulatur eciam ibidem fictor, quod 'Cristus
recedens ex hoc mundo, ne corpus suum ecclesie
militantis super terram esset acefalum, Petrum et
successores suos dedit ecclesie militanti pro
capite corporali super terram habendo usque ad
consumacionem seculi, dicens sibi: 'Tu es Petrus
et super hanc petram edificabo ecclesiam meam,'
et iterum dicens: 'Pasce oves meas.'"

17Ibid., pp. 243-244: "Consequencia autem sua
eciam apud laicos est invalida, puta ista: Christus dixit Petro: Tu es Petrus et super hanc
petram edificabo ecclesiam meam -- ergo Petrus est
caput corporale ecclesie militantis. Quomodo
autem intelligitur illud evangelium Cristi: 'Tu
es Petrus . . .', declaravi in tractatulo De
ecclesia, sanctorum ponens sentenciam, et pre-
sertim beati Augustini, . . . 'Super hanc petram,
quam confessus es, super hanc petram, quam cognovisti . . . Super me edificabo te, non me super
te. . . .' Hic Augustinus meliorem docens evangelii sentenciam quam fictor pro suo proposito
pretendebat; estimo enim, quod 'super hanc petram'
voluit intelligere 'super Petrum', et exinde
intulit, quod Petrus fuit caput ecclesie corporale."

18LB VI, 710 C-D: "Et Augustinus . . .
interpretatur, Christus erat petra, id est, petra
significat Christum: nec obstat quod hanc petram
dixerit spiritualem. Quicquid enim mysticum habet
sensum, spirituale dicimus. Bibebant aquam de

petra, non qualibet, sed de spirituali, quae
significabat illam unicam petram, unde salutem
hauriunt omnes credentes . . . ."

[19]EE III, 860, 381, 42-44.

[20]Holborn, p. 196, ll. 29-32: "Accedet hinc
quoque lucis nonnihil ad intelligendum scripturae
sensum, si perpendamus non modo quid dicatur,
verum etiam a quo dicatur, cui dicatur, quibus
verbis dicatur, quo tempore, qua occasione, quid
praecedat, quid consequatur."

[21]Holborn, p. 197, ll. 5-8: "Et quoniam totus
ferme Christi sermo figuris ac tropis obliquus
est, diligenter odorabitur theologiae candidatus,
quam sustineat personam is, qui loquitur, capitis
an membrorum, pastoris an gregis."

[22]Holborn, p. 197, line 33 - p. 198, line 8:
"Rursum cum suos interrogat: 'Vos quem me esse
dicitis?', capitis personam agit. Petrus totius
populi Christiani voce et vice respondet: 'Tu es
Christus, filius dei vivi.' Nullus enim est in
corpore Christi, a quo non exigatur ista confessio: 'Tu es Christus, filius dei vivi.'
Consimiliter quod Petro dicitur: "Tu es Petrus,
et super hanc petram aedificabo ecclesiam meam, et
tibi dabo claves regni caelorum,' ad universum
populi Christiani corpus pertinet." In later editions of his New Testament Erasmus will qualify
this position somewhat by adding "iuxta quorundam
interpretationem" toward the end of this comment.

[23]Holborn, p. 198, lines 8-12.

[24]Ibid., pp. 198-201.

[25]Ibid., p. 202, lines 1ff.

[26]Novum testamentum omne . . . (Basileae:
Frobenius, 1519), p. 56: "'pétros,' quemadmodum
et Cephas Syro sermone ut testis est Hieronymus
non hebraico soliditatem sonat." Erasmus seems to
be mistaken here: Jerome actually holds that

51

Cephas in both Hebrew and Syrian means "rock."
See PL 26, 366 B where in his commentary on
Galatians he writes: "Non quod aliud significet
Petrus, aliud Cephas: sed quod quam nos Latine et
Graece 'petram' vocemus, hanc Hebraei et Syri
propter linquae inter se viciniam, 'Cephan'
nuncupent."

[27]Novum testamentum (1519), p. 56: ". . . in
quem haud dubie competunt in primis velut in
Christianae fidei principem."

[28]EE IV, 1033, 103, 144-146; 104, 166-170:
"Ausus [Lutherus] est moderatius loqui de potestate Romani Pontificis, sed de qua isti nimis
immoderate prius scripserant; quorum praecipui
sunt tres Praedicatores, Alvarus, Sylvester, et
Cardinalis S. Sixti. . . .
De hoc pessime merentur qui per adulationem
illi tribuunt quod nec ipse agnoscit nec expedit
gregi Christiano. Et tamen nonnulli qui movent
has tragoedias, non faciunt studio Pontificis, sed
huius potestate ad suum quaestum suamque tyran-
nidem abutuntur."

[29]D. Martin Luthers Werke, vol. 2 (Weimar:
Hermann Böhlaus, 1884), p. 384: "Tu itaque,
beatissime pater, cui in primis omnium animarum
fidelium cura delegata est, qui ecclesiae sponsus
ac defensor existis, cuius sponsa super fide tanquam super adaequato constructa est fundamento
(Christo aiente 'Tu es Petrus, et super hanc
petram aedificabo ecclesiam meam'), exsurge tandem
leonino animo fidei christianae turbatores ex-
turbaturus."

[30]Novum testamentum (1519), p. 56: "At non in
hunc unum sed in omnes Christianos, quod elegantur
indicat Origeneshomilia prima, harum quas habemus."

[31]EE I, 165, 376, 9-11 and I, 181, 405, 38-41.

[32]Origen, ". . . In Matth. Homilia I," Opera,
[collected by J. Merlin] (Parisiis: J. Petit and

52

J. Badius Ascensius, 1512), fol. 1: "Interrogat Christus discipulos suos quem eum dicunt homines esse, ut ex apostolorum responsionibus nos discamus diversas opiniones fuisse tunc apud Iudaeos de Christo. Non solum hoc autem: sed etiam illud: ut nos qui volumus esse Christi imitatores: semperscrutemur qualis opinio sit apud homines de nobis."

[33]Ibid." "Forsitan si et nos dixerimus quod dixit Petrus: tu es Christus filius dei vivi: non in carne nobis et sanquine revelante: sed patre qui est in coelis mentem nostram illuminante: erimus Petrus: et eandem beatitudinem consequemur: quam ille: propter confessionem nostram similem confessioni illius."

[34]Ibid., aaa[r-v]: "Si ergo et nos patre nobis sicut diximus revelante: confitentes Jesum esse Christum filium dei vivi: facti fuerimus Petrus: utique et nobis dicetur a deo verbo. Tu es Petrus: et super hanc petram aedificabo ecclesiam meam: et caetera. Petra est enim omnis qui imitator est Christi: ex quo bibebant: qui bibebant de spiritali consequenti petra. Et super omni huiusmodi petra: aedificatur ecclesia dei. In singulis enim quibusque perfectis qui habent in se congregationem verborum: et operum: et sensuum omnium qui huiusmodi beatitudinem operantur: consistit ecclesia dei: cui portae non praevalebunt inferorum. Si autem super unum illum Petrum arbitraris universam ecclesiam aedificari a deo: quid dic de Iacobo: et Ioanne filius tonitrui: vel de singulis apostolis? Vere ergo ad Petrum quidem dictum est: tu es Petrus et super hanc petram aedificabo ecclesiam meam et portae inferorum non praeualebunt ei: tunc omnibus apostolis: et omnibus quibusque perfectis fidelibus dictum videtur: quoniam omnes sunt Petrus: et petrae: et in omnibus aedificata est ecclesia Christi:. . ."

[35]Origen, Origenes Werke, vol. 10, I Origenes Matthäuser-klärung: Die griechisch erhaltenen Tomoi, ed. E. Klostermann, Die griechischen

christlichen Schriftsteller der ersten drei
Jahrhunderte (Leipzig: Hinrich, 1935), Tom. XII,
11, p. 88, lines 6-13: "Καὶ εἴ τις λέγει τοῦτο
πρὸς αὐτόν, οὐ σαρκὸς καὶ αἵματος ἀποκαλυψάντον
αὐτῷ ἀλλὰ τοῦ ἐν τοῖς οὐρανοῖς πατρός, τεύξεται
τὸν εἰρημένον, ὡς μὲν τὸ γράμμα τοῦ εὐαγγελίου
λέγει πρὸς ἐκεῖνον τὸν Πέτρον, ὡς δὲ τὸ πνεῦμα
αὐτοῦ διδάσκει. . ."

[36]Origen, In Exodum Homilia V, PG 12, 329 C-D:
"Sed quis ita beatus est, qui sic tentationum
pondus expediat, ut nulla menti ejus cogitatio
ambiguitatis obrepat? Vide magno illi Ecclesiae
fundamento, et petrae solidissimae, super quam
Christus fundavit Ecclesiam, quid dicatur a Domino: 'Modicae, inquit, fidei, quare dubitasti?'"
Origen also refers to Peter on whom the church is
built in his commentary on John, fifth book,
section three.

[37]Novum testamentum, 1519, [e 5]: "Divus
Cyprianus in epistola primi libri tercia, videtur
accipere super Petrum esse fundata ecclesiam,
Petrus tamen inquiens, super quem ab eodem domino
fundata fuerat ecclesia. Nisi forte sic excusandus est Cyprianus, quod Petrum hic non pro homine
illo, sed pro typo accepit, quod propemodum
indicant quae sequuntur. Unus pro omnibus loquens, et ecclesiae voce respondens, ait, domine
quo ibimus? Itaque Petrus saxeus solidam ecclesiae fidem repraesentat." Note the double plu-
perfect -- a very typical Erasmian construction.

[38]Opera divi Caecilii Cypriani, ed. D. Erasmus
[Basileae: Frobenius, mense Februario, 1520], pp.
9-10: "Nec praepositum seruum deferi a quibusdam
miretur aliquis, quando ipsum dominum magnalia et
mirabilia summa facientem, et virtutes factorum
suorum dei patris testimonio comprobantem, discipuli sui reliquerint, et tamen ille non in-
crepuit recedentes, aut graviter comminatus est,
sed magis conversus ad apostolos suos dixit:
Nunquid et nos vultis ire? seruans scilicet legem
qua homo libertati suae relictus, et in arbitrio

54

proprio constitutus, sibimetipsi vel mortem appetit, vel salutem. Petrus tamen, super quem aedificata ab eodem domine, fuerat ecclesia, unus pro omnibus loquens, et ecclesiae voce respondens, ait: Domine ad quem ibimus? verba vitae aeternae habes, et nos credimus et cognovimus, quoniam tu es filius dei vivi: Significans scilicet et ostendens eos quia Christo recesserint, culpa sua perire, ecclesiam tamen quae in Christum credat, et quae semel id quod cognoverit teneat, numquam ab eo discedere, et eos esse ecclesiam, qui in domo dei permanent."

[39]Cyprian, "Ad Fortunatum," in Sancti Cypriani episcopi opera, pars I, ed. R. Weber, CCSL III (Turnholti: Brepols, 1972), XI, pp. 205-206, lines 106-108: "Cum septem libris plane copulatur et mater, origo et radix, quac ecclesias septem postmodum peperit, ipsa prima et una super Petrum Domini voce fundata."

[40]Cyprian, "De ecclesiae catholicae unitate," in Sancti Cypriani episcopi opera, pars I, ed. M. Benvenot, CCSL III (Turnholti: Brepols, 1972), pp. 251-252, lines 71-126.

[41]Novum testamentum 1519, [e 5]: "Non praevalebunt adversus eam. Notavit huius sermonis amphibologiam Origenes, quod pronomen eam, seu petram referre potest, seu ecclesiam. Verum id ad sententiam perparvi refert."

[42]Ibid.

[43]Desiderius Eramus, "Acta academiae Lovaniensis contra Lutherum" in Erasmi opuscula: A Supplement to the Opera omnia, ed. W. K. Ferguson (The Hague: Nijhoff, 1933), pp. 326-327, lines 122-126: "Omnia, quae hactenus in Lutherum sunt scripta, habent manifestam insaniam. Omnes turpissime adulantur Pontifici, quorum primus fuit Card. Caietanus, et Sylvester Prierias, tertius Thomas Todischus, quartus Augustinus Minorita quidam. Nam Louanienses, ni fallor, non edent

55

suas venias." According to Ferguson (p. 311),
this was written around the end of October or the
beginning of November, 1520.

[44]EE IV, 1183 (written January 28, 1521), 442,
133-139: "Quod hortaris ut Luthero me iungam, id
facile fiet, si illum videro in parte Catholicae
Ecclesiae. Non quod pronunciem illum ab hac
alienum, neque enim meum est damnare quenquam.
Domino suo stat ille aut cadit. Quod si res
devenit ad extremum tumultum, ut utroque mutet
Ecclesiae status, ego me interim in solida illa
petra figum, donec rebus pacatis liquebit ubi sit
Ecclesia; atque illic erit Erasmus, ubicunque
erit Euangelica pax."

[45]EE I, 296, 570, 157-158.

[46]Desiderius Erasmus, . . . Paraphrasis in
Evangelium Matthaei, per D. Erasmum Rot. nunc
denuo recognita . . . ([Basileae: Frobenius,
1522]), [r 6 - r 6ᵛ]: "Hac tam alacri, tamque
solida professione delectatus Iesus: Beatus es,
inquit, Simon fili Ioannis. Istam vocem non tibi
suppeditavit affectus humanus, sed pater coelestis, afflatu secreto suggessit animo. Nullus enim
digne sentit de filio, nisi patris instinctu, qui
solus novit filium. Atque ego vicissim, ne gratis
me tam magnifico testimonio ornaris, illud affirmo, te vere Petrum esse, hoc est, solidum lapidem:
non huc aut illuc vacillantem varijs opinionibus
vulgi, et huic saxo tuae professionis, superstruam
ecclesiam meam, hoc est, domum et palatium meum,
quam ita communiam inixam immobili fundamento, ut
nullae vires regni tartarei valeant illam expug-
nare. Multis machinis vos impetet Satanas, con-
citabit in vos impiorum spirituum cohortem, sed
meo praesidio stabit aedificum meum inexpugnabile,
tantum maneat ista solida professio. Regnum
coeleste est ecclesia: regnum diaboli est mundus.
Ab hoc non est quod quisquam sibi metuat, modo
Petrus sit, hoc est, tui similis. Atque huius
regni coelestis claves tibi sum traditurus.
Convenit enim ut ille primus sit autoritate,

primus est fidei professione et charitate. . . .
Ingredietur autem si apud te professus, quod tu
profiteris, per baptismum solvatur a peccatis:
. . ." According to P. S. Allen, it seems likely
that this octavo edition of the Matthew paraphrase
which I have just cited was printed in April or
May, 1522: EE V, introduction to letter #1255, p.
4. The edition I am working from is identical
regarding Mt. 16:18 with the earlier first editions published at Basel by Froben in March, 1522.

[47]Paraphrasis (1522) [r 5^V]: ". . . voluit
periculum facere, quantum profecissent discipuli,
ex tot sermonibus auditis, ex tot miraculis con-
spectis: et an aliquid sublimius de se sentirent,
quam vulgus."

[48]Paraphrasis (1522), [r 6]: "Hic Simon
Petrus, ut erat amantissimus Ieus, tanquam futurus
ordinis apostolici princeps, omnium nomine respondit: Tu es ille Christus, filius dei vivi, . . .".

[49]See previous note.

[50]The strong dualism here between the church/
heavenly kingdom and the world/kingdom of the
devil is rooted in Origen's dualism.

[51]Novum testamentum, 1527, p. 35.

[52]Erasmus, Annotationes in Matthaeum (1527),
f. 4^V: "In eam sententiam Theophylactus et
Chrysostomus, quam citat Catena aurea."

[53]P. S. Allen, EE VIII, 2239, 305, 52n.

[54]Theophylact, Theophylacti . . . in
quatuor evangelia ennarationes, diligenter
recognitae, tr. Joannes Oecolampad (Basileae:
Craiander, 1527), e 3^V: "Remunerat Petrum dominus,
mercedem illi dans magnam, quod super eum aedifi-
cauit ecclesiam. Quia enim confessus erat eum dei
filium Petrus, dixit, quod haec confessio, quam
confessus est, fundamentum erit futurum creden-

tium, ita ut omnis homo extructurus fidei domum,
hoc iacturus sit fundamentum. Nam licet innumeras
condamus virtutes, non habeamus autem fundamentum
rectam confessionem, inutiliter aedificamus. Quum
autem dixit, ecclesiam meam, ostendit se dominum
universi: deo enim serviunt omnia. . . . Si
igitur in confessione Christi confirmati fuerimus,
portae inferni, hoc est peccata non praeualebunt
nobis."

[55]Thomas Aquinas, . . . Opera omnia, vol. 16:
Catena aurea in Matthaei evangelium . . ., ed.
S.E. Frette (Parisiis: Vives, 1876), p. 295:
"Chrysostomus, hom. LIV Sup. Matth. Idest in hac
fide et confessione aedificabo Ecclesiam meam.
Hinc ostendit multos jam credituros quod Petrus
confessus fuerat, et erigit ejus sensum, et
pastorem ipsum facit."

[56]John Chrysostom, D. Ioannis Chrysostomi
. . . opera, vol. II (Basileae: in officina Frobeniana, 1530), f. 335: "Super hanc petram, non
dixit super Petrum: non enim super hominem, sed
super fidem aedificavit ecclesiam suam. Quid
autem erat fides? Tu es Christus filius dei vivi.
Petram vocavit ecclesiam, fluctus suscipientem, et
non titubantem. Etenim ecclesia tot suscipit
tentationes, non tamen vincitur. Quid est super
petram? hoc est, super confessionem, super sermones pietatis."

[57]John Chrysostom, . . . opera (1530), vol.
III, [CcC 6]: "Et ego dico tibi, quia tu es
Petrus, et super hanc petram aedificabo ecclesiam
meam, id est fidem atque confessionem. Hic aperte
praedixit magnam eorum qui credituri et erant et
sunt multitudinem fore, et sublimiora sapere ipsum
facit, et ecclesiae futurae pastorem constituit."

[58]Annotationes in Matthaeum (1527), p. 68:
"Idem libro retractionum priore, cap. 21 recenset
utranque sententiam, propensior tamen in hanc, ut
Petrus profitens Christum filium dei vivi typum
gerat ecclesiae, cui traditae sint claues.
Caeterum lectori liberum facit eligere, utram

voluerit."

[59]Augustine, D. Avrelii Augustini . . .
omnium operum . . . summa vigilantia repurgatorum
a mendis innumeris . . . vol. 1 (Basileae: [Fro-
benius], 1529), p. 21: "In hoc libro dixi in
quodam loco de apostolo Petro, quod in eo tanquam
in Petra fundata sit ecclesia, qui sensus etiam
cantatur ore multorum in versibus beatissimi
Ambrosij, ubi de gallo gallinateo ait, Hoc ipsa
petra ecclesia Canente, culpam diluit. Sed scio
me postea saepissime sic exposuisse quod a domino
dictum est, Tu es Petrus et super hanc petram
aedificabo ecclesiam meam, ut super hanc intelligeretur quem confessus est Petrus dicens, Tu es
Christus filius dei vivi, ac si Petrus ab hac
petra appellatus, personam ecclesiae figuraret,
quae super hanc petram aedificatur, et accepit
claues regni coelorum. Non enim dictum est illi,
Tu es petra, sed tu es Petrus, petra autem erat
Christus, quem confessus Simon sicut eum tota
ecclesia confitetur, dictus est Petrus. Harum
autem duarum sententiarum quae sit probabilior
eligat lector."

[60]Annotationes in Matthaeum (1527), p. 68:
"Similiter excusari possunt loca in quibus S.
Hieronymus in epistolis videtur dicere, super
Petrum fundatum ecclesiam Christi."

[61]Jerome, Lettres, vol. 1, edited by J.
Labourt (Paris: Les Belles Lettres, 1949), number
15, pp. 45-49.

[62]Jerome, Lettres, vol. 2, edited by J.
Labourt (Paris: Les Belles Lettres, 1949), number
41, pp. 87-90.

[63]Jerome, S. Hieronymi presbyteri opera, pars
I, opera exegetica 7: Commentariorum in
Matthaeum libri IV, CCSL LXXVII (Turnholti:
Brepols, 1969), p. 46, lines 1022-1024: "'Et non
cecidit; fundata enim erat supra petram.' Super
hanc petram Dominus fundavit ecclesiam. Ab hac

petra et apostolus Petrus sortitus est nomen,
. . ."

[64]Ibid., p. 141: "Sicut ipse lumen apostolis donavit ut lumen mundi appellarentur, et cetera quae ex Domino sortiti vocabula sunt: ita et Simoni qui credebat in petram Christum petri largitus est nomen, ac secundam metaphoram petrae recte dicitur ei: Aedificabo ecclesiam meam super te."

[65]Perhaps this was due to the publication of Estienne's critical edition of the Vulgate in 1528.

[66]Erasmus, Novum testamentum iam quintum accuratissima cura recognitum i Des. Erasmo Roter. cum Annotationibus . . . (Basileae: Frobenius, 1535), p. 71.

[67]Index Aureliensis . . ., vol. 5 (Baden-Baden: Foundation Index Aureliensis, 1974), p. 303.

[68]Atlas zur Kirchengeschichte . . . ed. H. Jedin et al (Freiburg im Breisgau: Herder, 1970), 68 B C2.

[69]Valery Andreas, Bibliotheca belgica (Lovanii: Iacobus Zegers, 1643), p. 68; reprint edition: Monumenta humanistica belgica, 5 (Nieuwkoop: B. de Graaf, 1973).

[70]Lucas Wadding, Scriptores ordinis minorum . . . (Romae: ex typographia Francisci Alberti Tani, 1650), p. 34.

[71]Anton Broickwy, . . . in quatuor evangelia annarationum . . . (Coloniae: Quentell, 1539), fo. cxx.

[72]Ibid., fo. cxx[v]: "Hic Simon Petrus, ut erat amantissimus Iesu, tanquam futurus ordinis apostolici princeps, omnium nomine respondit: Tu es Christus, . . ."

[73]Ibid., fo. cxx^v-cxxi: "Et ego affirmo te esse Petrum, hoc est, solidum lapidem, non huc aut illuc vacillantem varijs opinionibus vulgi: et huic saxo tuae professionibus, superstruam ecclesiam meam."

[74]Ibid., fo. cxxi: "Multis machinis impetet vos satanas, sed meo praesidio stabit aedificium meum inexpugnabile, tantum maneat ista solida professio."

[75]Ibid.: "Convenit enim, ut ille primus sit autoritate, qui primus est fidei professione et charitate."

[76]Ibid., fo. cxx^v: "Debitam fidem digna mercede remuneravit."

[77]Ibid., fo. cxxi.

[78]Ibid.: "Hierony. Sicut ipse lumen, apostolis donavit ut lumen mundi appellarentur, caeteraque ex domino fortiti sunt nomina, ita et Simoni qui credebat in petram Christum, Petri largitus est nomen, ac secundum metaphoram petrae, recti dicitur ei, aedificabo ecclesiam meam super te."

[79]P. Feret, La Faculté de théologie de Paris et ses docteurs le plus célèbres, vol. 1: xvie siècle, phases historiques (Paris: Picard, 1900), p. 75.

[80]Sisto da Siena, Bibliotheca sancta (Cologne, 1586), p. 257 as cited in Feret, La Faculte . . ., p. 76.

[81]Richard Simon, Histoire critique des principaux commentateurs du Nouveau Testament . . . (Rotterdam: n. p., 1693), p. 591.

[82]Ibid.: "Pro gloria Evangelii et integritate fidei fortiter incumbis, ut haeretici et haereticorum fautores ultri cibus flammis adurantur et de medio tollantur."

[83]I have not consulted these editions.

[84]For this reason Richard Simon classified d'Arbres as more of a theologian than a critic or commentator in his Histoire critique, pp. 590-591.

[85]Jean d'Arbres, Primus tomus theosophiae . . . (Parisiis: Simon Colinaeus, 1540), p. 171: "Ecclesia fundata est super Petram, et non super Petrum."

[86]D'Arbres, . . . theosophiae . . ., p. 171^V: ". . . in eadem tamen homilia sentire videtur Christum aedificavisse suam Ecclesiam super Petrum, sed vocat Petrum eo in loco fidem Petri et confessionem. Etiam id dixit per Tropum."

[87]Ibid., p. 172^V: "Ex omnibus doctorum sententiis quae pugnare videntur, tametsi non pugnent, brevi colligemus epilogo, Ecclesiam simpliciter et aptissime fundatam esse super petram, et super Petrum, significatione quadam et tropo."

[88]Ibid., p. 171^V: "Ex hac August. doctrina possumus colligere ecclesiam esse in Christo per proprietatem, et Petrum in petra per significationem: maius autem est et excellentius esse in Christo per proprietatem, quam esse in petra per significationem, quare absolutius et longe verius dicimus Ecclesiam esse petram, quam Petrum petram."

[89]Ibid., p. 172^V: "Consideremus deinde Ecclesiam nullo alio quam fidei, inniti fundamento, super quod et spem et charitatem, suam sedem habere dicimus, et ab hac emergere virtute, cui innitendum est, et ab optimo fidei propugnaculo, honestae vitae, bonorumque operum subsidia pendent. Quod si sustuleris fidem, et Ecclesiam subvertes."

[90]Jean François, Bibliothèque générale des écrivains de l'Ordre de Saint Benoit, vol. 1 (Bouillon: Société Typographique, 1777), p. 204;

reprint ed. (Louvain-Heverle: Bibliothèque S.J., 1961).

[91]H. Hurter, Nomenclator literarius . . ., vol. IV: Theologia catholica tempore medii aevi ab anno 1109-1563 (Oeniponte: Libraria academica wagneriana, 1899), p. 1260.

[92]Concilium tridentinum, vol. 5: actorum pars altera, 2nd ed., edited by S. Ehses (Friburgi Brisgoviae: Herder, 1964), p. 149: "Don itaque Isidorus abbas nomine aliorum oravit; ostendere conatus est, studium sacrae scripturae praecipue ad monachos pertinere, . . . Consuluit tamen, esse in decreto cavendum, ne monachi contentiosis et scholasticis lectionibus implicentur, . . ."

[93]Isidoro Chiari, Novi testamenti vulgata quidem aeditio . . ., vol. 2 (Venetijs: Schoeffer, 1541), p. 70.

[94]Ibid., p. 72.

[95]Vulgata aeditio veteris ac novi testamenti, vol. 3 (Venetijs: Schoeffer, 1542), p. 17; Biblia sacrosancta, 2nd edition (Venetiis: Iuntas, 1557, 1564), p. 408[v]; I have been unable to consult his Novi testamenti vulgata published in Antwerp, 1544.

[96]Marcella and Paul Grendler, "The Survival of Erasmus in Italy," Erasmus in English 8 (1976), p. 4.

[97]Venetia: Gio dal Griffo (Grifio), 1547; see Z iv[v] for Mt. 16:18. The Grendlers in "The Survival of Erasmus in Italy," p. 4, discuss Tomitano's problems with the Venetian Holy Office.

[98]Johannes Wild, In sacrosanctum Iesu Christi evangelium secundum Matthaeum commentariorum libri quatuor . . ., 2 vols. (Moguntiae: Behem, 1559), p. 217: "En haec ["Tu es Christus . . .] est fides Petri: imo non tantum Petri, sed et

Pauli, aliorumque apostolorum, imo totius Ecclesiae."

[99]Ibid., p. 217^V: "Sed nunc Christum audiamus: 'Beatus es, inquit Simon Bariona.' Vides hic quod Petri confessionem omnibus alijs praetulit, ac summe colladavit."

[100]Ibid., p. 219.

[101]Ibid.: "Unum hoc dico, potestatem Petri, quam a Christo accepit, ego toto corde et veneror et amplector: neque enim vane sunt verba Christi. Illud tunc etiam ingenue fateor, si successores Petri eo modo potestate sua usi essent quo Petrus, nemo Christianus eam potestatem impugnasset: quia autem plerique; hac potestate abusi sunt, (quemadmodum nemo est qui nesciat) haec causa et seminarium est huius tumultus; neque spes aliqua est tumultum hunc cessaturum, nisi tollatur causa."

[102]Ibid., p. 219^V: "Vides Petrum sic appellatum esse propter fidei confessionem."

[103]Ibid.: "Scriptura petram nonnumquam accipit pro robore, et firmitate, vel securitate."

[104]Ibid., p. 220: "Ex hoc claret, quod Christus Ecclesiam suam non super Petrum, aut quemcumque alium hominem aedificavit: nullus enim homo tam firmus et constans, qui non possit moveri, id quod etiam in Petro manifeste videmus."

[105]Ibid.: "Petra igitur primarie Christus est, cui tota Ecclesia superaedificata est."

[106]Ibid.: "Deinde quia per veram fidem Christo coniungimus, ac sic quodammodo et nos petrascimus, (si sic licet loqui) et ipsa igitur fides Christiana, et veritas Evangelica firma et inconcussa petra illa est, super quam Christus aedificavit Ecclesiam suam."

[107]Ibid.: "Ad Matthaeum revertamur. 'Super hanc, inquit, petram aedificabo Ecclesiam meam.' Petram, cui Ecclesia innititur, supra diximus esse Christum, vel potius fidem veram, id quod ex verbis Christi manifeste colligitur." Italics my own.

[108]Ibid.: "Et subdit, 'Et super hanc petram' super hanc scilicet fidei confessionem, per quam petra effectus es, aedificabo Ecclesiam meam."

[109]Ibid.: "Qui hanc fidem nescit, ad Ecclesiam non pertinet, etiamsi videatur primus esse in Ecclesia."

[110]Antonio R. Rodriguez Monino, La biblioteca de Benito Arias Montano (Budajoz: Impr. de la Diputacion provencial, 1929).

[111]Benito Arias Montano, . . . elucidationes in quatuor evangelia . . . (Antwerpiae: Plantinus, 1575), p. 55: "h. 'Tu es Petrus' Simon non antea dictus est Petrus, quam hoc testimonium protulit a patre Deo revelatum. Et firmitudo Ecclesiae Christi non aedificatur super testimonium de ipso, quatenus propheta est, quamis maximus propheta habeatur, sed quatenus Christus filius Dei vivi est. Id testimonium quoniam Simon vere a Deo doctus primus protulit; Petrus est appellatus primus omnium qui Iesum esse Christum Filium Dei vere agnoverunt et testati sunt. Atque primus habuit promissionem virtutis et efficentiae huius testimonij, non solum in se, sed etiam erga alios. Nam cum Petrus revera et experimento ipso habuit testimonium Dei in se, claves regni caelorum accepit a Christo iam ex hoc loco et tempore promissas."

[112]Ibid., L 1 3[v].

[113]Arias, Liber Ioseph . . . (Antwerpiae: Plantinus, 1572) p. 112: "Petram etiam firmissam illam Christi notitiam exponimus, quam habent ij, qui divini spiritus virtute illustrati sunt, super

quam aedificatur ecclesia Christ, firmissimam; cuiusmodi notitia quia Simon auctus fuit, Petrus a Christo est appellatus."

[114]R. Konetzke, "Valdés, 2, Juan de," Die Religion in Geschichte und Gegenwart, third edition, volume 6 (Tübingen: Siebeck, 1962), p. 1224.

[115]José C. Nieto, Juan de Valdés and the Origins of the Spanish and Italian Reformation (Genève: Droz, 1970), p. 181.

[116]Ibid., pp. 154-158.

[117]Ibid., p. 156, citing Oddone Ortolani, Pietro Carnesecchi . . . (Firenze: Felice le Monnier, 1963), p. 203.

[118]Juan de Valdés, . . . Commentary upon the Gospel of St. Matthew, tr. J. T. Betts (London: Trübner, 1882), p. 15.

[119]Juan de Valdés, El Evangelio según San Mateo . . ., ed. E. Boehmer (Madrid: Libreria Nacional y Extranjera, 1880), pp. 301-302: "Muchas cosas hay en estas palabras, dignas de mucha consideracion, para la intelligencia de las cuales convendria que el hombre estuviese desnudo y despojado de toda afecto humano, de toda opinion humana y aún de todo discurso de prudencia humana."

[120]Ibid., pp. 307-308: "Estos es lo que al presente entiendo en ostas palabras, las cuales son de tanta importantia que, aunque me parece quedar satisfecho con esta inteligencia, todavía quedo con deseo de alcunzar otra mejor, y así ruego á Dios, me la dé ó por sí mismo ó por medio de algun siervo suyo, pero en cuanto ha de servir para gloria suya y de su unigénito hijo Jesu Cristo nuestro Señor."

[121]Ibid., pp. 304-305: "Como gratificando y confirmando Cristo la confession de San Pedro entiendo que dice: 'y yo tambien te digo á tí que

etc., como si dijese: Tú me has confesudo á mí por
Mesía hijo de Dios vivo, y yo te doy á tí este
nombre de piedra por la firmeza que hay en esta tu
confession que es como piedra, y te digo más que
sobre esta piedra edificaré mi iglesia etc.
Adonde entiendo que dice Cristo que habia de
edificar su iglesia sobre la confesion de San
Pedro, entendiendo que, el fundamento de la iglesia es confesar á Cristo por Mesía, hijo de Dios
vivo, . . ."

[122]Ibid., p. 305:   "De esta manera entiendo
que la iglesia cristiana está fundada sobre creer
de Cristo lo que acquí confiesa San Pedro."

CHAPTER II

"PETRA" AS CHRIST

The interpretation of "petra" as Christ,
present in the patristic period and dominant in
medieval exegesis,[1] continues in various ways in
the commentaries on Matthew of John Major, Jacques
Lefevre d'Etaples, Frans Titelmans and François
Vatable.

John Major's "In Matthaeum ad
literam expositio" (1518)

John Major (ca. 1467-1550)[2] wrote two
commentaries on Matthew's gospel. The first
commentary was published by Jean Cranion at Paris
in 1518.

Before commenting on "petra" Major emphasizes that Peter in confessing Jesus as the
Christ responds for all the apostles; he stresses
that Jesus' question was asked of all the apostles
and that Peter was their chief ("praecipuus
Apostolorum").[3] The significance of "praecipuus"
will later be examined in discussing the historical context of Major's 1518 commentary.[4]

Major's position regarding "petra" is
straightforward: the "rock" is what Peter confessed; the qualifying adjective "hanc" does not
point to Peter but to Christ who is the rock.[5]
As evidence for this position Major cites I Cor.
10:4 and Augustine's Retractiones:

'I said in a certain place about the
apostle Peter that on him as on a rock
the church was built.' But I realize

69

that at a later time I frequently so
explained what was said by the Lord,
'Thou art Peter, . . .' that 'on this' he
understood as that which Peter confessed
saying 'Thou art the Christ . . .' . . .
and if Peter was called by this rock he
represents the person of the church,
which is built upon this rock. For 'Thou
art the Rock' was not said to him but
'Thou art Peter'; moreover 'the rock was
Christ' whom Peter confessed, just as the
whole church confesses.[6]

It is important to note what Major does
not cite from Augustine. He omits altogether
Augustine's passing nod to Ambrose's reference to
Peter as the rock upon which the church is built.
He omits Augustine's phrase with reference to
Peter "et accipit claves regni coelorum," perhaps
because in Major's eyes the keys were given to all
the apostles. Finally, Major, like Erasmus, omits
Augustine's stated desire to leave to the reader
the decision whether "petra" is to be understood
as Christ or Peter.

Major also uses as evidence for the position that "petra" is Christ what he calls the
"glossa marginalis" and the "glossa interlinearis":

And the marginal gloss commenting on this
passage holds the same position, thus
saying, 'Peter from me the Rock, so that
I may retain for myself the dignity of
the foundation; you upon me will set in
order the clean stones and reject the
unclean ones.' And the interlinear gloss
says with reference to the word Church,
'that is, Christ in whom you believe.'[7]

Two further questions will be posed of
this commentary: what is the overall structure of
Major's argument? and what is the significance of
his comments on "petra."

70

The structure of Major's commentary seems influenced by the procedures operative in scholastic circles in Paris. He divides chapter sixteen of Matthew into four parts.[8] Jesus' questions in chapter sixteen furnish us with the practice of inquiry; this is significant because Major normally steers far away from the exemplary sense of scripture.[9] After the exposition of chapter sixteen up to and including verse nineteen follow certain "dubitationes" (most of which concern the pope and not the rock);[10] Major relies to a great extent on logical categories in answering these. Following immediately upon these, Major's commentary resumes with Mt. 16:20. This scholastic structure is not surprising, given that Major not only taught but also published commentaries on Peter Lombard's Sententiae during his first teaching stint at the colleges of Montaigu, Navarre, and the Sorbonne at the University of Paris (1509-1517). In fact the College of Montaigu preferred lectures on the Sententiae to lectures on the Bible.[11] This latter emphasis is clearly seen in the "Dialogus de materia Theologo tractanda" between Gawin Douglas and David Cranston, a disciple of Major, attached to Major's commentary of 1519 on the first book of Lombard's Sententiae. To the charge that more theologians are reading Aristotle than the doctors of the church David replies:

> Regarding current subjects writers now at one time introduce the Philosopher, at another time the doctors of the church; using the one they do not omit the other so that this shows that theology, the goddess of the sciences, does not deviate from true philosophy. Through these instructions they nourish the little ones in the faith just as the eloquence of Saint Peter has it: always be prepared to make a defense to everyone calling you to account for that hope which is in you.[12]

71

To the charges that theologians busy themselves
with innumerable frivolous positions and that such
discussions do not help theology but in fact
hinder it, David replies -- and here indicates the
way in which exegesis was regarded within the
Major school:

> Writers have observed this way of writing
> on the Sentences for three hundred years.
> And if you feel that this was done ir-
> rationally, remember the saying that
> custom makes the error common [?] for
> several are desirous for the bible and
> the easier parts of theology [italics
> mine]; others pick out hidden and in-
> tricate calculations. Now according to
> the opinion of the Apostle the theologian
> is indebted to Greeks and barbarians.
> However those questions which they think
> futile frequently provide the ladder of
> intelligence an opportunity to engage in
> sacred letters. Rather, in the front of
> this group our Major is of the same mind
> with his introduction to the fourth book
> of the Sentences as I have frequently
> heard and continue to hear from his
> mouth.[13]

With respect to this scholastic emphasis Major
has sometimes been classified as belonging to the
school of the "Termini" or to "Terminist Scotism."[14]
The clearest statement from Major himself appears
in his preface of 1519 to his In Quartum Sententiarum where he states that although he is em-
ploying Nominalist principles he intends to go
beyond Nominalism by treating theological matters,
thus reconciling Realism and Nominalism.[15]

The historical context for this 1518
commentary will be briefly indicated. The commentary itself was dedicated to James Beaton,
archbishop of Glasgow, who in 1518 induced Major
to leave Paris and to become professor of philosophy and divinity at the University of Glasgow;

Beaton will later play a prominent role as regards Major's second commentary on Matthew (1529). The influence of French conciliarism is also evident in the commentary of 1518. The fourth inquiry added to his commentary on Mt. 16:19 concerns the question whether the Roman pontiff is above the whole church or a universal council representing the church. There he cites two views: that of the canonists, the authorities of the pope and Italy (responding positively to the question) and that of the Council of Constance, the University of Paris and all of France (responding negatively to the question).[16] Although Major up to and beyond this commentary on Matthew took a very minimalist view of the papacy,[17] the strength of his conciliarism cannot match that of the fifteenth century. While Major argued for a qualified monarchial constitution for the church, as late as 1484 prestigious papal electors were still calling for an aristocratic constitution.[18] Also the 1518 commentary on Matthew itself manifests the distance between his own view of the papacy and those of Wyclif and Hus. On the question whether the pope may be called "holy," Major responds that the pope may be called "the Holy Father" since he represents a holy society; he adds that Wyclif and Hus should not scoff at this title.[19] Finally a remark taken from his Sentences commentary of the following year indicates a willingness to acquiesce to the judgment of the Roman church and to the faculty of theology at Paris.[20]

John Major's "...In quatuor Evangelia..." (1529)

Major's second Matthew commentary appeared in 1529 as . . . In quatuor Evangelia expositiones luculente et disquisitiones et disputationes contra hereticos plurime . . .[21] Aside from the scholastic character of this title the preface to the commentary on Matthew itself reflects the scholastic concern to synthesize by

occasionally asking brief questions.[22] The
structure of the body of this commentary comprises
a citation of a segment of the gospel text, an
exposition of that text, with sometimes an "inquiry" added. The commentary concludes with four
"very appropriate" questions: whether the law of
grace is the only true law; what are the degrees
of catholic truth; and discussions of the number
of the evangelists and the site of the Promised
Land.

The text that Major is following is not
that of Erasmus but the common Vulgate rendering
with the significant capitalization of "petra":
"Et ego dico tibi: quia tu es Petrus, et super
hanc Petram aedificabo ecclesiam meam: et portae
inferi non praevalebunt adversus eam."[23]

Major's commentary again stresses that
Peter responds for all; however, more importance
is attributed to Peter -- he was more observant
and less hesitant to speak.[24] After a discussion
of "Beatus tu Simon" one is surprised to find no
exposition of "super hanc petram." Finally at the
end of his comment on locsing and retaining Major
stresses that the papacy has been instituted by
divine law and this institution cannot be rejected
by human powers.[25]

Major then breaks off the continuous
commentary of Mt. 16 in order to pose three questions, the first of which concerns what Jesus
meant by the pronoun "hanc," "Thou art Peter," and
"upon this rock I will build my church."[26] He
proceeds to distinguish different meanings regarding "hanc." The Glossa interlinearis cites
Christ, as does the Glossa ordinaria.[27]
Chrysostom, on the other hand, favors "faith" and
"confession." Chrysostom was easily accessible in
western Europe at this time[28] and thus his rendering of "petra" in terms of "fides" and "confessio" would have been widely known. As in the
earlier commentary Augustine is mentioned; however, Major abbreviates Augustine still further

here. He cites Augustine's rendering of "petra" in terms both of Peter and Christ; the part that he omits deals with Peter as a figure of the church confessing the true Rock of the Church, that is, Christ.[29] The next opinion cited is that of Pierre d'Ailly (died 1420), chancellor of the University of Paris, later bishop and cardinal, and thoroughgoing Occamist. Major points out that Pierre d'Ailly in his "vespers" follows Augustine's interpretation of "petra" in terms of Christ.[30] However, one looks in vain for this position in d'Ailly's "Questio vesperiarum";[31] therefore Major must be thinking of d'Ailly's "Recommendatio sacrae scripturae . . . ." This little sermon delivered at d'Ailly's inaugural lecture as a "magister" deals entirely with Mt. 16:18. He cites the diversity of understanding among the fathers, showing that "petra" was taken both as Peter and as Christ.[32] He himself favors the Christological interpretation, citing I Cor. 10:4.[33] Later he allows and concedes for the sake of concord that although Christ is the principal foundation of the church, several foundations can be built upon Christ.[34] D'Ailly also distinguished between two senses of scripture and applied this to Mt. 16:18: if according to the literal sense we can understand either Peter or Christ with respect to "petra," then according to the spiritual sense we can understand divine scripture and the holy teaching of Christ.[35]

Major then cites the variety of opinions in his own day: "not a few eminent in lives and letters are divided, some affirming that Christ indicated Peter by the pronoun 'hanc'; it seems to several others that both Christ and Peter are indicated, Christ himself first as the foundation in place of which no one can put another, and then with Christ indicating by hand ("progrediente manu") Peter as the vicar and future leader of the church."[36] Although Major does not specify here whom he has in mind by those eminent in lives and letters, it seems probable that he was thinking of some of his colleagues at the College of Montaigu

in Paris.[37] Regarding those who took "hanc" in
terms of Peter by 1529, certain Romanists would
have to be mentioned: Juan de Torquemada, Tommaso
de Vio, and Leo X. The other position held by
some prominent men ("hanc" refers to Christ
primarily and Peter secondarily) had already
become a prominent Roman Catholic way of dealing
with Luther's claims that the rock was Christ.[38]

Major then proceeds to give an explanation
for this last position (something he had not done
with respect to the other positions): "For if
Jesus had wanted to indicate himself alone, in
vain would he have addressed Peter, and if Jesus
had wanted to indicate Peter alone he would have
not have said 'this' but 'that,' but saying 'this'
he indicated the one power of each of them, although in such a way that he and not Peter builds
the church."[39]

Major's final comment amidst all this
diversity of opinion is that the particular position one adopts on "petra" is not all that important; what is important is that "we hold that the
governance of the church was promised and given to
Peter"; holding this position, for Major, is identical to rejecting the opposing heretical view.[40]

What explanation can be given for the
definite change of position on the rock in the two
commentaries? One suggestion is that the anti-
Lutheran climate in Paris contributed to the
change.[41] Certainly there is something to this.
The theological faculty of the University of Paris
on April 15, 1521, condemned certain views of
Martin Luther especially as excerpted from his
De captivitate Babylonica ecclesiae (1520); among
other charges, the Paris theologians found Luther's
writings destructive of the hierarchical order and
heretical. Although no reference to Luther's exegesis of Mt. 16:18 or views on papal power is
contained in the statement, the text explicitly
opposes Luther's view that the keys of the church
belong to all Christians.[42] It should be noted

76

that Major did not take part in this condemnation
for he was by then back teaching in his native
Scotland. There are clear signs also of the anti-
Lutheran climate in Scotland at this time. The
Scottish Parliament in 1525 (by which time Major
had returned to Paris) condemned Luther, his
followers and their theological positions; this
Act also forbade the importing of Luther's books
by ships and the teaching of Luther's positions.[43]
Those violating these statutes were subject to
forfeiture of ships and goods and imprisonment;
nobles especially were singled out in an addition
to this Act on September 5, 1527.[44]

Major's own writings of the 1520's witness
to this new climate. The prefatory letter to the
1529 commentary on Matthew which was addressed to
James Beaton, then archbishop of Saint Andrews,
primate of Scotland and papal legate, states that
one of the purposes of his commentary was "to
safeguard the ancient translation and the catholic
traditions according to the doctrine of the Roman
church and received through the doctors."[45] He
also saw his commentary as clearly opposed to "the
Wycliffites, Hussites, and following close behind
them, the Lutherans."[46] This preface calls
special attention to Beaton's efforts to eradicate
heresy from Scotland: he is praised for having
uprooted the Lutheran heresy in Scotland and
especially for "having removed an unfortunate
follower of Lutheran heresy and treachery."[47]
Major is thinking specifically of the burning of
Patrick Hamilton at Saint Andrew's in 1528.
Hamilton, a student of Major's, had personally met
both Luther and Melanchthon in 1527 and may
definitely be identified as a Lutheran. Upon his
return to Scotland and the publication of his
Loci communes Hamilton encountered the wrath of
the archbishop. Although his Loci communes contains no mention of Mt. 16:18 and no remarks
concerning the pope, an observer mentions that,
among other charges, the archbishop objected to
Hamilton's holding that the Pope is the Antichrist.[48] Major's later works mention similar

77

Lutheran castigations. One in particular mentions that the Parisian theologians have been so occupied with sacred letters in order to fight Luther and his views that the investigation of the Sentences has lapsed; "ordinary matters" now rule the day.[49]

Another possible explanation for the change regarding "petra" may be attributed not to the reformation in Germany and Scotland but rather to the reformation in England. At least one English bishop and supporter of Henry VIII stated in 1531 before the House of Commons that "John Majoris, a great doctor of Paris, who had composed a book on this question [the marriage between Henry and Catherine of Aragon] in favor of the dispensing power of the Pope [Henry VIII opposed this in 1531], had confessed to him that he had so concluded in order more to please the Pope, and favor the authority of the Holy See; . . ."[50] This bishop of London was arguing for the position that the marriage was illegal and he was citing in favor of his position various European universities and calling into question the position of those such as Major who argued in favor of the pope's jurisdiction over such cases. If all this true, then Major moved to a pro-papal position in opposition to Henry VIII's claims and thus adapted his comments on Matthew accordingly to support the power of the pope rather than the jurisdiction of universities or secular rulers. But this is the lone evidence and it was called into question by Chapuys, ambassador of Charles V to the English court, who characterized the testimony of the earlier named bishop as a lie.[51]

Although the evidence for an anti-Lutheran explanation of Major's change is substantial, nevertheless, there is still one more possibility to consider and it is this: Major's change regarding Mt. 16:18 can be seen as a return to the scholastic mode of arguing in which the magister is concerned to present both sides of an argument, sometimes giving his own view, but sometimes not.

For example, compare the exposition we have just
investigated with Major's discussion of taxation
in his Historia maioris Britanniae of 1521. There
he presents arguments both for and against taxation, de-emphasizing his own opinion in favor of
the merits of the case itself:

> Here the question of taxes presents
> itself for debate and we examine each
> side. Foremost against the manner of the
> governor proceeding, that is, taxing I
> argue thus . . . . For the same position
> I argue so: . . . Thirdly, I argue in
> such a way . . . . Fourthly I argue
> so . . . . The opposing side is argued
> so . . . . But to this objection it can
> be responded . . . . Scarcely without
> the ill will of the other side someone
> can here respond analytically and clear-
> ly. The clever person can perceive from
> what has been said my own opinion (which
> I leave to the judgment of the prudent
> one to take a part).[52]

Jacques Lefèvre d'Etaples' "Commentarii initiatorii . . ." (1522)

Jacques Lefèvre d'Etaples (ca. 1460-1536)[53]
probably received the masters degree from the
University of Paris in 1480; he had no theological
training as such. From 1508 to 1520 he was involved in scholarly work at the Abbey of Saint-
Germain-des-Prés. In spring of 1521 he was
called to Meaux to assist Bishop Guillaume Briçonnet with a comprehensive program of diocesan
reform. The Biblical commentaries of Lefèvre were
thus authored and directed toward reform of a
church which was described by Bishop Briçonnet as
"arid and dry," one whose waters of "life, doctrine and virtue" had been dried up by "the heat
of avarice, ambition and voluptuous living."[54]

Lefèvre's commentary on Matthew was prepared in 1521 and published in June of 1522.[55]

The opening "Praefatio," written in 1521, is
significant for an understanding of all of Lefèvre's Biblical commentaries. First, there is a
strong emphasis on the "primaeva ecclesia," that
is the church as it existed before the reign of
Constantine: that church is a model of believing,
that church practiced "evangelium solum," that
church's image is the hoped for goal of the
contemporary age.[56] Although Lefèvre's commentary
omits all references to the age of this primitive
church, nevertheless the tone of his comments
hearkens back to the patristic age. Secondly, the
"Praefatio" stresses the need for singlemindedness
regarding the sufficiency of the "verbum Dei";
Lefèvre's emphasis on the "verba mea" of Matthew
7:24-25 in exegeting Mt. 16:18 will reflect this
emphasis.[57] Thirdly, the prefatory letter stresses
the priority of believing over understanding; the
Mt. 16:18 exegesis will also stress not what
Jesus' contemporaries understood about him, but
rather what Peter believed about Jesus.[58]
Fourthly, the letter sheds light on the nature of
the commentary that Lefèvre is writing: his commentary dispels darkness and prepares the way for
the breaking in of God's light. His commentary is
thus purgative and initiatory in distinction from
commentaries of illumination and perfection.[59]
Lefèvre ends this note by describing the arrangement of the commentary: he gives the Vulgate
rendering (even though Erasmus' translation was
known by him), followed by brief annotations which
deal mainly with textual criticism and the commentary itself, also concerned with "purgation."[60]
His mathematical interest is also present in the
commentaries in that he is the first to use numbers in the outer margin and in the text itself to
refer the reader to the "commentary" and "annotations" respectively.

Lefèvre's commentary, like many others
that we have already seen, stresses that Peter
speaks for all and that he utters divine truth,
not human opinion.[61] The divine character of
Peter's response is then indicated: Peter's

response was infused by God himself and Christ's consequent word of blessing says much more about the revelation of the heavenly Father than about Peter himself (Peter is blessed because of the Father's activity). Then he adds that the Father alone is blessed.[62] Lefèvre stresses that this solid confession of faith is firmer than any rock.[63] On this rock and faith of this unshakeable truth (that Jesus is the Christ, the son of the living God) Christ the Lord founded his church.[64]

Lefèvre then defines what the rock is: Christ and the Word of God (which are identical for him). The reason for this is the text of Mt. 7:24 ("Therefore everyone who hears these my words and does them will be like the wise man who built his home above the rock").[65] Lefèvre is well aware of how he is interpreting "petra" here for he calls the reader's attention to his interpretation in the following remark: "Note the manner in which Jesus calls himself and his word 'the rock,' and certainly a firm rock, upon which the unshakeable home that is the church is built, lest someone say that Peter is the rock upon which the church is founded."[66] Lefevre is making a unique contribution here to commenting on "petra" in the sixteenth century: He is the only sixteenth century exegete to make the movement from the "petra" of Mt. 16:18 back to the "petra" of Mt. 7:24-25. Medieval commenting on the rock of Mt. 16:18 also had in mind the rock of Mt. 7:24-25.[67] Previous exegesis going back to Origen had made the movement in the other direction, that is, from Mt. 7:24-25 to Mt. 16:18.[68]

What also is going forward here is Lefèvre's concern to stress clearly that the "petra" is Christ and not Peter;[69] the reason that Peter is neither a rock nor a firm rock is that the Lord afterwards calls him Satan.[70] This remark is reinforced later in his commentary when he again clearly differentiates Peter from "petra": "And if it is said (as certain people want to say) that

81

'Peter' comes from 'rock' just as 'Christian' comes from 'Christ,' it must also be said that the individual Christian is not Christ and Peter is not the rock."[71]   Between these references to Peter, Lefèvre inserts another argument for exegeting "petra" in terms of Christ, that is, Paul's testimony that Christ is the rock.[72]

The Christological interpretation is repeated later in his commentary on Matthew 16. He points out that the keys belong not only to Peter but to all those who in faith are built upon Christ.[73]   And at the end of his discussion of the keys he stresses that the doctrine (Jesus is the son of the living God) objectively refers to Christ himself "who is that rock and unshakeable foundation of the entire church" and subjectively refers to the divine infusion of the eternal Father in us.[74]

Note that in this whole discussion of our text no church father was mentioned, although we have noticed a similarity between Lefèvre and Augustine regarding the Petrus a petra argument. It has been argued that Lefèvre is working under the inspiration of Augustine in his comments on Mt. 16:18-19;[75] but this does not seem to be the case.   Although there is a certain identity between Lefèvre's position and one of Augustine's positions on "petra," Augustine does not use Matthew 7:24-25 in explaining the rock of Mt. 16:18.   The identity between Lefèvre's position and that of Guillaume Briçonnet, Bishop of Meaux and Lefèvre's sponsor, has been correctly noted.[76] However, the bishop's correspondence before the publication of Lefèvre's Commentarii does not mention the "petra" of Mt. 16:18; rather the bishop's understanding of "petra=Christus" does not occur until later.

This investigation of Lefèvre's exegesis has shown an intense emphasis on the verbum Dei and the verba Christi as key interpretative categories for Mt. 16:18.   How this would relate

in turn to suggestions regarding the Begriffflich-
keit of Lefèvre's writings (for example,
"humanist Aristotelianism"[77] and theological
humanism[78]) is the subject of a wider study.

Titelmans' "Elucidatio paraphrastica sancti evangelii secundum Matthaeum" (1545)

Frans Titelmans was born around 1502 in
Hasselt (Belgium). In 1526 he entered the Franciscans of the Observance at Louvain. There from
1526 to 1535 he taught philosophy and theology
(mainly courses dealing with New Testament books)
and lectured on Scripture at the Convent School.
He distinguished himself by his knowledge of
Biblical languages, although he defended the
Vulgata editio against the reforms of Valla,
Lefevre and Erasmus. In 1535 he was drawn to Rome
by the ideals of the Capuchin reform and in 1536
joined the Capuchins there. He is generally
thought to have died in 1537. His commentary on
Matthew was published posthumously: Antwerp,
1545, 1576; Paris, 1546; Lyons, 1547, 1556.

His Matthew commentary is fashioned
along the lines of theology and philology: first
comes the elucidatio of the text by way of paraphrase and expansion (the text itself being high-
lighted in the inner margin); then occur brief
annotationes on the chapter under discussion.

As in almost every commentary thus far
considered, Peter answers and brings forth the
confession of truth in the name of all the apostles, indeed as the mouthpiece of the apostles.[79]
This same leveling of Peter's uniqueness is seen
in the paraphrase of Peter's confession: "we
believe and profess . . ."[80] The content of
Peter's confession reflects the church's later
credal and conciliar statements about Jesus: ". .
. the Christ, the son of the living God, . . .
true man and God, consubstantial son and coequal
of God the Father who is the true and living

83

God."[81] But Titelmans is not adopting a conciliarist position by these remarks, for he later
stresses that Peter alone is established in power
because of his "confessio veritatis" and that a
certain enduring authority will be entrusted to
Peter and his successors.[82]

        Titelmans then paraphrases our rock
passage: "And on this rock, upon this truth of
faith which you have confessed and which you have
brought forth, saying 'Thou art the Christ . . .,'
likewise ("item") as well upon me the firmest
rock, which you have confessed in this statement,
I will build and construct the edifice of my
church, which I want to build for my Father."[83]
In support of this position that the rock is the
"veritas fidei" and Christ, Titelmans paraphrases
I Cor. 3:11: "For no one can establish any other
foundation than what I establish since I truly am
Christ Jesus . . ."[84] This movement from the
"petra" of Mt. 16:18 to the "fundamentum" of I
Cor. 3:11 was not unique to Titelmans. The
Dominican cardinal Hugo de Sancto Charo (died
1263) glosses "et super hanc petram" with "that is
upon this foundation . . . . I Corinthians 3
. . .:"[85] Titelmans adds by way of explanation
and perhaps to separate the "confessio veritatis"
of Peter from the "veritas fidei et confessionis"
which is Christ: "and the very truth of faith and
confession about me will be the foundation of the
whole building."[86]

        His annotations on Matthew 16 make no
mention of "petra."

François Vatable's Annotations
on Matthew's Gospel

        François Vatable was born at Gamaches in
the Picardy region of France around 1493.[87] His
early life was spent in close association with
Lefèvre: in 1516 he was described as Lefèvre's
"discipulus";[88] he later lived with Lefèvre at
Saint-Germain-des-Prés and accompanied him to

84

Meaux where they both participated in Bishop
Briconnet's reform; this association lasted
through 1528. Vatable was regarded as one of the
finest Hebraists in Europe, although he was by no
means deficient in Greek. When Francis I established the College de France in 1530 he was
installed as "royal professor of Hebrew letters."
Soon after this the attacks from the Sorbonne
faculty began under Beda's instigation; the content of the charges was that Vatable and others
were neglecting and casting doubts about the
Vulgate edition by their emphasis on Greek and
Hebrew letters.

Though he published nothing of his own
during his lifetime, he translated much of Aristotle into Latin and edited some of Lefevre's
philosophical works (1528-1536).

From 1539 to 1545 at Paris Robert
Estienne published a Bible containing the annotations of Vatable on both Testaments, together
with the Vulgate translation and the new version
of Leon de Juda. These annotations drew on lecture notes taken by Vatable's students and were
later inveighed against by the Sorbonne faculty
and even disowned by Vatable himself. In 1552 or
1553[89] was published his Annotationes in Novum
Testamentum. The notes are very brief and consist
of paraphrases of the Latin comments on syntactical points, giving the Vulgate and other ren-
derings of a particular word, short explanations
of the meanings of particular words and the Hebrew
background for words and ideas. To "Quia tu es
Petrus, etc." is affixed: "I have named thee
Peter because finally you were about to proclaim
that I am the Rock ("Petram"), a very solid one
("rupem")."[90] This is significant in that according to Vatable Jesus calls Peter "Peter" not
in view of his earlier confession but in antici-
pation of Peter calling Jesus "petra." The rock
beats Peter to the punch.

Other posthumous editions of Vatable's
notes appeared in the 1557 Geneva edition, the

1564 Basil edition, the 1584-1585 Salamanca edition (reprinted in 1605 and 1729), and a 1599
Leiden edition. The Salamanca edition of 1584-
1585 was purged by the university theologians
there and was published with the approval of the
Spanish inquisition.

Conclusion

        The petra=Christus interpretation of Mt.
16:18 occurs four times between 1518 (Major) and
1553 (Vatable), sometimes with slight nuances:
Christ and his word, the truth of faith ("veritas
fidei") and Christ. The exegetes holding to this
view share no common school and indeed represent
very different sixteenth century movements (scholasticism, conciliarism, humanism) and views
(defenders and critics of the Vulgate edition).
They share with the petra=fides position the
notion that Peter is speaking on behalf of all the
apostles and not on his own. They also share a
common argument for their position: the firmness
and solidity of the rock mentioned in Mt. 16:18
can point only to Christ and certainly not to the
very fluctuating and unstable Peter; this argument
stands in clear continuity with the medieval
argument for petra=Christus. Other supports for
this interpretation also continue medieval lines,
specifically the practice of interpreting Mt.
16:18 in terms of Mt. 7:24 (Vulgate: "Every one
therefore that heareth these my words and doth
them shall be likened to a wise man that built his
house upon a rock"), and I Cor. 3:11 (Vulgate:
"For other foundation no man can lay, but that
which is laid: which is Christ Jesus"). While not
continuing the medieval reliance on Ephesians 2:20
(Vulgate: "Built upon the foundation of the
apostles and prophets, Jesus Christ himself being
the chief corner stone:"), I Cor. 10:4 is utilized:
(Vulgate: "And they all drank the same spiritual
drink: And they drank of the spiritual rock that
followed them: and the rock was Christ"). These
exegetes together make but one reference to a

patristic writer (Augustine) in support for their position and although they continue the dominant medieval interpretation, only Pierre d'Ailly is explicitly mentioned in this regard.

One should note, however, that this interpretation is the weakest (in terms of numbers) strain within sixteenth century Roman Catholic exegesis, unlike that of the middle ages where the petra=Christus position was the most popular one. John Major's shift from a solely Christological interpretation to one including both Christ and Peter might be the key to understanding the decline of this interpretation; Major, among other factors, seems to have been influenced by the anti-Luther climate in France and Scotland and by his concern to protect Peter's governance of the church.

[1]Fröhlich, Formen, pp. 159-160

[2]The precise date of Major's birth is controverted: see A. MacKay, "Life of the Author," in John Major, A History of Greater Britain as well England as Scotland . . . (Edinburgh: Edinburgh University Press, 1892), p. xxix and James H. Burns, "New Light on John Major," Innes Review 5 (1954), pp. 83-100.

[3]Joannes Major, In Matthaeum ad literam expositio, una cum recentis et octo dubijs et difficultatibus ad eius elucidationem admodum conducentibus passim insertis quibus perlectis pervia erit quatuor evangelistarum series (Parisiis: Granion, 1518), f. 59^v; reprinted in Opera omnia Joannis Gersonii, ed. L. du Pin, 5 vols. (Antwerpiae: sumptibus Societatis, 1706), II: 1146 D - 1147: "Quaestio movebatur omnibus Apostolis, respondit Petrus pro omnibus . . . . . . Quando quaesivit quid sentirent Apostoli, Petrus pro omnibus respondit, quia Apostolorum erat praecipuus: . . ."

[4]Major's commentary also seems to minimize Peter in that there is no comment on "Tu es Petrus."

[5]Ibid., p. 1147 A: "'Et ego dico tibi, quia tu es Petrus, et super hanc Petram,' quam confessus es, 'aedificabo Ecclesiam meam.' . . . Hoc pronomen 'hanc,' non demonstrat Petrum, sed Christum qui est Petra: . . ." The 1529 commentary will show that here Major is following Pierre d'Ailly.

[6]Ibid., p. 1147 A-B: ". . . 'Petra autem erat Christus. Primae Corinthiorum x.4. Et Augustinus, in Libro Retractionum sic inquit: 'Dixi in quodam loco de Apostolo Petro, quod in illo tanquam in Petra aedificata est Ecclesia.' Sed

scio me postea saepissime sic exposuisse quod a
Domino dictum est, 'Tu es Petrus, et super hanc
Petram aedificabo Ecclesiam meam' ut, 'super hanc'
intelligeretur quem confessus est Petrus dicens:
'Tu es Christus Filius Dei vivi' . . . ac si
Petrus ab hac Petra appellatus, personam Ecclesiae
figuraret, quae super hanc Petram aedificatur.
Non enim dictum est illi, Tu es Petra, sed 'Tu es
Petrus: Petra autem erat Christus,' quem confessus
est Simon, sicut tota Ecclesia confitetur." Major
was not using the editio princeps of Augustine's
works published at Basel in 1506 and at Paris in
1515.

[7]Ibid., p. 1147 B: "Et Glossa marginalis
illud exponens idem tenet, sic inquiens, 'Petrus a
me Petra, ita ut mihi retineam dignitatem fundamenti: tu super me ordinabis lapides mundos et
abjicies leprosos.' Et Interlinearis in verbo
'Ecclesiam,' dicit 'id est, Christum, in quem
credis.'" Alexandre Ganoczy in his "Jean Major,
exégète gallican," Recherches de Science
religieuse 56 (1968), p. 462, n. 18 holds that
Major was using the Bible published by Froben at
Basel during 1498-1502. This Bible also contained
the commentary of Nicolas of Lyra who glossed
"petram" with "quam confessus es, id est, super
Christum."

[8]Ibid., p. 1145 C: "Hujus capitis decimi
sexti quatuor sunt principales partes."

[9]Ibid., p. 1146 C: "Hic [Mt. 16:13] datur
nobis exemplum quaerendi, quae opinio in vulgo de
nobis habetur, ut si invenerimus malam, et mali
tali societate fiamus, eam fugiamus; si bonam, in
illa continuemus . . ."

[10]Ibid., p. 1147 C: "Circa hanc literam
dubitatur . . ."

[11]Augustin Renaudet, Préréforme et humanisme
à Paris pendant les premières querres d'Italie
(1494-1517), 2d ed., rev. and corr. (Paris:
Librairie d'Argences, 1953), p. 470.

[12]"Dialogus de materia Theologo tractanda," in Joannes Major, In primum Sententiarum (Paris: [Ascensius], 1519), p. [a ii]: "Secundum materias occurrentes nunc philosophum nunc doctores ecclesiae scribentes introducunt: unumque facientes aliud non omittunt: ut theologiam scientiarum deam a vera philosophia non deviare ostendant: et ut parvulos per manuductiones in fide alant: secundum beati Petri eloquium: parati semper ad sanctificationem omni poscenti vos rationem de ea quae in vobis est spe."

[13]Ibid.: "Hunc modum scribendi in sententias a trecentis annis scriptores observavere: et si praeter rationem id factum esse censeas ius (ut vulgariter aiunt) communis error facit. bibliam et faciliores theologiae partes nonnulli exoptant. abscensas et intricatas calculationes alii: modo (secundum apostoli sententiam) Graecis et Barbaris debitor est theologus. Eae autem quas existimant quaestiones futiles crebro scalam intelligentiae ad sacras literas capessendas praestant. Quinetiam in fronte huius primi Maior noster eiusdem est mentis cum exordio quarti. sicut frequenter ab eius ore accepi, et accipio."

[14]MacKay, "Note on the School of the Terminists to which John Major Belonged," in John Major, A History of Greater Britain, p. cxxv.

[15]John Major, ". . . in exordio praelectionis lib. quarti sententiarum ad auditores propositio," In Quartum Sententiarum (Paris: Badius, 1519) in John Major's History, p. 438: "Insuper nominalium adhuc vidi neminem qui opus in Quartum ad umbilicum calcemque perduxerit: quod in eos tanquam probrosum alii retorquent dicentes nominales logice et philosophie sic implicari ut theosophiam negligant: et tamen varia sunt theologica quae metaphysicam praesupponebant. Conebor ergo nominalium principiis adhibitis in singulas distinctiones Quarti unam quaestionem vel plures scribere quas et reales si advertant facile capient. Utrinque enim viae theologica (circa

quam praecipue versabor) erit communis."

[16]Opera . . . Gersonii, II: 1150 A-B: "Unus, quem Canonistae, authoritatibus Pontificis Maximi stipati tenent cum Italia, quod Pontifex est etiam supra Concilium rite congregatum, quod repraesentat universalem Ecclesiam. Alius est modus, qui Constantiae conclusus est, omnino illi oppositus: unde nostra Universitatis, et Gallia tota insequitur oppositum." Ganoczy in "Jean Major, exégète gallican," p. 464 suggests that this commentary manifests conciliarist preoccupations in the line of Gerson; he emphasizes that Major's reference to Peter as "praecipuus" not "principalis" reflects Gerson's distinction between having the power of the church and having power over the church. Here we might note that Julius II while addressing French cardinals and prelates with his "Salvator dominus noster" of 1512 refers to Peter as ". . . coelestis regni clavigero, apostoloque principi, . . ." (See Mansi, vol. 32, col. 574.)

[17]In his comments on distinction twenty-four of the fourth book of the Sentences (1509), Major says very little about the pope and what he does say is either very situational (whether it is proper for a pope to allow an indidivual to hold several benefices) or very restrictive of the pope's power ("papa nec est deus nec conditor nature sed eis subiectus . . ."). See John Major, Quartus Sententiarum . . . (Parisiis: Ponchetus, 1509), f. 139-140.

[18]Cesare Baronio, Odorico Rinaldi, and James Laderchi, Annales ecclesiastici, 37 vols. (Barri-Ducis: Bertrand, 1877), 30: year 1484, n. 28.

[19]Opera . . . Gersonii, II: 1149 C: "Ex hoc patet, quod potest talis loqutio admitti: Papa est Pater Sanctus, licet fit in mortali, quia praeest uni sanctae Societati. Wicleff et Huz illum modum loquendi non debuerunt irridere, cum habeat sensum sufficienter verum."

[20]John Major, ". . . in exordio praelectionis lib. quarti sententiarum ad auditores propositio," In Quartum Sententiarum (1519), p. 439: "Caeterum si in hoc opere vel in alio in lucem emisso vel emittendo erraverim sacrosanctae Romanae ecclesiae et aliis facultatis theologiae Parisiensis matris meae acquiesco indicio: et quod ille approbant vel reprobant hoc ipsum approbo vel reprehendo."

[21]Parisiis: Badius, 1529.

[22]John Major, In Matth. in Major's History, p. 447: "Denique ut summatim dicamus, nullum locum vel mediocriter docto ambiguum indiscussum praetermisimus, intermiscentes subinde breves quaestiunculas; . . ."

[23]John Major, In quatuor Evangelia expositiones, f. 64.

[24]Ibid., f. [64^V]: "Omnium vice respondet Petrus. Tu es Christus filius dei vivi. Serijs in rebus (ut credere par est) Apostoli inter sese sermocinabantur. Simon reliquis serventior nec ad loquendum tardus pro omnibus respondit."

[25]Ibid., lines 91-92: "Attamen divino iure summus potificatus est institutus, nullis humanis viribus antiquandus."

[26]Ibid., lines 94-95: "Hic nonnulla disquiremus. Primo quid Christus demonstravit per pronomen hanc, Tu es Petrus et super hanc petram aedificabo ecclesiam meam."

[27]Ibid., lines 98-100: "Commentarius interlinearis per hanc petram dicit Christum in quem Petrus credidit demonstrari. Ac marginalis glossa ait: a me Petra, ita ut mihi retineam dignitatem fundamenti, tu super me ordinabis lapides mundos et abijcies leprosos."

[28]Editions of his works appeared in 1466, 1470, 1475, 1476, 1482, 1487, 1494 and 1520.

[29]Ibid., lines 101-104: "Dixi in quodam loco de Apostolo Petro quod in illo tanquam in Petra aedificata est ecclesia, sed scio me postea saepissime sic exposuisse quod a domino dictum est. Tu es Petrus et super hanc Petram aedificabo ecclesiam mean. Ut super hanc intelligeretur quam confessus est Petrus, dicens: Tu es Christus filius dei vivi."

[30]Ibid., lines 104-105: "Quamviam Aliaccensis in suis vesperijs imitatus est: . . ."

[31]There the question d'Ailly is examining is "Utrum petri ecclesia lege reguletur." While Mt. 16:18 is employed twice, in neither place is he concerned with defining the sense of "hanc." See Pierre d'Ailly, Questiones . . . super primum, tertium et quartum sententiarum . . . Theologiae laudes una cum principio in cursum bibliae. Questiones in vesperiis . . . (n.p.: Johannes Petit, n.d.), f. cclxxvii-cclxxx.

[32]Pierre d'Ailly, "Recommendatio sacrae scripturae. . ." in Questiones, f. cclxix: "Ubi ex variis sanctorum dictis magna oritur prolixitas quaestionis."

[33]Ibid.: ". . . non tamen videtur quod in petra petrus. sed in petra christus sit intelligendus de quo agit apostolus. petra autem erat Christus prima Corinthios. 10."

[34]Ibid., f. cclxix^V.

[35]Ibid.: "Sed salva omnino christi salvatoris sententia: sive in petra petrum: sive in petra christum secundum litteralem sensum intelligere valeamus. tamen secundum spiritualem intellectum per hanc petram divinam scripturam et sacram christi doctrinam signare possumus."

[36]Major, In quatuor Euangelia expositiones, f. [64^V], lines 105-108: ". . . nec pauci alii literis moribusque praestantes diversificantur affirmantes alii Christum per pronomen hanc Petrum

94

indicasse. Nonnullis videtur utrumque indicasse, se primum tanquam fundamentum praeter quod nemo aliud potest ponere, et deinde progrediente manu, Petrum, tanquam vicarium et ecclesiae futurum principem." I have been unable to trace the roots of the interesting phrase "progrediente manu."

[37]Major's prefatory address to Noël Beda, Pierre Tempeste and other scholastics at Montaigu ends "Ex Montisacuti collegio literis et moribus decorato..." See Major, In secundum Sententiarum disputationes denuo recognitae et repurgatae (Parisiis: Parvus and Badius, 1528); reprinted in A History of Greater Britain . . ., p. 441.

[38]John Fisher is an excellent example of this. Some fifteenth century writers such as Thomas Netter also adopted the double position.

[39]Ibid., f. [64^V]-65: "Nam si se solum indicaret, frustra Petrum compellasset, et si solum Petrum, non hanc sed istam dixisset, dicens autem hanc, unam indicat utriusque potestatem, sic tamen ut ipse non Petrus aedificet."

[40]Ibid., f. 65: "Sed non magnopere interest, modo teneamus habenas ecclesiae Petro promissas atque collatas: quem modum ubique fovemus oppositum tanquam haereticum exsufflantes."

[41]Ganoczy, "Jean Major," p. 457; he also feels that the new position does not reflect the deepest conviction of Major (p. 459).

[42]Caesar Bulaeus, Historia universitatis Parisiensis . . ., 6 vols. (Parisiis: Noel, 1665-1673), 6:119: "Claves ecclesiae sunt omnibus communes."

[43]The Acts of the Parliaments of Scotland, (Edinburgh: Record Comm., 1814-1844), 2:295.

[44]Ibid.

[45]Major, Preface to In quatuor Evangelia expositiones; reprinted in his A History of Greater Britain . . ., p. 447: ". . . antiquam praeterea servare tralationem et catholicas iuxta Romanae ecclesiae doctrinam per Doctores receptos traditiones."

[46]Ibid.: "Wiclevitarum item et Hussitarum et eorum sequacium Lutheranorum pestiferas zizanias e bono dominici agri semine, quantum potuimus, evellimus: . . ."

[47]Ibid., pp. 447-448: "Nomini quidem, nam et Jacobus nobis supplantatorm significat: tua autem praestans virtus Lutheranam haeresim, ut mox apertius dicam, ita in Scotia supplantavit, ut sperare liceat eam nunquam istic repululaturam: . . . Denique moribus maxime tuis, nam ut dicere occoepimus, non sine plurimorum invidia in primis sed infelicem Lutheranae haereseos et perfidiae sectatorem viriliter sustulisti: ut secundum nomen tuum sit et laus tua."

[48]See John Foxe, Actes and Monuments . . ., (London: Day, [1563]; reprinted in 8 vols., New York: AMS Press, 1965), IV: 559; he cites the supposed views of Hamilton objected to by Beaton "That the pope hath no power to loose and bind; and that no pope had that power after St. Peter. . . . That the pope is Antichrist, and that every priest hath the power that the pope hath."

[49]Major, Prefatory note to John Major Eck, ... in Primum magistri Sententiarum disputationes et decisiones nuper repositae . . . (Parisiis: Parvus and Badius, 1530), in A History of Greater Britain . . ., p. 450: "Accessit praeterea a duodecim (si rite recordor) annis fidei catholicae nova et detestanda calamitas, Martini Luteri, et qui ab eo os ponendi in caelum temeritatis ansam acceperunt, execranda haeresis: ad quam confutandam, omnes theologiae studiosi Luteciae ad sacras sese literas, neglectis sententiarum definitionibus, accinxerunt, ita ut nostra Academia Sor-

bonica obtutum mentis omnem ad materias cuilibet
captu faciles fixerit, positionesque Sorbonicas
ingeniosis animis dignas, in materias maiorum
ordinarium (ut vulgato more loquar) commutarint."

[50]Eustace Chapuys to Charles V, April 2,
1531, Letters and Papers Foreign and Domestic
of the Reign of Henry VIII preserved in the
Public Record Office, the British Museum, and
Elsewhere, 21 vols., edited by J. Gairdner (London: Her Majesty's Stationery Office, 1880; reprint ed., Vadux: Kraus, 1965), 5:84.

[51]Ibid.

[52]Major, Historia maioris Britanniae, . . .
([n.p.] Ascensius, [1521]); r i - r ii: "Hic
vectigalium quaestio ad disputationem sese offert
et utrinque disputabimus. In primis contra
gubernatori modum procedendi, Argumentor sic. . . .
Ad eadem partem argumentor sic: . . . Tertio
arguit sic. . . . Quarto argumentor sic. . . .
In oppositum arguitur sic. . . . Sec huic ob-
iectioni responderetur. . . Sine alterius partis
malivolentia vix quispiam resolutorie et clare
potest hic respondere: verum meam particularem
opinionem (quam prudentum iudicio discutiendam
relinquo) ex dictis ingeniosus percipere potest."

[53]For a rather full bibliography on his life
see E. F. Rice, "Introduction," in The Prefatory
Epistles of Jacques Lefèvre d'Etaples and
Related Texts, ed. by E. F. Rice (New York:
Columbia University Press, 1972), pp. xxiv-xxv.

[54]Guillaume Briçonnet to Marquerite d'Angoulême, Meaux, December 22, 1521 in . . . Correspondance (1521-1524), vol. 1 Années 1521-1522, ed.
C. Martineau et M. Veissière (Genève: Droz, 1975),
p. 85: "L'Eglise est de present aride et seche
comme le torrent en la grand challeur australe.
La challeur d'avarice, ambicion et voluptuese vie
a deseché son eaue de vie, doctrine et exem-
plarité." For further discussion of the social

97

context of Lefèvre's commentary see Henry Heller, "Reform and Reformers at Meaux: 1518-1525" (Ph.D. dissertation, Cornell University, 1969).

[55]The Bibliotheque National of Paris contains the manuscript notes of the commentary dated 1521. The references will be to the June 1522 edition published at Meaux; I have not consulted the 1523 edition (Basel), the 1526 ("denuo recogniti", Basel), the 1531 and 1541 editions (Cologne).

[56]The Prefatory Epistles, p. 437: "Et utinam credendi forma a primaeva illa peteretur ecclesia . . . quae nullam regulam praeter evangelium novit, . . . Et quidni saecula nostra ad primigeniae illius ecclesiae offigiem redigi opturemus, . . ."

[57]Ibid., p. 436: "Verbum Dei sufficit. Hoc unicum satis est ad vitam quae terminum nescit inveniendam. Haec umica regula vitae aeternae magistra est; cetera quibus non adlucet verbum Dei quam non necessaria sunt, tam nimirum superflua."

[58]Ibid.: "Non proposit Christus, dux vitae et eiusdem largitor aeternae, intelligendum evangelium, sed credendum, . . ."

[59]Ibid., p. 439: "De quorum tamen genere hosce commentarios, quos primum ad Dei gloriam, deinde ad evangelicae veritatis cognitionem, postremo ad omnium utilitatem in evangelia conscripsimus, nequequam esse dicimus; sed de eorum qui mentis tenebras discutiant et eam luci perviam quoquo modo efficiant . . . . Proinde hos commentarios ne stellae quisdem lucenti per noctem assimilari volumus, sed aeriae potius purgationi. Tria namque sunt quae maiores nostri posuere: katharismòs, phōtismòs, kaì teleíōsis ĕte teleiótēs, id est purgatio, illuminatio, et perfectio, . . . quo in genere commentarios nostros, qualescumque sunt, collocamus et proinde purgatorios, id est initiatorios nuncupamus."

[60]Ibid., p. 440: "At ne vos lateat quo pacto
hi commentarii sint purgatorii, paucis tandem vos
ordinis admonebo. Primo loco vetus occurrit
editio. Deinde annotationes breves, . . . Quae
omnia tum mentium tum veteris litterae purgationem
efficiunt. Tertio loco sequitur commentarius
exactius consimilia efficiens, id est, interdum
veteris litterae, interdum mentium, interdum
utrorumque illius mendas, harum caligines deter-
gens."

[61]Jacques Lefèvre d'Etaples, Commentarii
initiatorii in quatuor evangelia . . . (Meldis:
Colinaeus, 1522), f. 66r: "Petrus autem pro
omnibus: veritatem, non opinionem, respondit."

[62]Ibid.: "El haec vera fides: et veritatis
non ab homine, sed a deo infusae, confessio. . . .
Haec beatitudo Petro tribuitur: non quatenus a
Petro, sed quatenus a patre caelesti provenit. in
hoc enim beatus est: quod pater coelestis provenit. in hoc enim beatus est: quod pater
coelestis illi revelare dignatus est. Neque ulla
beatitudo aliter ulli tribuenda est: quam illius
contemplatione a quo est. A quo enim esse potest:
nisi a deo, qui solus beatus est, et solus potens
rex regnantium et dominus dominantium."

[63]Ibid.: "Et ab hac solida veritatis confessione quae a deo patre est, et omni petra
firmior: . . ."

[64]Ibid.: ". . . et super hanc petram, in-
concussibilisque veritatis fidem quod Christus est
filius dei vivi, fundavit dominus ecclesiam suam."

[65]Ibid.: "Et petram pro Christo et verbo dei
accipi, manifestat dominus cum ait cap. 7 huius,
hoc modo. Omnis ergo qui audit verba mea haec et
facit ea: assimilabitur viro sapienti qui aedificavit domum suam supra petram. Et subiungit.
Et descendit pluvia et venerunt flumina, et
flaverunt venti et irruerunt in domum illam: et
non cecidit. fundata enim erat supra firmam

petram." In commenting on the "petra" of Mt.
7:24-25 Lefèvre writes "Petra: Christus, sermoque
eius" (f. 31^v).

[66]Ibid.: "Ecce quo pacto se et verbum suum
vocat petram, et firmam quidem petram, supra quam
nimirum inconcussibilis domus id est ecclesia
aedificatur, ne quis dicat Petrum esse petram
supra quam fundata est ecclesiam."

[67]Fröhlich, Formen, p. 51 recognizes this when
he writes that ". . . anderseits sprechen die Aus-
leger [i.e. medieval exegetes] von Mt. 16, 18
selbst immer wieder von der 'firma petra' und
zeigen damit, dass sie Mt 7, 25 im Ohr haben."

[68]Origen held that the prudent man of Mt. 7
is the Lord who builds his church on the rock,
that is, on his own strength and vigor. See GCS
41, p. 76. "ei dè legéi perì toũ alēthõs phro-
nímou andròs toũ oikodomésantos autoũ tèn oikían
epì tèn pétran, oũtos, ó kúrios ó oikodomésas,
autoũ tèn ekklēsían epì tèn pétran toutéstin epì
tèn eautoũ sterrótēta kaì eutonían."

[69]Ibid.: ". . . ne quis dicat Petrum esse
petram supra quam fundata est ecclesia."

[70]Ibid.: "nam quod Petrus non sit petra, et
tanto quoque minus firma petra: dominus paulopost
satis detexit, cum dixit ei. Vade retro Satana,
scandalum es mihi: quia non sapis ea quae dei
sunt, sed ea quae hominum."

[71]Ibid.: "Et si dicitur (ut quidam volunt)
Petrus a petra, ut Christianus a Christo, Christianus autem non est Christus; neque ergo Petrus
petra." Here there is a strong similarity to
Augustine's argument in his . . . Operum, ed. D.
Erasmus, vol. X (Basileae: ex off. Frobeniana,
1529), sermo xiii, d. 2: "Quia enim Christus
petra, Petrus populus Christianus. Petra enim
principale nomen est, ideo Petrus a petra, non
petra a Petro, quomodo non a Christiano Christus,
sed a Christo Christianus vacatur."

[72]Ibid.: "Et Paulus Christum petram esse interpretatur, cum ait. Bibebant autem de spiritali consequente eos petra. petra autem erat Christus."

[73]Ibid.: "Neque eas solus a domino accepit Petrus: sed etiam caeteri omnes qui in fide aedificaverunt supra Christum, iuxta Christi domini voluntatem, ecclesiam."

[74]Ibid.: f. 66^r-67: "verum Christus de hac fide quod ipse esset filius dei vivi quae est una clavium caelestis doctrinae, hic loquitur, et quam voluit in ecclesia sua esse fundamentariam. Quae quid aliud est in obiecto, quam Christus ipse, qui est ipsa petra, et totius ecclesiae inconcussibile fundamentum: in nobis autem, quam aeterni patris infusio."

[75]Guy Bedouelle, Lefèvre d'Etaples et l'intelligence des Ecritures, p. 212.

[76]Bedouelle, Lefèvre, p. 212, n. 1, citing Ph.-Aug. Becker, "Les idées religieuses de Guillaume Briçonnet, évêque de Meaux," Revue de Théologie et des Questions religieuses (Montauban) IX (1900), pp. 318-358, 377-416.

[77]Rice, "Introduction", pp. xvi-xvii.

[78]Noël Beda, Annotationum . . . in Iacobum Fabrum Stapulensem libri duo: . . . (Parisiis: Ascensius, 1526), sig. Aa, iv as cited in Rice, "Introduction," p. xxiv, n. 36.

[79]Elucidatio paraphrastica sancti evangelii secundum Matthaeum . . . nunc primum edita (Paris: Mace, 1545), f. 53^v: "Statim omnium nomine, tanquam omnium Apostolorum os, Petrus respondens, absque hesitatione veritatis confessionem protulit, dicens: . . ."

[80]Ibid.: "Nos credimus et profitemur, . . ."

[81]Ibid.: ". . . sed Christam filium Dei vivi, . . . verum hominem et Deum, filium consubstantialem et coaequalem Dei patris, qui est verus et vivus Deus."

[82]Ibid.: f. 54: ". . . constituam te qui hanc veritatis confessionem protulisti, cum plenitudine potestatis, meum in terris vicarium, . . . Tanta erit tua authoritas, et eorum qui in tuum locum successuri sunt usque ad consummationem saeculi. Omnino enim ad consummationem usque saeculi perdurare debet in tuis successoribus tradenda tibi potestas, quomodo in consummationem usque non deficiet Ecclesia."

[83]Ibid.: ". . . super hanc fidei veritatem quam es confessus, et quam protulisti, dicens: Tu es Christus filius Dei vivi, item et super me petram firmissimam, quam in praedicto verbo confessus es, ego aedificabo atque superstruam aedificium Ecclesiae meae, quam aedificare volo patri meo."

[84]Ibid.: "Fundamentum enim aliud memo potest ponere, nisi quod ego ponam quod ero [sic] ego Christus Iesus: . . ." The Vulgate renders this verse "Fundamentum enim aliud nemo potest ponere praeter id quod positum est, quod est Christus Iesus."

[85]Hugo de Sancto Charo, Biblia latina, vol. 6: Postilla super evangelium secundum Matthaeum (Basileae: Amerbachius, 1498-1502), i 4: "id est super hoc fundamentum . . . Eiusdem c.3 Fundamentum aliud nemo potest ponere praeter id quod positum est: quod est christus iesus."

[86]Elucidatio paraphrastica, f. 54: ". . . et veritas ipsa fidei atque confessionis de me, erit fundamentum totius aedificii."

[87]Rice, Introduction to Letter 83, The Prefatory Epistles of Jacques Lefèvre d'Étaples, p. 249.

102

[88]Thomas Grey to Erasmus, August 5, 1516 in Correspondance des réformateurs dans le pays de langue francaise . . ., edited by A. L. Herminjard, volume 1 (1512-1526) (Genève: Georg, 1866), p. 23.

[89]Critici sacri . . ., ed. John Pearson et al (London: Boom, 1698), vol. I, n.p. and x.

[90]Critici sacri. . ., vol. VI, p. 557: "'Quia tu es Petrus, etc.] i. Cognominavi te 'Petrum' propterea quod aliquando pronunciaturus esses me esse Petram et rupem solidissimam."

CHAPTER III

"PETRA" AS PETER

One exegetical novelty of the sixteenth
century was the exegesis of "petra" in terms of
Peter and his successors the popes. This position
will be examined in the commentaries of Tommaso de
Vio (Cajetan), Matthias Bredenbach, Sisto da
Siena, Cornelius Jansen, the authors of the notes
to the various editions of the Rhemes New Testament, Juan Maldonado, and Sebastian Barradas.

Cajetan's "Evangelia cum commentariis" (1532)

In 1524 Cajetan's Jentacula novi testamenti . . . appeared at Vailly-sur-Aisne; this
work contains a "literal exposition" of sixty-four
passages, but does not discuss Mt. 16:18.[1] His
commentary on Matthew was completed by November
12, 1527 and was published three years later at
Venice by Iuncta.[2] This commentary was dedicated
to Pope Clement VII; in his dedication, one dis-
covers that it is Cajetan's intention to stress
the "literal sense"[3] and to allow the doctrine of
the papal see to be a determinant of the meaning
of the text.[4]

The actual commentary, unlike the others
already examined, may be described in terms of
Petrus solus: Peter alone responds to Jesus'
question without consulting the other apostles;[5]
Peter alone received divine revelation from the
Father;[6] Peter alone receives Jesus' response of
blessing.[7]

Cajetan then proceeds to exegete "et super
hanc petram":

Note in what regard you are 'Peter,' in
what regard you are 'stone' ("saxum"):
with respect to the office, namely, of
foundation. Indeed the pronoun 'this'
illustrates the stone under discussion;
moreover the pronoun was said about no
other stone and the following discussion
concerns nothing else than Peter.
Therefore according to the plain context
of the literal sense Peter himself is
intended by the pronoun 'this.' This is
the same as if Jesus said more openly
'you are a stone ("saxum") and upon this
stone ("saxum").'[8]

The nuanced character of Cajetan's remarks is
important; his interpretation of "petra" in terms
of Peter is a qualified one, that is, the rock is
not simply Peter but Peter with respect to the
continuing office of foundation within the church.
In support of this position his exegesis employs
syntactical arguments. His discussion of the
demonstrative pronoun "hanc" involves him in a
discussion of how such a pronoun is properly used
and to whom must it apply in this passage. The
concern with the literal sense of the passage
follows from the discussion of the demonstrative
pronoun and further indicates that "literal sense"
has to do with contextual meaning and logical
reference.[9]

Cajetan proceeds to a brief comment on
"aedificabo ecclesiam meam":

You, being now a rock, I will make the
foundation in building my church upon
you. Jesus promises Peter the first
place itself in the church, and such a
foundation he maintained in the building.
Jesus promises that he will make Peter
the foundation of the church, since he
predestined his church (which will be
tempted) upon the firmness of Peter's
foundation. See the mysterious depths of

this selection discussed more fully in
our little work De institutione pontificatus a Iesu Christo, lest we should
say the same thing over again here.[10]

Clearly this reinforces the already mentioned
notion of Peter as "petra." What also seems to
be stressed is the Christological emphasis of the
Matthean passage, that is, the idea of Christ as
the one who builds, which in turn and secondarily
involves the notion of that upon which Christ
builds (Peter).

A key expression is "the firmness of
Peter's foundation." In what does this firmness
consist? Here it would be helpful to consult
Cajetan's remarks on Matthew 16:23 (Vulgate: "Who
turning, said to Peter: 'Go behind me, Satan:
thou art a scandal unto me, . . .'"). His commentary there first adopts a universalist interpretation suggested by Origen and not found in
Cajetan's Mt. 16:18 exegesis (where Peter is
definitely not taken in a universal sense). That
is, he interprets "Satan" in terms of everyone who
opposes Jesus and his mission.[11] Then he proceeds
to make a sharp distinction between Peter as
Satan, a scandal, and not knowing divine things
and Peter as blessed and recipient of divine
revelation; for Cajetan this is the same as
distinguishing Peter according to himself and
Peter supported by divine grace.[12] Such an emphasis on the Father revealing adds to the Christological emphasis we have already seen a theological dimension and further reduces the
"Peter-centeredness" of his commenting on "petra."

There is something else astonishing about
the last quoted comment: Cajetan refers the
reader to one of his earlier works, De institutione pontificatus a Iesu Christo, for a deeper
discussion of Matthew 16:18. Note that for
Cajetan what goes on in a Bible commentary can
also occur in a dogmatic treatise!

107

Cajetan's "De divina institutione pontificatus Romani pontificis super totam ecclesiam a Christo in Petro" (1521)

This tract was published in three different places in 1521 (Rome, Cologne, Milan). Cajetan dedicated it to Leo X but was also thinking of Luther since the questions Cajetan takes up are ones that Luther had already discussed in his *Resolutio lutheriana super propositione sua decima tertia de potestate papae* (1519). Specifically the tract is concerned with Matthew 16:17f. and John 21:15ff so as to see what light they shed on the "mystery" of the primacy of Peter and Roman pontiffs over all churches.[13] With reference to both texts he brings sixteenth century questions and disputes: "whether the words of Christ were said to Peter alone, . . . whether through these words the pontificate of the entire church was commissioned by Christ to Peter alone, . . . whether here the pontificate of the entire church committed by Christ to Peter was given by the same Lord to the successor of Peter . . . whether here the pontificate was given by Christ to the Roman pontiff."[14] More specifically, his discussion of the Matthean text is concerned to answer those positions which minimize the singularity of Peter.[15]

Given this context, how does Cajetan interpret "petra" and what reasons does he give for his position(s)? To answer these questions, one must pay close attention to the framework within which Cajetan is writing.

Cajetan seems to argue consistently in terms of the larger structure of the promises made to Peter by Christ; his position on "petra" must thus be appreciated within this broader concern. With regard to the first promise "petra" has to do with a certain divine event in which Christ the actor (not Peter) establishes the church in faith by providing for a certain foundation; Peter is crucial here not because he is considered as an individual but insofar as he is "petra."

First, then, the context of the promises
made to Peter must be appreciated. Here Cajetan
is concerned to stress the differences between the
promise made to Peter in verse eighteen and that
made to Peter in verse nineteen; these promises
are not of the same type but differ.[16] The first
promise concerns the construction of the church,
while the second concerns the question of authority in the church.[17] The first promise concerns
the substance of the church while the second
concerns office in the church.[18]

Later Cajetan distinguishes between the
two promises with more distinct reference to
Peter: the first promise is not made to Peter
unconditionally but insofar as he is "Rock"; the
second promise is made unconditionally to the
person of Peter.[19] His explanation of this difference makes clear that the first promise is
qualified by the use of "Petrus," "hanc" and
"petram" while the second promise simply uses
"tibi" in an absolute way.[20] The second difference mentioned here by Cajetan is that in the
first promise the emphasis is on Christ as the
main actor in promising Peter the office of
sustaining the church, whereas in the second
promise Peter becomes the sole actor.[21] From
these differences Cajetan then draws the distinction between the office of Peter with respect
to the active power of using the keys and his
office of sustaining the church in faith. The
office of the keys is entrusted to a man while the
office of sustaining the church in faith pertains
to both Christ and Peter: Christ considered as
the actor, the rock considered as the method of
sustaining the church, and Peter considered as the
foundation and undergirding.[22] Later Cajetan
repeats the distinction between the promises and
in this context emphasizes that Peter is "Petrus"
in faith, just like a rock ("petra") as Leo the
Great, Gregory the Great and Bede have set forth.[23]
Later on again in discussing the first promise
Cajetan stresses that Matthew 16:18 deals with
Peter as the foundation of the church in relation

to the design for a pastor of the whole church, a design which excludes the other apostles.[24]

Cajetan's position is further nuanced in that "petra" must also be interpreted in terms of the Roman pontiffs considered as successors of Peter (and not as simply individuals -- the pope as individual may be either an unbeliever or a heretic) and as oriented toward Christ's promise of the firmness of faith of the entire church:

> When he said 'You are Peter,' the Lord referred to solid faith both in Peter and in his successors considered according to their proper persons. He meant this for the present, and when he said 'I have prayed for you that your faith be not deficient,' he meant it as well for the future. When he said 'upon this rock I will build my church' and 'Strengthen your brethren' the Lord truly referred to the same faith as pertaining to the church . . . It follows from the solid- ity in faith of the person of the Roman pontiff as pertaining to the church that he is not able to err in defining axio- matically Christian faith, since in a definition of this sort the faith of the universal faith is built up, and through this faith is built the church of Christ upon the rock of the apostolic see.[25]

It remains to be seen how Cajetan also grounds all that he has said about the first promise in what he understands by the literal sense, which for him is also the sensus historicus, ecclesiasticus et catholicus. A three-fold under- standing may be seen in the "hanc petram" of Mt. 16:18: Christ, Peter and Peter's confession of faith.[26] However, Cajetan goes on to affirm that only one of these understandings is faithful to the literal sense and this understanding has to do with Peter: "however if we should investigate more deeply, one and one alone is the literal

110

sense, that is, that by 'this rock' is meant Peter."[27] Augustine is then cleverly employed, or rather the liberty that Augustine leaves to the reader in his Retractiones is taken up by Cajetan for his argument in favor of Peter![28] His argument here is that Peter has to be the correct understanding because his analysis of the words shows that if Christ had been speaking of himself he would not have said "I will build" but "I am building." "I will build" refers to his making Peter out of Simon.[29]

The second argument that Cajetan gives for this interpretation is the connection between "hanc petram" and "tu es Petrus": the prominence which the gospel gives to the expression "tu es Petrus" is lost unless it be complemented and explained in terms of Christ's action upon the rock.[30] He advances Jerome's exegesis in favor of this manner of argumentation: "according to the metaphor of the rock it is correctly said to Peter: I will build my church upon you."[31] What Cajetan fails to mention is that Jerome's commentary on Mt. 16:18 also refers to Christ as the rock in whom Peter was believing.[32] Here he also appropriates Chrysostom's position on "petra" (Peter's confession of faith) by saying that this confession is identical "with the solidity or firmness of faith which Peter denotes; for the confession of faith does not differ from its solidity or firmness except insofar as the act differs from its habit; and again it is fitting that the church have more for its foundation (habitual) faith rather than the confession of faith."[33] The latter remark, implying a distinction between the habitus of faith and its confession, most likely is influenced by Cajetan's reading and understanding of Romans 10:10 ("Corde enim creditur ad iusticiam, ore autem confessio fit ad salutem"). Having returned to his position of identifying "Petrus" with "petra" according to the literal sense, Cajetan returns to the history of previous exegesis and seeks to take up all previous interpretations in his literal sense:

111

However to speak more exactly, say 'this' rock, that is the rock with respect to you, the solidity of faith with respect to you, Christ believed and Christ confessed with a view to you, so that you may embrace all the exegesis of the fathers; for considered separately all are true, but they only reveal part of the truth, exegeting 'faith' or the 'confession of faith' or 'Peter' or 'Christ.' But when each position is simultaneously ("simul") joined so that it is explained what the persons of Peter and of Christ and faith mean simultaneously ("simul"), the whole truth and the whole sense is gotten of the letter of the text which says not 'on the rock' but 'on this rock! And indeed the metaphorical rock is individuated and becomes 'this rock,' because it exists in this designated subject, just as anything else existing in Peter is particularized and becomes 'this', since it belongs in the very person of Peter.[34]

Thus Cajetan is able on the one hand to affirm all the patristic interpretations of "petra" by simultaneously affirming them with particular reference to the individuated rock, that is, Peter. The element of individuation is crucial for Cajetan; he implicitly rejects the Origenist position that "petra" can refer to any and all believer(s).[35]

Cajetan's final chapter in this treatise mentions the authorities he sees as affirming his thesis that the office of pontiff over the entire church has been instituted on Peter and on the Roman bishop as successor of Peter. Exegetes mentioned there include Chrysostom, Ambrose, and Jerome. The first of these comes from Chrysostom's fifty-fifth homily, which is concerned with chapter sixteen of Matthew: "Jesus establishes Peter as the pastor of the future church."[36]

112

Though citing correctly Chrysostom's position in
this homily,[37] only later does Cajetan acknowledge
that Chrysostom in the same homily interprets
"petra" in terms of "faith" and "confession," but
he qualifies this interpretation by adding that
Chrysostom later specified Peter in terms of the
rock: "And even if he had earlier glossed 'And
upon this rock I will build my church' with 'that
is, faith and confession' nevertheless he says
later 'I say to you that thou art Peter and I will
build my church upon you.'"[38] Cajetan here is
citing a Chrysostom text which differs significantly from the reading found in modern editions:
"From all his words notice Christ's power. 'I say
to you that thou art Peter; I will build the
church; I will give you the keys of heaven.'"[39]

The second element from the exegetical
tradition that Cajetan mentions comes from one
whom Cajetan knows as Ambrose:

> Ambrose in his forty-seventh sermon,
> which is concerned with the faith of
> Peter the apostle and which is cited in
> distinction fifty of the canon 'Fide-
> lior,' says of Peter: 'As the good
> pastor received the flock to be guarded
> so that he who had earlier been incon-
> stant might become the support for all,
> and so that he who had wavered under the
> trial of interrogation might establish
> the rest in the solidity of faith.
> Therefore for the solidity of devotion of
> the churches is Peter called rock, just
> as the Lord says "Thou art Peter, and
> upon this rock I will build my church";
> for Peter is called rock because he as
> the chief will have established the
> foundations of faith among the nations
> and as an immovable rock holds together
> the scripture and bulk of the entire
> Christian work.'[40]

Cajetan here is following a variant of the Roman
edition of Gratian's Decretum, specifically

Prima pars, distinctio fifty, canon fifty-four.[41]
In fact this sermon is not from Ambrose but from
Maximus, Bishop of Turin. Maximus' sermon is
longer than the one Cajetan is thinking of and
attributes "petra" to both Peter and Christ, but
for different reasons: Peter may be said to be the
rock with respect to his ministry, while Christ is
called the rock in the sense of I Cor. 10:4, that
is, with respect to strength.[42]

       Cajetan then cites an Ambrosian hymn which
speaks of Peter as the rock: "And Ambrose in the
liturgical hymn refers to Peter as the rock of the
church, saying: 'When the cock crowed, Peter the
rock of the church cried away his guilt.'"[43]
Cajetan is thinking of the hymn "Aeterne rerum
conditor" sung on Sundays at Lauds or Matins; the
hymn's central concern is with Christ as cosmic
creator and ruler of the times and seasons.

       There is still another reference to
Ambrose's use of "petra:"

> And Ambrose in sermon eleven which is
> concerned with the miracles of Jesus:
> 'Therefore the Lord got into this single
> ship of the church, in which Peter was
> established as chief when the Lord said
> "Upon this rock I will build my church."
> This ship so floats into the depth of
> that time that as the world perishes it
> receives all those and guards them
> unhurt. For we see a figure of this
> church in the Old Testament. For just as
> the ark of Noah at the time of the
> destruction of the world had received all
> those and preserved them safe and sound,
> so the church of Peter with the age going
> up in flames embraces all those and will
> represent them. And just as in Noah's
> time with the cessation of the flood a
> dove brought to his ark a sign of peace,
> so with the judgment of world accom-
> plished Christ brings the joy of peace to

the church of Peter, since Christ is the
dove himself, that is peace.'[44]

Modern research has shown this to be the work not
of Ambrose but again of Maximus of Turin.[45] The
sermon is actually concerned with the two boats
mentioned in Lk. 5:2. The emphasis on Peter in
the sermon derives in part from the Biblical
stress that it was Peter's boat that Jesus got
into and not the other one. The conclusion of
this sermon is significant in that the importance
of faith for a secure boat and tranquil sea is
stressed.[46]

The last reference to previous exegetical
tradition is contained in an allusion to Jerome:
"Jerome says on the Matthean text: 'To Simon who
was believing in the rock Christ was imparted the
name of Peter, and according to the metaphor of
the rock it is correctly said to him: "I will
build my church upon you."'"[47] This is a fairer
representation of Jerome's position than we saw
earlier in this treatise where the reference to
the rock Christ was not mentioned.[48]

No other patristic exegesis or use of Mt.
16:18 is mentioned by Cajetan, although he was
familiar with the exegesis of Cyprian's De
catholicae ecclesiae unitate.[49]

Mathias Bredenbach: Introduction

Mathias Bredenbach was born in 1499 in the
village of Kerspe which was part of the duchy of
Monte (Berg). His early schooling was in Münster
and later he received the Master's degree in arts
and philosophy from Cologne in 1524. His entire
career was spent in teaching at Emmerich in Kleve;
he was appointed rector there due to his bril-
liance as a "trilinguist" (Latin, Greek and
Hebrew). He was often consulted on academic
matters, especially by his Jesuit friends in
Cologne. With the reformation in Germany he

became very much involved in polemical and controversial writings, especially against the
Lutherans in Germany. He died at Emmerich in 1559
and was survived by his two sons, Theoderic and
Tilmann. His exegetical writings were published
together by these sons at Cologne and Antwerp in
1560: commentaries on the first sixty-nine psalms
and on Matthew's gospel.

Bredenbach's ". . . In sanctum Christi Evangelium secundum Matthaeum, pia ac catholica commentaria" (1560) [50]

The dedicatory letter which prefaces this
work gives some interesting information as to the
prehistory of the text. Theodoric and Tilmann
Bredenbach, sons of Matthias, in dedicating this
volume to Robert, Bishop of Leoden, relate that
their father, anxious that his students read books
which would be both useful and enjoyable, selected
out of each testament one book -- the Psalms and
the Gospel of Matthew -- and added commentaries on
each.[51] The sons in turn took the unpublished and
unpolished notes, submitted them to the judgment
of the professors of theology at Cologne and then
published them.

The text that Bredenbach is following is
that of the Vulgate; that is somewhat surprising
for he was familiar with Greek and with Erasmus'
New Testament emendations.[52] Some indication of
Bredenbach's position on "petra" is indicated in
his remarks on Mt. 16:13 where he mentions that at
Caesarea Phillipi Peter is designated high priest
of the church and pope[53] and on Mt. 16:16 where
Peter is referred to as the most beloved by Jesus
and the future leader of the apostolic order.[54]

His actual exegesis of Mt. 16:18 begins
with his affirmation that "petra" has been understood in many ways: Christ, faith/confession, and
Peter:

Augustine in his homily on this passage
understands rock in terms of Christ
himself. Indeed in the tenth treatise on
the epistle of John he interprets rock as
faith. Several think that rock is used
of the profession of faith which Peter
makes here. Most assert that Peter
himself is called rock by the Lord in
this place, the rock upon which he would
build his church.[55]

The first reference to Augustine comes from his
sermon on Mt. 14:24-33 in which Peter is said to
represent the Christian populace and he derives
his name from the rock Christ who builds the
church not on Peter but on himself.[56] The second
reference to Augustine comes from Augustine's
treatise on the first letter of John where Augustine does speak of "petra" in terms of Peter's
faith that Jesus is the Christ; the emphasis,
though, is on distinguishing Peter's loving faith
from the unloving faith of the demons.[57] Neither
Bredenbach nor any other sixteenth century exegete
has thus far dealt with distinguishing Peter's
faith from the faith of the demons; this seems
especially strange because we have already seen a
significant number of exegetes who interpret
"petra" in terms of faith. Next we should note
that Bredenbach as late as the late 1550's notes
that "several" (seemingly referring to contemporary opinion) interpret "petra" in terms of
faith; but in the next breath he mentions that
more, in fact most, of his contemporaries understand "petra" in terms of Peter.

He then proceeds to a short discussion of
these "three views." He affirms that all of these
views have a certain authority and that all can be
grounded in a pious understanding of the verse.[58]
The first position, besides having Augustine's
authority to recommend it, recalls other Scrip-
tural verses which refer to Jesus as the rock: I
Cor. 10:4, Mt. 21:42 (not mentioned by any exegete
which held "petra" to be Christ), and I Cor.

117

3:11.[59] The second and third views (which Bredenbach understands in terms of faith and Peter) seem
to be substantiated by the writings of Chrysostom
and Theophylact.[60] Bredenbach seems to be twist-
ing the position of Theophylact a bit, for Theophylact's passage, when quoted more fully, clearly
stresses the identity between "petra" and "confessio," a "confessio" which is not restricted to
Peter alone.[61]

    Bredenbach then discusses the third view
(petra=Petrus). What recommends this position is
that it has the most authorities behind it, indeed
the weightiest ones; this position also comes from
those who sometimes speak of "petra" with reference to the first or second positions.[62] Further-
more, all these diverse interpretations can be
taken up into one, and this due to Bredenbach's
confidence that there can be no radical dissension
and disagreement among the "holy doctors" of the
church and his hope that the interpreter will
bring a sense of piety to his work.[63] He then
begins to cite the authorities for the position
petra=Petrus: Augustine, Basil, Ambrose, Cyprian,
Tertullian, and Clement. His source for the many
places in which Augustine posits an identity
between "petra" and "Petrus" is John Fisher's
Assertionis Lutheranae confutatio.[64] Fisher cites
Basil in the context of responding to Luther's
charge that the Roman pope is not the successor of
Peter and is not the vicar of Christ over all the
churches and thereby was not established by Christ
with reference to Peter; Basil is cited to bring
forth an authority, although his words stress
Peter's faith as much as Peter's person.[65]
Bredenbach also relies on Fisher for references to
pseudo-Ambrose and Cyprian.[66] Bredenbach, too,
follows Fisher in bringing forth the authority of
Tertullian: "And more ancient than Cyprian is
Tertullian in his book De praescriptionibus
haereticorum: he says, 'Was anything hidden from
Peter, called the rock of the church to be built,
who attained to the keys of the kingdom of heaven
and the power of loosing and binding in heaven and

on earth.'"[67] Neither Bredenbach nor Fisher
allude to the context of Tertullian's remarks in
which he is responding to certain Gnostics who
claimed that the apostles were somewhat ignorant
regarding the saving truths handed on by Jesus.[68]
Bredenbach also mentions epistles from Clement and
Anacletus as authorities for the position petra=
Petrus;[69] since neither are properly called
exegetes their position will not be analyzed.
Bredenbach concludes the patristic listing in
favor of his position by saying that "there is no
one of the orthodox camp . . . who has shrinked
from this interpretation."[70]

Having said this Bredenbach turns his
attention to the position that petra=Christus.[71]
His answer is one that we have already seen in
Cajetan: it is possible that Christ and Peter be
both rock and foundation in the sense of the
collation between John 1:9 and Mt. 5:14. Both
Christ and the apostles may be said to be the
light of the world without any disadvantage
accruing to either of them.[72] Jerome is quoted as
a source for this view.[73] Leo the Great is also
cited for this position that the basis of both
being "petra" lies in Christ's power which he in
turn communicates to Peter.[74] He then turns to
Origen's position vis-à-vis the rock. Although
acknowledging that Origen universalized the
notion of "rock" so as not to apply it to Peter
alone but to all Christian believers, nevertheless
he holds that Origen's exegetical work as a whole
does not militate against the primacy of Peter in
the church.[75] Rather Origen himself does discuss
and uphold this primacy according to Bredenbach:

In homily seventeen on the gospel of
Luke, Origen says 'therefore all the
others were brought to stumble insofar as
Peter, as the leader of the apostles, de-
nied the Lord three times.' And towards
the end of his fifth book on Paul's
epistle to the Romans Origen says 'since
the supreme power of feeding the sheep is

handed over to Peter, and on Peter just
as on earth the church is founded, the
confession of no other virtue is demanded
of him except charity.' And in the fifth
homily on Exodus: 'To the great foundation of this church and to the very solid
rock upon which Christ founded his church,
see what is said: "Oh you of little
faith, why do you doubt?"'[76]

Bredenbach's reference to Origen's homily on Luke
2:35 is correct in that Origen does refer to Peter
as "apostolorum princeps," but there seems to be
some distance between the idea of all stumbling in
Peter's threefold denial and the later developed
notion of the primacy of Peter.[77] The reference
to Origen's commentary on Romans is cited correctly, although there again Origen is not ex-
pounding Peter's primacy but rather discussing the
excellence of charity.[78] The third reference to
Origen comes from his homily on Exodus 14:11-12
where Origen is discussing "the burden of temptations"; Peter serves as an example that even a
prominent individual may succumb to temptation and
doubt.[79] Bredenbach recognizes that these passages of Origen are not self-evident in their
support of Peter's primacy and may be taken in
other ways; thus he adds that since Origen was erroneous in some of his views, one must be referred
to the wider context of not only Origen's positions but of others too.[80]

    This wider context is fleshed out by a
reference to Jerome which Bredenbach uses as
another argument for his position that <u>petra=
Petrus</u>:

    The church is founded upon Peter, even if
    in another passage the very same is said
    of all the apostles, and all of them
    receive the keys of the kingdom, and the
    strength of the church is made solid
    equally among them; nevertheless from
    among the twelve one is to be chosen, so

that, with a head established, the occasion for schisms might be taken away.[81]

Here especially the context needs to be noted: Jerome is speaking against the disparagement of virginity in the church against the charges of Jovinian; the quote cited above is actually presented as a counter-argument ("At dicis") to Jerome's own argument for the excellence of John's virginity, and the pre-eminence of John even over Peter.[82] Jerome's mention of schism invites Bredenbach into a short discussion of the importance and necessity of the primacy as a defense against schism, heresy and the devil, which seek to destroy the church and to transmute it into innumerable sects, a phenomenon not absent from his own time Bredenbach notes.[83]

Having established what seems to be appropriate evidence for the patristic foundation for petra=Petrus,[84] Bredenbach moves on to a more direct discussion of the text. The two arguments that he will bring forward are based on what he calls the power of Jesus' words themselves in the passage and the most evident sense of the passage. He holds that there is a natural movement from Jesus' efficacious speaking to Peter becoming that which Christ efficaciously says to him:

How greatly does that force and succession of the Lord's words and of the matter itself which is under consideration naturally invite us. Simply consider, reader, the power of the words. Jesus says 'I say to you. I, who possess the power of executing and bringing about what I say, say to you and not to anyone else standing around here. And what do I say? That you are Peter. And not only are you called Peter, but you actually are Peter. And upon this rock, certainly, which I make strong with these my efficacious words and which I make solid and immoveable so that this rock may be

121

an invulnerable foundation; in other
words, I will build my church upon
you.'85

Having formulated this basic thesis that
petra=Petrus, he begins with the objection that
"Petrus" and "petra" are different, that one and
the same thing cannot be both "Petrus" and "petra"
for "Petrus" is derived from "petra."86 He responds first by referring the reader to Jn. 1:42
(Vulgate: "Et adduxit eum ad Iesum. Intuitus
autem eum Iesus dixit: Tu es Simon filius Ioana;
tu vocaberis Cephas, quod interpretatur Petrus.")
in order to prepare for his philological argument
for the identity between "petra" and "Petrus."87
Thus having established the identity between
Cephas and "Petrus" he moves on to show the identity among terms in different languages: "petrus=
saxum (Latin) = pétra (Greek)"; that is they all
mean "rock."88 He comes full circle by aligning
these terms with Cephas. Here he refers to
Jerome's philological equating of the Hebraic/Syrian
"cepha" with "petra" in Latin and Greek.89
Bredenbach thus corrects the errors made in this
regard by Erasmus in his editions of 1516 and
1519. To confirm Jerome's and his own position he
turns to two contemporaries, a rabbi of Constan-
tinople, Elias ben Benjamin Ha - Levi (died after
1540) and a Christian Hebraist, Paul Büchelin
(1504-1549). Elias is cited for a passage in his
Thesbites:

> 'Kepha': Simon son of Kepha was one of the
> disciples of Jesus the Nazarene, and
> they say in the gospel that at first his
> name was Simon Bar Jona and Jesus called
> his name 'Kepha' (fortress). The inter-
> pretation of that word 'Kepha' is 'strong.'
> In many places he hints he alone will be
> the head and strength of his faith and so
> he called him 'Kepha.' And so 'and for a
> stone of offense' is interpreted 'leKepha
> Mathkela' (Rock of assembly, of calling
> together, of the church) and so his name

in Roman is Peter, and in Italy stone is
pronounced 'perida.'[90]

It should be noted here that Bredenbach is the
first Christian-Hebraist that we have encountered
in our investigation of commenting on Mt. 16:18;
perhaps he himself is aware of this in a certain
sense because he turns to a fairly accurate[91]
translation of Elias' Hebrew by Paul Büchelin.

> 'Cephah': Simon son of 'Kepha' was one of
> the disciples of Jesus the Nazarene; they
> report about him in the gospel that his
> first name was Simon son of Jona, and
> that Jesus called him 'Kepha' which sig-
> nifies 'strength' and 'fortification.'
> For the interpretation of the Hebrew word
> SEHLA' is KEPA', and is employed in the
> sense of 'strength' in many places.
> Besides, Christ wanted to indicate here
> that he would be the head and strength of
> his faith and accordingly he (Christ)
> called him KEPA'. Again where the Hebrew
> text has 'for a stone of offense' the
> interpretation has LeKEPA' MATK^eLA'.
> Similarly he is called 'Petrus' in the
> Roman tongue. And besides the Italians
> call 'rock' 'pereda.'[92]

Having attempted to show the identity between
"Petrus" and "petra" from the arguments of a
Jewish scholar and his Christian interpreter,
Bredenbach adds his own view along similar philological lines: Jesus did not use Greek or Latin
in naming Peter but rather Syrian (more specifically KEPA') which means "pétra;" this in turn the
Evangelist or his translator translated "pétros"
and not "pétra," not because the two words are
different in regard to Peter but because the
masculine form would be more appropriate; the
other apostles as well as the evangelists themselves sometimes call Peter by the Greek name,
sometimes by the Syrian one.[93] He then reinforces

this argument by appealing to the Hebraic origin
of Matthew's gospel which would have had Jesus
saying "Thou art the Rock and upon this rock I
will build my church."[94]

Bredenbach then advances his second
exegetical argument, the one drawn from the total
context of verse eighteen:

> Since the Lord Jesus in this passage
> proclaims Peter to be blessed and wishes
> to indicate (and to recite the reasons)
> his very own motives of so distinguished
> an utterance about Peter. The first of
> these is the revelation which was made to
> him by the heavenly father; the next of
> these reasons was that Jesus himself was
> about to give Peter the keys of the
> kingdom of heaven. What would have been
> more out of place and more absurd than to
> interrupt this so concise a statement by
> another one in which he announces that he
> is about to build upon himself? For why
> would he say this more to Peter than to
> the others? But since we understand the
> rock to be Peter himself everything hangs
> together most appropriately and every-
> thing flows in the most beautiful order.[95]

The force of Bredenbach's argument here is to ask
who could be more appropriate (contextually
speaking) a candidate for "petra" than Peter
himself? He relies on an <u>inclusio</u> argument, that
is, both before and after verse eighteen Peter is
the subject of what Jesus is saying and verse
eighteen, no matter what one's interpretation, is
spoken to Peter.

Having presented his two exegetical arguments, Bredenbach engages in the sort of discussion usually associated with a treatise on the
papacy -- he attempts to show the need for one
bishop to have a certain primacy over all the
bishops of the church for the sake of unity and

peace (Bredenbach the Christian-Hebraist adds an example from the primacy of the priesthood in Deuteronomy 17:8-13).[96]

Sisto da Siena's "Bibliotheca sancta" (1566)

Sisto da Siena was born of Jewish parents in Siena, Italy in 1520; as an "adolescent"[97] he converted to Christianity. He later joined the Franciscans who sent him to study under Ambrosius Catharinus (Lancelot Politi) at Siena. After 1550[98] the Roman inquisition charged him with heresy and condemned him to death; however, Michele Ghislieri, the commissary-general of the inquisition (later to be Pius V), through daily visits and many tears and intercessions, obtained a recantation on the part of Sisto, who by 1555 joined Ghislieri's order, the Dominicans.[99] In 1559 he was appointed censor of Hebrew books. Sisto died prematurely at Genoa in 1569. His most influential work is the Bibliotheca sancta first published at Venice in 1566 in two volumes containing eight books.[100]

Sisto's analysis of Matthew 16:18 comprises two separate annotations. The first of these begins by referring to Augustine's sermon on Mt. 14:24-33 in which the church is not founded on "petra . . . Petrum" but "Petram, quae Christus est."[101] Sisto also mentions the treatise on John where Augustine, heavily relying on I Cor. 3:11, again holds that the "petra" is Christ.[102] The reason for beginning with Augustine and especially with an Augustine who employs Paul in explaining "petra" is that "the heretics of our time," in Sisto's own words, use both Augustine and Paul to laugh at the Roman Catholic explanation of "petra" in terms of Peter.[103]

The remainder of this annotation is concerned with responding to these charges of the "heretics." Sisto argues that the cited passages

125

from Augustine are indeed revered and that the
Roman Catholic position advanced here is also
grounded in the exegesis of Augustine; his <u>Retrac-
tiones</u> statement is advanced as approving of both
interpretations while preferring neither.[104]
To the charge that to take "petra" in terms of
Peter is necessarily to set up another foundation
for the church in place of Christ, Sisto responds
that no new foundation is being established.
Rather he affirms that Christ is the one foundation ("fundamentum") upon whom other rocks (note
the plural here) can be superimposed - that is,
Peter and the other apostles. In this last
statement Sisto is self-consciously and cleverly
moving from the "petra" of Mt. 16:18 to the
"fundamenta" of Rev. 21:14.[105]

Sisto then strives to buttress his positions by affirming that they are supported by the
"ancient fathers": Clement of Rome, Origen,
Basil, Theophylact [!], Jerome, Chrysostom, and
Hilary.[106] Some elements are new here. Where
Erasmus and many others used Origen's homily on
Matthew to prove that "petra" needs be taken as
faith, Sisto points to a confusing passage from
this same homily which speaks of Peter as deserving to be the "foundation of the church."[107]
The reference to Hilary is also new, not only in
terms of those writers who interpreted "petra" in
terms of Peter, but also in the sense that this is
the first mention of Hilary by a sixteenth century
exegete. However, Sisto seems much less inter-
ested in Hilary's actual words in his commentary
on Mt. 16:18 (he never cites them) than in rescu-
ing Hilary from the hands of the long-dead but
still influential Erasmus:

Hilary on the canon with reference to
Matthew, chapter sixteen, exegetes these
words in the same way as the previous
exegetes, although Erasmus argues that
his words be given another meaning, when
he adds a note to this effect in the
margin: faith is the foundation of the

126

church. By these words Erasmus wished
that Hilary be interpreted as if he
thought faith was the foundation and
rock, and not Peter. Hilary nevertheless
speaks quite openly of Peter, as is clear
to anyone who reads his words.[108]

To prove further Erasmus' error in his discussion
of Hilary, Sisto appeals to Hilary's remarks on
Psalm 103 where Peter is again referred to as "the
one upon which Christ was about to build his
church" and as "the foundation of the church."[109]

        Sisto's second annotation dealing with Mt.
16:18 is entirely concerned with the proper response to Origen's contention that "petra" should
be taken in the broad sense of every imitator of
Christ. Rather than give his own argumentation as
a response to Origen, Sisto turns to a contemporary, Johannes van den Bunderen (1481-1557), and
his work Compendium concertationis . . . published
in Venice in 1548, a work written in support of
papal authority and one which was later praised by
Roberto Bellarmino. Sisto notes that Bunderen was
writing against the Lutherans who used Origen's
commentary in their attack on Peter's primacy.[110]
Sisto also agrees with Bunderen that Origen's
exposition is "typical and allegorical, which uses
are not customarily employed for confirming
dogmas"; proof for this may be seen, according to
this view, in Origen's explanation of the "gates"
and "keys" of Mt. 16:18 in terms of sins and
virtues.[111]

Cornelius Jansen's ". . . commentariorum
in concordiam et totam historiam
evangelicam" (1571-1572)

        Cornelius Jansen (1510-1576), not to be
confused with the later and more renowned Cornelius Jansen (1585-1638), was born in Hulst,
Flanders. After studies at Ghent and Louvain he
taught Scripture at the Premonstratensian Abbey of

Tongerloo until 1542. He later attended the Council of Trent as the delegate of the University of
Louvain of Philip II of Spain. The last nine
years of his life were spent at Ghent where he was
bishop.

Jansen wrote on many Biblical books, among
them Proverbs, Ecclesiasticus, Psalms, Wisdom, and
Luke. His . . . commentariorum in suam concordiam,
ac totam historiam euangelicam, partes IIII first
appeared in 1571-1572 and was reprinted many times
during the last quarter of the sixteenth century
in Lyons, Venice, Louvain, and Paris.

Jansen's remarks betray a notable polemical character. In contrast to the "contentious
innovators" of his time who hold that the primacy
of Peter is neither necessary nor authentic with
respect to Mt. 16:18, he opposes his own, and more
importantly in his eyes, patristic, position that
the "petra" is indeed Peter who holds a certain
primacy over the other apostles, a primacy which
his successors participate in by hereditary
right.[112] More specifically, the "innovators"
rely especially on Augustine's remarks in his
Retractiones and his treatise on John 21 (Jansen
cites more Augustine than Sisto) in order to claim
his non-identity between "petra" and "Petrus."
According to Jansen, the "innovators" are not
concerned with Augustine's identity between
"petra" and Christ, because this seems forced and
thus they generally understand "petra" in terms of
"fides."[113] Jansen then notes that the "innovators" were able to bring forward patristic
support for their identification of "petra" with
"fides," (Hilary, Cyril, Chrysostom, Theophylact)
and "rationes" as well (Paul's identification of
"petra" with Christ in I Cor., the fact that
"Petrus" and not "petra" was said to Peter, and
the fact that the text has "hanc petram" rather
than "hunc Petrum").[114]

To this position, Jansen compares his own
arguments which are meant to answer the Protestant

arguments and which are to prove that petra=
Petrus. His first argument we have already seen
in Cajetan's exposition: the "hanc" of Mt. 16:18
can only refer to Peter who is the object of the
discourse and this is the plain context of the
literal meaning.[115] Jansen like Bredenbach adds a
linguistic remark: in the Chaldean bible "Cepha"
is generally found where in the Hebrew bible there
is SLᶜ.[116] Thus what Christ really said was "Thou
art 'Cepha' and on this 'Cepha' I will build my
church"; this reading represents the Syriac gospel
behind the present Greek text; this reading is the
equivalent of saying in Latin "Thou art rock
("saxum") and on this rock ("saxum") I will build
my church."[117] This linguistic insight allows
Jansen to appropriate and correct Augustine: "If
master Augustine would have weighed this carefully
he would not have judged that what must be understood by 'petra' is open to doubt. Rather he
would have held most certainly that "petra" ought
to be understood as "Peter."[118] Augustine's
confusion on this point was compounded by those
Greeks who translated the Syriac "Cepha" with the
masculine "ó pétros" rather than the feminine "é
pétra," although either of these is appropriate.
Certainly according to this way of thinking Peter
may be called "é pétra," even though the Greek
interpreter of Matthew chose to use the masculine
rather than the feminine.[119] Jansen also sees
that this linguistic approach to Mt. 16:18 is
indicated by the literal context, well-founded in
its idiomatic peculiarity, and confirmed by the
common consensus of the fathers. Here he refers
to the ever increasing phenomenon in sixteenth
century literature of drawing up lists of patristic positions seemingly in favor of the Romanist
position -- see Albert Pigges' Hierarchiae
ecclesiasticae assertio, Book Three (Cologne,
1551) as a brilliant example of this.[120]

        Jansen then proceeds to list examples of this
patristic concord: Tertullian, Origen, Cyprian,
Basil, Ambrose and, according to Jansen, too many
others to mention.[121] For all these writers and

their respective citations Jansen is indebted to Pigges' Hierarchiae ecclesiasticae assertio, Book Three, Chapter 3; both he and Pigges are concerned to demonstrate that the universal patristic opinion equates "petra" with Peter. What also prompts the appeal to these sources is that these authorities are old and therefore this position has been present from the beginning of the church. The reference to Origen is difficult to pinpoint. Cyprian's letter to Iubaian, the Mauretanian bishop who disagreed with Cyprian over baptism, does loosely speak of "petra" in terms of Peter; however, the context of the letter is the conflict over the baptism of the heretic Novatian and his followers. Cyprian is concerned to point out that there is only one baptism which gives a remission of sins; Peter is cited in relation to the rock of Mt. 16:18 as a sign of the unity of the church, a church with prelates established by evangelical law and by the Lord's ordination; only in such a church that licit baptism and remission of sins occur.[122] The other reference in this letter to Peter and the rock occurs in the context of Cyprian's asking which is the source of living water, the heretics or the one church which guards and holds the Lord's own power.[123]

Neither is Basil actually doing exegesis in book two of his polemic against Eunomius. Rather he is responding to the view that since there are different names there are necessarily different substances. He opposes this in saying that different names point to different properties but all men participate in the same substance. Peter (and Paul) are brought forward as examples; thus when we hear the name "Peter" we do not think of his substance or essence but rather of his properties, one of which is that since he was outstanding with reference to faith "he received the building of the church upon himself."[124] The reference to "Ambrose" is actually to a sermon given on the feast of Peter and Paul by Maximus of Turin. Maximus certainly does attribute the "petra" of Mt. 16:18 to Peter:

We have frequently said that Peter himself was called 'rock' by the Lord when
he says, 'Thou art Peter and upon this
rock I will build my church.' Therefore
if Peter is the rock upon which the
church is built, rightly he first heals
the foot. So that just as he contains
the foundations of faith in the church,
so also he strengthens the foundations of
the members [the feet] in man. It is
correct to say that he first cures the
feet in the Christian, so that now
neither troubled nor incapacitated, but
robust and strong, one can step upon the
rock of the church.[125]

However, one should also note that this sermon
also goes on to speak of Paul as a "vessel of
election" ("vas electionis") on a parallel and
equal footing with the rock of Peter.[126]

Jansen then returns to those patristic
writers whom his adversaries brought forward as
evidence for the position petra=fides. According
to Jansen, Augustine never excluded the "Peter"
interpretation of "petra," but rather left the
final decision up to the freedom of the reader.[127]
Jansen adds that the reasons Augustine seems to
favor the Christ interpretation seem "too little
effective." Had he been more appreciative of the
underlying Syriac version he would not have been so
disposed to the Christ interpretation. Further,
his use of I Cor. 3:11 does not exclude Peter and
the other apostles being foundations upon the
primary foundation Christ.[128] As to the other
patristic authorities that "the adversaries" bring
forward, not only do these speak of Peter as the
"petra," but also even in those places where
"petra" is described in terms of faith and confession, the patristic writers with their locating
of faith in terms of Peter alone and with their
emphasis on the coinherence of faith and Peter
differ substantially from the adversaries with
their broadening of faith to refer to the faith of

any man or faith in general.[129] There are certain
new elements introduced here into the "petra"
argumentation. Jansen uses Chrysostom's remarks
about the keys being given to Peter as evidence
that the rock cannot stand for faith in general;
otherwise Peter would not have been singled out
for the honor of the keys.[130] In order to rescue
Hilary from the adversaries, Jansen appeals to
Hilary's commentary on our passage (remarking with
more subtlety than Sisto that someone added
falsely a marginal note in the Froben/Basel edition of Hilary that faith is the foundation of the
church):

> Having been found to be worthy, Peter
> first recognized what of God was in
> Christ. Oh, in the announcement of the new
> name the fortunate foundation of the
> church and in its building a worthy rock
> who destroys the infernal laws, the gates
> of Tartarus, and all the confinements of
> death. Oh, blessed doorkeeper of heaven,
> to whose judgment the keys of eternal
> entrance are handed over?[131]

Although the parallelism between the image of
Peter as rock and foundation and the consequent
image of Peter as possessing certain authoritative
judgment has been recognized,[132] what also needs
to be stressed is that Hilary sees these laudatory
words of Peter as his reward ("praemium") for his
confession of faith.[133] Jansen does not discuss
the particulars of the Hilarian passage supposedly
brought forward by the adversaries to interpret
"petra" in terms of faith.[134] Then he moves on to
a discussion of Cyril. While not discussing in
detail the adversaries' use of Cyril's De
trinitate, book 4,[135] he does appeal to Cyril's commentary on John, specifically to his remarks on
Jn. 1:42: "Jesus foretells that the present name
Simon will not be for himself, but Peter, sig-
nifying appropriately by the name itself that on
him just as on a rock and very firm stone he was
about to build his church."[136]

132

Jansen adds at the end of his comment that Peter became the rock through his singular faith and this unique event differentiates Peter from his own successors in the Roman See. That is, what is said about building the church upon Peter pertains only to Peter and not to his successors.[137] And although the successors of Peter at Rome may be said to be the "heads of the entire Christian church" and "foundations and primary stones upon which the church of their respective times is founded," nevertheless Peter "is not only the foundation of the faithful who were with him on earth, but also entirely of the entire church of the faithful who either have believed in Christ after Peter or are about to believe."[138] And although everything that is said after Mt. 16:18 does pertain equally to Peter and his successors, the "rock" passage pertains properly to Peter "just as the name Peter is proper to him and not shared in by his successors."[139]

The Rhemes New Testament of 1582

Certain Roman Catholic scholars exiled from Elizabethan England journeyed first to Douay in the Spanish Netherlands where they established an English College. When driven from Douay they moved to Rhemes in northeastern France. There they published the first English version of the New Testament authorized by the Roman church. The polemical and controversial intent of this writing is evident throughout; the writers are self-consciously responding to certain Protestant translations and interpretations of the New Testament. In this response the authors seek to be enlightened by "Apostolike tradition, the expositions of the holy fathers, the decrees of the Catholike Church and most ancient Councils."[140]

The exegesis of chapter sixteen of Matthew is interesting in many respects. Besides repeating certain points already set out in earlier Roman Catholic exegetica, the authors incorporate some new information and ideas of their own. First they specify more fully the liturgical days on which Mt. 16:13-19 was used as a gospel reading: the feast of Saints Peter and Paul (June 29th), the feast of the Chair of Peter at Rome (January 18th), the feast of the Chair of Peter at Antioch (February 22nd), the feast of Peter's Chains (August 1st), "and on the day of the creation and coronation of the Pope, and in the Anniversarie thereof."[141] Secondly, while clearly identifying the "petra" of Mt. 16:18 with Peter in the annotations on this verse (and this self-consciously against the "Adversaries"), they suggest an English translation of Mt. 16:18 already prepared for in earlier exegesis of petra=Petrus, that is, "Thou art Peter, and upon this peter Will I build my Church . . . ."[142] Thirdly, in differentiating the headship or foundation of the church they stress a certain kenosis on Christ's part which in effect allows Peter to be both head and foundation of the church: ". . . which was not to make him self [Jesus] or to promise him self to be the head or foundation of the Church. For his father gave him that dignitie, and he tooke not that honour to him self, nor sent him self, nor tooke the keies of heaven of him self, but al of his father. He had his commission the very houre of his incarnation: . . ."[143]

The Rhemes New Testament also advances new authorities for the position that Peter is the rock without discussing or even citing the actual words of these authorities: Augustine's Ennarationes in psalmos, Sermo 49 on John's gospel, Sermones 15 and 29 on saints' feasts, and Adnotationes in Iob, chapter thirty, Ambrose's Expositio euangelii secundum Lucam, Jerome's Commentarii in Isaiam, Epiphanius' Ancoratus, Leo the Great's Epistola 89, Gregory's "Li 4 ep. 32 ind. 13," and Theodoret's Compendium haereticarum fabularum, book 5 (section 28).[144]

Augustine does clearly identify Peter with "petra": ". . . et in illa confessione appellatus
erat Petra, supra quam fabricaretur ecclesia
. . ."[145] Augustine's commentary on Job contains
no references to Peter or to the rock![146] The
passage from Ambrose's Expositio concerns Luke
9:20 and speaks of Christ, Peter, faith, and the
individual Christian as a "petra."[147] Jerome does
see Peter as the "petra:" "Unde et super unum
montium Christus fundat Ecclesiam, et loquitur ad
eum: 'Tu es Petrus . . .'"[148] Epiphanius uses
"petra" of Peter while he is discussing saints as
the temples of God.[149] Leo the Great's letter
contains no references to Mt. 16:18.[150]
Theodoret in discussing penitence refers to Peter
as the "primum Ecclesiae fundamentum."[151]

　　　　Finally with respect to the question of
Peter and his successors the Rhemes New Testament
affirms that the great privileges ascribed to
Peter in Mt. 16 should not die with Peter but be
perpetuated in the church through Peter's
successors.[152] Augustine's Psalmus contra
partem Donati and Leo's letter 89 (again) are
cited in support of this.[153]

　　　　　　Juan de Maldonado's "Commentarius
　　　　　　in IV evangelia" (1596-1597)

　　　　Juan de Maldonado (1534-1583) was born in
Casas de la Reina, near Estremadura, Spain. He
studied at Salamanca and Rome under such prominent
theologians as Soto, Cano, Vittoria and Tolet. He
entered the Society of Jesus in 1562. All of his
Biblical commentaries were composed at Bourges.
By 1582 his commentary on Matthew was finished;[154]
it was first published in his Commentarius in IV
evangelia at Pont-à-Mousson in 1596-1597 (later
editions include: Venice, 1597 and Lyons, 1598;
his commentary was still being reprinted in the
nineteenth century).

　　　　Maldonado in beginning his commentary on
"et super hanc petram . . ." points out that some

patristic writers have interpreted "petra" in
terms of the faith or confession of faith mentioned earlier in the chapter or in terms of
Christ himself (these were frequently cited by
certain Calvinists):   Gregory of Nyssa's Contra
Judaeos; Chrysostom's Adversus Iudaeos oratio 2;
pseudo-Ambrose's commentary on Galatians 4;
Augustine's treatise on John.[155]

After this standard exegetical beginning,
Maldonado declares his own position: the "petra"
of Mt. 16:18 is no one other than Saint Peter.[156]
He gives two reasons for this position: 1) the
demonstrative pronoun "hanc" functions as a
relative pronoun modifying Peter and this linkage
is appropriate, contrary to Calvin, because
Matthew was writing in the Syriac tongue; 2)
Christ was speaking of the foundation of a building and it is more common to speak of such buildings in terms of the feminine than in terms of the
masculine which is rarely used.[157]

He then turns to specific objections and
errors of the Calvinists regarding his interpretation. To the question why did Jesus not say
"super te," Maldonado responds that Christ was
speaking of the foundation of a building and a
building is founded upon rocks, not upon men.[158]
Later in answering the Calvinist question why
Jesus singled Peter out for the blessing and why
this text pertains to Peter speaking for himself
alone Maldonado writes:

> In any case it was appropriate in these
> matters that just as Christ was choosing
> the twelve apostles according to the
> likeness of the twelve patriarchs, so
> also he choose one like Abraham, who
> because of his greater faith, was the
> head of all, and just as Abraham was the
> foundation of the Old Testament, so Peter
> was the foundation of the Church of the
> Gospel. For all things are equal in
> both. Abraham excelled in faith, Peter

136

excelled in faith. Abraham's name was
changed since he was to be the father of
many nations, . . . and Peter's name was
changed since he was to be the father and
head of all Christians.[159]

Maldonado is also concerned to address those other
biblical passages used by the Calvinists to argue
against the divine foundation of the Church upon
Peter. The arguments he advances regarding I Cor.
3:11 and Eph. 2:20 have already been made by
earlier exegetes.

He interrupts the series of questions and
objections by inserting a brief discussion of the
patristic authorities who hold that the Church was
built upon Peter. Among those writers he lists
without discussing their actual positions are:
Hippolytus' De consummatione mundi, Tertullian's
De pudicitia, Gregory Nazianzen's Oratio de
moderatione disputationibus servanda, Basil's
Homilia de poenitentia, pseudo-Ambrose's commentary on Galatians 2, Leo's Sermo two, his
Epistula to the Vienna bishops and Epistula to
Geminianus (?), the Council of Chalcedon, Juvencus, and Michael Psellus' Apud Theodoretum and
his In Cantica, book three.[160] Hippolytus' work
does not discuss Mt. 16:18 directly but does refer
to Peter as "fidei petra."[161] Tertullian does
indeed understand "petra" in terms of Peter; in
fact he paraphrases Jesus' words in terms of
"super te." Maldonado conveniently omits all
references to the context of Tertullian's Montanist position of denying to a church authority
what belongs to Peter alone.[162] Gregory Nazianzen
in giving examples of order and discipline within
groups cites Peter as the one who was called
"Petra."[163] The author of Homilia de poenitentia
does refer to Peter as the rock; however he also
sees Christ as a more primary rock.[164] Pseudo-
Ambrose in his commentary on Galatians 2 does not
discuss Mt. 16:18 but in explaining verses seven
and eight does attribute to Peter a limited primacy intended "for the establishing of the [Jew-
ish] church."[165] Leo does interpret "petra" in

137

terms of Peter and his successors.[166] Neither in
its definition of faith nor in its various canons
explicitly did the Council of Chalcedon remark on
Mt. 16:18; however, the Council's definition of
faith does refer to Leo the Great's "Flavian Tome"
as "the great confession of that Peter" which has
served as a "sure pillar" for the true faith.[167]
Iuvencus in his Evangelica historia does poeti-
cally connect up the name "Petrus" and "saxum."[168]
The two references to Michael Psellus seem inap-
propriate here; though classified as an "autor
vetus" by Maldonado, he lived in the eleventh
century (1018-c. 1078). His expositions on the
Canticle of Canticles contain no references to Mt.
16:18.[169]

Maldonado also lists some writers (with
accompanying citation) who were thought by some to
have interpreted "petra" in a sense other than
Peter. Among those in this category is Chrysostom's second Homilia on Psalm 50.[170] However he
never discusses the positions of those writers
mentioned at the beginning of his comments on this
passage. He is especially concerned to show that
this last group (those who interpret "petra" in
terms of "fides") is not linked with the "heretics" of his own day; in order to establish such
distance he suggests that what these early writers
really meant was that the church was built upon
the faith and confession of Peter, that is, upon
Peter because of his faith and confession.[171]
Soon thereafter he adds that these writers did not
deny what the heretics now deny, that is, that
Peter is the foundation of the church.[172]

Maldonado ends his commentary by posing
this question: what is it that is granted unique-
ly to Peter by these words, especially since
others (apostles, prophets) may be said to be the
foundation of the church?[173] Peter is like
Christ and unlike the other foundations in that
after Christ Peter is the first foundation of the
church, Peter takes Christ's place in his absence,
and the whole church, not just a part, relies on
him.[174] Peter is unlike Christ in that while

Christ is the foundation by his own power, Peter
is the foundation because of Christ's power.[175]

Sebastian Barradas " . . . commentariorum in concordiam et historiam quatuorum euangelistarum" (1599)

Sebastian Barradas was born in Lisbon,
Portugal in 1543. He entered the Jesuits in 1558;
later he taught exegesis at Coimbra and Evora
(1581-1589). He died in 1615.

Toward the end of the sixteenth century
the commentaries by Roman Catholics on this verse
become longer and longer, incorporate more patristic authorities, and attempt to advance more
reasons in support of the petra=Petrus position.
Barradas' commentary is an excellent example of
this phenomenon. His work also demonstrates the
reason for this phenomenon, that is, the chapter
which contains the exegesis of Mt. 16:18 is entitled "The promise of the highest pontifical
office made to Peter."[176]

Barradas acknowledges right at the beginning that previous interpretation of "petra"
has been ambiguous since many of the Fathers took
"petra" in terms of confession, faith, or Christ
(Hilary, Ambrose, Gregory of Nyssa, Cyril, Augustine, Chrysostom). Although he will return to
these men later in his discussion he does not
discuss these petra≠Petrus passages at all. What
is new here are the references to Ambrose's work
on Eph. 2 and Gregory of Nyssa's commentary on the
seventh penitential psalm (142).[177]

But then after having acknowledged such
diversity he argues in favor of "petra" being
taken in the sense of Peter.[178] He sees this
interpretation borne out in the very "structio" of
the verse and its context.[179] By this he refers
to certain arguments already seen in this chapter:
Jesus speaking in Hebrew, that is Syriac; the

force of the demonstrative pronoun "hanc"; the
larger context of verse eighteen where statements
are made to Peter (thus also verse eighteen).[180]
The new elements that Barradas adds are these:
First, "petra" is the "ratio" which stands behind
and explains Peter's new name, just as the angel
gives the "ratio" for Jesus' name in Matthew 1,
and just as the name Abraham is explained in
Genesis 17 -- what is being given in all three
cases is the "ratio nominis".[181] Secondly, to the
argument that since the preceding and following
statements are made to Peter, therefore verse
eighteen must be applied to him, Barradas adds
that this would be true even if Christ had used
the name "Simon" because the "sense" would be the
same.[182]

Here he interrupts the listing of "rationes" in order to address those "inexperienced"
individuals who say that since Christ is the
"foundation" of the church, there can be no other
foundation and, consequently, Peter is neither
"rock nor foundation."[183] Barradas responds to
this position by differentiating types of foundations:

Let these learn from buildings that there
is no one stone of foundation as such but
many. Therefore just as in buildings so
in the church -- the greatest stone and
principal foundation is Christ. The
church is primarily founded upon Christ.
On him Peter depends as the second rock
of foundation. . . Just as the foundations of the prophet and apostle [Ephe-
sians 2] and just as Christ Jesus the
foundation, is there nothing further than
this? How are we to think except as
Christ is openly called the holy of the
holy ones: and thus figuratively the
foundation of the foundations. Therefore
if you think in terms of the sacraments,
Christ is the holy of the holy ones; if
you think of a flock gathered together,

140

Christ is the pastor of the pastors; if
you think of architecture, Christ is the
foundation of the foundations . . .[184]

Barradas then turns to those patristic
writers (even those cited earlier, he notes) who
held Peter to be both rock and foundation. Certain new elements are found in this discussion.
Hilary is brought forward in that book of his De
trinitate as supporting the notion of Peter as
"petra."[185] Chrysostom is also listed, first for
his Homilia 4 on Isaiah 6:1, for his Homilia on
Mt. I, and for a section of his fifty-fifth
Homilia on Mt. heretofore unnoticed by other
exegetes.[186] Barradas also appeals to Augustine's
seventh treatise on John's gospel.[187] Among the
other patristic texts he cites these are new:
Basil's comments on Isaiah 2,[188] Epiphanius'
Panarion,[189] Cyprian's De simplicitate
praelatorum and De habitu virginum,[190] and
Jerome's Dialogus adversus Pelagianos.[191]

The Isaiah Homilia by Chrysostom does not
directly discuss Mt. 16:18 but simply indicates
that Peter was married![192] Augustine does interpret "petra" in terms of Peter with reference to
his seventh treatise on John's gospel.[193] Basil
does refer the "petra" to Peter in his Enarratio
in prophetam Isaiam: ". . . Petrus, supra quam
petrum pollicitus fuerat Dominus suam se aedificaturum Ecclesiam."[194] Epiphanius while writing
against the Cathari heresy speaks of both Peter
and faith as the rock.[195] Cyprian's treatise on
virginal dress while recommending spiritual goods
and qualities does refer to Peter as the rock.[196]
Finally, it is true that Jerome's anti-Pelagian
dialogue speaks of Peter as the rock; however
Barradas omits mentioning that the Pelagian
Critibulus is speaking here of Peter as an example
of ecclesiastical simplicity.[197]

Barradas then returns to his overall
reason why Peter is "fundamental rock and chief."
The reason is that Christ, leaving the earth,

141

needed one vicar, moderator, and head to ward off
schismatics and heresiarchs.[198] Barradas adds
that both Peter and his successors in the Roman
chair, including the present pope Clement VIII,
functioned and function in this role of unity.[199]

Barradas ends his comment with a final
encouragement to the reader to note that the
"petra" of Mt. 16:18 does not signify any stone
whatsoever ("lapis") but a Rock ("Rupes") in the
sense of Isaiah 2:10, 7:19 and 51:1, that is, a
concrete rock in which one might hide or a concrete rock from which material comes.[200] Peter
is this very rock, that is, foundation, pastor,
head and chief of the church.[201]

Barradas' note on "aedificabo ecclesiam
meam" returns to the unity theme already advanced
earlier: the oneness of the church demands the
best type of rule, that is a monarchial one.[202]

CONCLUSION

The Roman Catholic commentaries which
explain "petra" in terms of "Petrus" date from
Thomas de Vio's commentary in 1532. By the
1550's, Bredenbach can assert that petra=Petrus is
the dominant Roman Catholic position; the subse-
quent commentaries substantiate this claim. With
respect to these commentaries four areas deserve
comment. First, they are all self-consciously
exegeting out of conflict situations in which they
see themselves defending the petra=Petrus position
against the counter positions of "heretics,
adversaries, innovators and/or Calvinists."
Secondly, their understanding of "petra" is an
institutional "petra" in terms of a continuing
officium in the church necessitated by Christ's
departure or absence. Jansen is a notable exception here in that he excludes Peter's successors from consideration as "petra." Thirdly,
this group of commentaries shows a critical
concern for the actual language of the text as

revealing Matthew's intent; Bredenbach stands out
in this regard for he is the first sixteenth
century exegete to stress the Aramaic background
and rendering of Mt. 16:18. Finally, all these
exegetes are concerned to appropriate and to
bring to a certain unity all earlier exegesis in
terms of petra=Petrus=Roma; Cajetan's "simul"
approach is most characteristic of this tendency.
In so doing these exegetes clearly bring out the
patristic positions regarding Peter, both
petra=Petrus and petra=Petrus=Roma. However,
they are generally unconcerned to uncover the
contextual character of the various patristic remarks. The only two medieval writers mentioned
are Theophylact and Michael Psellus, but these
are mentioned in patristic terms and groupings.
In fact the majority of medieval exegetes opted
for positions distinctly different from the
position adopted by the exegetes in this chapter;
the predominant medieval positions were
petra=Christus and petra=fides.

144

NOTES FOR CHAPTER THREE

[1]I have consulted the 1537 and 1538 editions published at Lyons.

[2]The edition used here was published in 1532.

[3]Cajetan, Evangelia cum commentariis ([Parisiis]: Ascensius, Parvum, Roigny, 1532), f. iv: "Fuit autem intentio mea sensum litteralem tantummodo prosequi."

[4]Ibid.: "Qualiacumque autem haec scripta sint apostolatus tui iudicio subiicio: quemadmodum et mea reliqua. Nihil enim in Christi ecclesia tutum est quod apostolicae sedis doctrinae non quadrat."

[5]Ibid., f. xlviir H: "Iesus omnes interrogavit, non tamen omnes respondent: nec Petrus consultat cum aliis responsionem, sed ut postea dominus testatur, tactus interna revelatione statim respondet."

[6]Ibid., K: "'Tibi.' Non dicit vobis. soli enim Petro significatur revelatio haec facta."

[7]Ibid., f. xlviii A: "'Dico tibi.' Non vobis. 'Quia tu.' Non vos."

[8]Ibid.: "'Et super hanc petram.' Ecce ad quid es Petrus, ad quid es saxum: ad officium scilicet fundamenti. Pronomen siquidem hanc demonstrat saxum de quo est sermo: de nullo autem saxo praemissus est aut sequitur sermo nisi de Petro: ipse igitur Petrus secundum planum contextum literae demonstratur per pronomen 'hanc.' Ac si apertius diceret. 'tu es saxum and super hoc saxum.'"

[9]Cajetan's emphasis on the literal sense brought him into no little controversy with his

145

Roman Catholic contemporaries; he was numbered
among the heretics in Gabriel du Preau's De
vitis, sectis, et dogmatibus . . . (Coloniae,
1569) for supposedly holding that the Genesis
story about Eve being formed from the rib of Adam
must not be taken literally (here understood as a
statement about what really happened). Others
such as Alphonse de Castro regarded such positions not so much heretical but as erroneous.

[10]Ibid., A-B: "'Aedificabo ecclesiam meam.'
Te qui iam es saxum, efficiam fundamentum in
aedificando ecclesiam meam super te. Principatum
ecclesiae se Petro promittit, qualem fundamentum
obtinet in aedificio. Fundamentum ecclesiae
Petrum facturum se Iesus promittit: quia sui
tentandam praedestinavit ecclesiam super firmi-
tatem sedis Petri. Vide huius lectionis mysteria
per nos latius discussa in opusculo de institutione pontificatus a Iesu Christo: ne eadem repe-
tamus."

[11]Ibid., xlviii[r] I: "'Satana.' Non est
diaboli nomen proprium Satanas: sed in genere
significat adversarium. Omnis enim qui adver-
satur, Satanas est. . . ."

[12]Ibid., K: "Confer Petrum Satanam, scandalum et non sapientem divina sed humana, cum
Petro beato, cui Pater revelavit quod Iesus est
Christus filius dei vivi: et discernes Petrum
secundum seipsum a Petro divina fulto gratia: et
intelliges non suffragari percaepta divinae
gratiae dona, si postea non perseverat assis-
tentia eiusdem divinae gratiae."

[13]Cajetan, De divina institutione pontificatus Romani pontificis, (1521), ed. F. Lauch-
ert, CC 10 (Münster in Westfalen: Aschendorff,
1925), p. 2, lines 12-15: "Quia vero ex sacris
litteris pendet omnis questionis huius veritas,
et duo sunt praecipui textus, scilicet Matthe.
xvi et Io. ultimo, expresse de hoc mysterio
loquentes, ideo primo iuxta utrumque textum

investigandum est . . ."

14Ibid., lines 15-20: ". . . an soli Petro
verba Christi dicta sint. Secundo, an per haec
soli Petro pontificatus totius ecclesiae a
Christo commissus sit. Tertio, an hic totius
ecclesie pontificatus Petro a Christo commissus,
sit ab eodem Domino datus successori Petri.
Quarto, an sit a Christo hic pontificatus datus
Romano pontifici ut Petri successori."

15Ibid., lines 20-25: "Ut autem primi clara
sit absolutio, Matthei textus prius discutiendus
sic est, ut in primis tractetur opinio dicentium
verba Christi non Petro, sed persone qualificate,
deinde dicentium non Petro, sed ecclesie, postea
dicentium Petro et apostolis aliis, demum negan-
tium soli Petro, quia ecclesie dicta esse."

16Ibid., page 10, lines 12-13: "Ubi adverte
non solum diversas, verum non unius sed diver-
sorum generum promissiones Petro factas esse; . . ."

17Ibid., lines 13-16: ". . . nam prima
promissio constructionem respicit ecclesie:
'edificabo ecclesiam meam'; secunda autem auctori-
tatem: 'dabo claves regni coelorum,' 'et quodcum-
que solveris' etc."

18Ibid., lines 16-18: "Illa ad ecclesie
substantiam, ista ad officium respicit, tantum
que inter se differunt, quantum est inter substantiam et officium distantia."

19Ibid., p. 12, lines 31-34: "Duplex autem
advertenda est inter has promissiones differentia: prima est quod esse fundamentum ecclesie non
promittitur persone Petri absolute, sed quatenus
est Petrus seu petra; claves autem regni coelorum
promittuntur persone Petri absolute."

20Ibid., p. 12, line 34 - p. 13, line 9:
"Et habes hanc differentiam ex evangelio, dum de
primo dicitur: 'et super hanc petram edificabo

147

ecclesiam meam,' et non dixit: super te edificabo ecclesiam meam; per 'hanc' enim 'petram'
demonstravit totum quod dixerat: 'tu es Petrus';
nam 'petram' reddidit ad li Petrus, et articulum
'hanc' reddidit ad pronomen tu, tanquam si
diceret: tu es Petrus et super te Petrum edificabo ecclesiam meam. De clavibus autem regno
coelorum non dicitur: et tibi Petro, neque:
huic petre, sed simpliciter et absolute: 'tibi
dabo claves'; monstrans per hoc quod dixit
'tibi', quod persone, non qualitati per petram
significante, puta fidei, promittebat claves.
Persone ergo qualificate promissum est fore
Christi ecclesie fundamentum, persone vero nude
promisse sunt claves regni coelorum." Earlier
Cajetan had argued for the identification of
"petra" with "Petrus" on the basis that "no other
rock, indicated or named, is found in the gospel."
Ibid., p. 12, lines 3-7: "Significantissime
siquidem ille articulus 'hanc' exprimit eandem
monstrari petram, de qua tunc erat sermo, quae et
per pronomen: 'tu es Petrus' monstrabatur, et
hoc tanto clarius, quanto nulla alia petra tunc
monstrata aut nominata invenitur in evangelio."

[21]Ibid., lines 9-17: "Altera differentia
est, quod in prima promissione Petro promittitur
ecclesiam sustinendi officium, non se Petro sed
Christo actore; nam non dixit: et super hanc
petram edificabis ecclesiam meam, sed dixit;
'super hanc petram edificabo ecclesiam meam,'
tanquam si diceret: tu sustinebis tanquam petra
me edificante ecclesiam meam super te petra. In
promissione vero clavium aperiendi officium et
claudendi non sibi reservavit Dominus, sed se
daturum claves promisit, ut ille cui dantur agat
aperiendo vel claudendo regnum coelorum."

[22]Ibid., p. 13, lines 17-23: "Hae ex evangelii plano sensu differentie constant. Ex
quibus evidenter colligitur differentia inter
officium Petri quoad potestatem utendi clavibus
et solvendi atque ligandi, et officium eiusdem ad
sustenendam ecclesiam in fide, dum officium

148

clavium homini committitur, officium vero sustinendi ecclesiam in fide ad Christum ut actorem,
ad petram ut rationem sustinendi, ad hominem vero
Petrum ut fundamentum suppositumque spectare
dicitur."

[23]Ibid., p. 14, lines 14-21:   "Ad alias
obiectiones, ex illis verbis: 'tu es Petrus, et
super hanc petram edificabo ecclesiam meam,'
dicitur, quod haec quidem spectant ad pontifi-
calem gradum, non secundum officium clavium, sed
secundum officium fundamenti. Et ex proposito
Dominus dixit, non: tu vocaberis Petrus, sed:
'tu es Petrus,' ut affirmaret: tu es Petrus re
et nomine, hoc est, tu es solidus, firmus, constans etc. in fide tanquam petra, ut Leo, Gre.,
Bedaque exponunt."

[24]Ibid., p. 36, lines 1-11:   "Et obiectis
quidem contra primam promissionem Petro factam,
ut foret fundamentum ecclesie, responderetur,
quod esse ecclesie fundamentum simpliciter id est
totaliter proprium est Christo, esse autem fundamentum ecclesie secundum aliquod tempus vel
secundum aliquam rationem particularem, communi-
catum est aliis. Et sanctis quidem, quibus
revelata est doctrina fidei pro ecclesia, com-
municatum est esse fundamentum sub rationibus
apostolorum et prophetarum, Petro autem ultra
predictam rationem promissum est fore fundamentum
secundum rationem pastoris totius ecclesie
Christi, secundum quam rationem non convenit
aliis apostolis esse fundamentum." Finally,
Cajetan again discusses Peter as the rock of the
church in the context of the two promises on p.
53, lines 20-29:   "Quocirca iungendo ambas promissiones, quum ex prima Petrus futurus sit
fundamentum ecclesie catholice (ubi in Petro
officium sustinendi ecclesiam catholicam in fidei
soliditate statuitur, et parieter ecclesie
catholice necessitas inherendi Petro ut fundamento imponitur; edificationis enim ratio expo-
scit, ut edificium necessitatem habeat inherendi
petre, super quam fundatum est), ex altera vero

149

Petro ecclesie potestatis plenitudo pollicita
sit, manifeste liquet promissum huiusmodi verbis
Petro ecclesie catholice pontificatum esse; haec
enim duo praecipua esse in totius christianae
ecclesie pontifice constat."

[25]Ibid., p. 83, lines 5-10, 20-24:   "Fidem
enim solidam in Petro et successoribus suis
secundum proprias personas significavit Dominus
et dicens 'Tu es Petrus'; in presenti, et dicens
'Ego rogavi pro te, ut non deficiat fides tua,'
in futuro. Fidem vero eiusdem in ordine ad
ecclesiam significavit Dominus et dicens 'Super
hanc petram edificabo ecclesiam meam,' et dicens:
'Confirma fratres tuos.' . . . Ex soliditate
autem in fide persone Romani pontificis in ordine
ad ecclesiam provenit, ut errare non possit
sententialiter diffiendo de fide christiana,
quoniam in huius modi diffinitione construitur
fides universalis ecclesie, et per eam edificatur
ecclesia Christi ab ipso Christo super petram
sedis apostolice." See also p. 84, lines 5-7
where again the emphasis is on Christ and not
Peter or the Roman pontiffs building the church
upon the apostolic seat.

[26]Ibid., p. 10, lines 18-20:   "Et licet in
prima promissione triplex inveniatur intellectus,
exponendo per 'hanc petram' vel Christum vel
Petrum vel confessionem Petri, ut Chriso.
exponit, . . ." The reference to Chrysostom does
not indicate that he held all three of these interpretations; rather, as Cajetan will point out
later, he interpreted "petra" in terms of "fides"
and "confessio"; see chapter one for the actual
citations.

[27]Ibid., lines 20-22:   ". . . si tamen
subtilius perspexerimus, unicus est sensus
literalis, hoc est, quod per 'hanc petram' demonstratur Petrus."

[28]Ibid., lines 22-27:   "Aug. enim in libro
primo retractionum cap. xxi. lectoris iudicio

150

relinquit, quae duarum sententiarum sit probabilior, Petrus ne an Christus demonstretur per
'hanc petram.' Unde hac libertate freti, ex ipso
evangelii textu dicimus per 'hanc petram' Petrum
demonstrari, . . ."

[29]Ibid., lines 26-32: ". . . ut patet ex
eo, quod Dominus dixit: 'super hanc petram
"edificabo".' Si enim seipsum demonstrasset, non
dixisset: edificabo, sed: edifico, quoniam tunc
vere super se ipsum edificabat, faciendo de
Symone Petrum; super Petrum autem non tunc, sed
post resurrectionem edificare cepit, et propterea
dixit in futuro: edificabo, ac si aperte diceret:
te quum nunc facio Petrum postea faciam fundamentum ecclesie meae."

[30]Ibid., p. 10, line 32 - p. 11, line 3:
"Confirmaturque hic sensus, quia aliter imper-
tinenter premisset: 'tu es Petrus,' quum tamen
pro maxima re hoc Petro dictum evangelium in-
sinuet, quum Dominus quasi reddens vices Petro
(ut predictum est) dixerit: 'tu es Petrus'; quid
enim tam magnum sonaret esse Petrum, aut quorsum:
'tu es Petrus,' nisi subsequenter demonstraretur:
'et super hanc petram ecclesiam meam'?"

[31]Ibid., lines 3-5: "Unde Hierony. exponens hunc locum ait: 'Secundum autem metaphoram
petre recte dicitur ei: edificabo ecclesiam
meam.'"

[32]S. Hieronymi presbyteri opera, pars I,
opera exegetica 7: Commentariorum in Matthaeum
libri IV, CCSL LXXVII (Turnholti: Brepols, 1969)
p. 141, lines 72-77: "'Quia tu es Petrus et
super hanc petram aedificabo ecclesiam meam.'
Sicut ipse lumen apostolis donavit ut lumen mundi
appellarentur, et cetera quae ex Domino sortiti
vocabula sunt ita et Simoni qui credebat in
petram Christum petri largitus est nomen, ac
secundum metaphoram petrae recte dicitur ei:
Aedificabo ecclesiam meam super te."

151

[33]Ibid., p. 11, lines 5-9: "Expositio autem
Chriso. de confessione fidei in idem redit,
quoniam confessio fidei in idem redit cum soliditate seu firmitate fidei quam denotat Petrus;
non enim differt ab ea, nisi tanquam actus ab
habitu; et rursus constat quod ecclesia magis
habet pro fundamento fidem quam fidei confessionem."

[34]Ibid., p. 11, lines 10-21: "Unde relin-
quitur, quod ad litteram per 'hanc petram' demonstratur Petrus. Exactius autem loquendo dic
'hanc' petram, id est in te petram, in te soliditatem fidei, in te Christum creditum, in te
Christum confessum, ut complectaris omnes sanctorum expositiones; nam singule verae quidem
sunt, sed partem tantum veritatis explicarunt,
fidem seu fidei confessionem aut Petrum vel
Christum exponentes. Quum autem utrumque simul
iungitur, ita quod et Petri personam et Christi
seu fidem simul significari exponitur, integra
veritas, integer sensus habetur littere, dicentis
non super petram, sed super 'hanc' petram.
Individuatur siquidem metaphorica petra et fit
'haec', quia est in hoc demonstrato supposito,
sicut quodlibet aliud in Petro existens individuatur et fit 'hoc,' quia est in ipsa Petri
persona."

[35]Ibid., p. 15, lines 3-6 and p. 17, lines
1-4.

[36]Ibid., p. 89, lines 6-8: ". . . Chriso.
omel. lv. super Matth. exponens illud: 'Super
hanc petram,' dicit: 'Petrum ecclesie future
pastorem constitutit.'"

[37]John Chrysostom, . . . Opera, vol. III
(Basileae: in officina Frobeniana, 1530), [CcC
6]: "Et ego dico tibi, quia tu es Petrus, et
super hanc petram aedificabo ecclesiam meam,) id
est fidem atque confessionem. Hic aperte praedixit magnam eorum qui credituri et erant et sunt
multitudinem fore, et sublimiora sapere ipsum

152

facit, et ecclesiae futurae pastorem constituit."

[38]Ibid., lines 14-17: "Et licet superius
glosaverit: 'Et super hanc petram edificabo
ecclesiam meam,' 'id est fidem atque confessionem,' inferius tamen ait 'Ego dico tibi, tu es
Petrus, et ego super te edificabo ecclesiam
meam.'"

[39]PG 58, 535: "Ex his omnibus ejus poten-
tiam animadverte. 'Ego tibi dico, tu es Petrus;
ego aedificabo Ecclesiam; ego tibi dabo claves
coelorum.'"

[40]Ibid., p. 93, lines 16-24: "Ambrosius in
sermone xlvii. de fide Petri apostoli, et habetur distinctione 1. ca. 'Fidelior,' dicit de
Petro: 'Tanquam bonus pastor tuendum gregem
accepit, ut qui sibi infirmus ante fuerat, fieret
omnibus firmamentum, et qui ipse interrogationis
tentatione nutaverat, ceteros fidei soliditate
fundaret. Denique pro soliditate devotionis
ecclesiarum petra dicitur, sicut ait Dominus:
"Tu es Petrus, et super hanc petram edificabo
ecclesiam meam"; petra enim dicitur eo quod
primus in nationibus fidei fundamenta posuerit et
tanquam saxum immobile totius operis christiani
compagem molemque contineat.'"

[41]CIC 1, 198.

[42]Maximi episcopi Taurinensis Sermones, ed.
A. Mutzenbecher, CCSL, 23 (Turnholti: Brepols,
1962), sermo LXXVII, p. 320, no. 1, lines 14-17:
"Petra ergo pro devotione Petrus dicitur, et
petra pro virtute dominus nuncupatur, sicut ait
apostolus: 'Bibebant autem de spiritali sequenti
eos petra; petra autem erat Christus'"; this
Sermo is also found in PL 57,353.

[43]Ibid., p. 94, lines 1-2: "Et idem in
hymno dominicali Petrum petram ecclesie appellat,
dicens: 'Hoc ipsa petra ecclesie canente culpam
diluit.'" See PL 16,1473.

[44]Ibid., p. 94, lines 4-14: "Et in sermone xi. de mirabilibus: Hanc igitur solam ecclesie navem ascendit Dominus, in qua Petrus magister est constitutus, dicente Domino: Super hanc petram edificabo ecclesiam meam. Que navis in altum seculi istius ita natat, ut pereunte mundo omnes quos suscipit servet illesos. Cuius figuram iam in veteri videmus testamento. Sicut enim Noe arca naufragante mundo cunctos quos susceperat incolumes reservavit, ita et Petri ecclesia conflagrante seculo omnes quos amplectitur representabit illesos. Et sicut tunc transacto diluvio ad arcam Noe columba signum pacis detulit, ita et transacto iudicio ad ecclesiam Petri Christus gaudium pacis referet, quia ipse columba vel pax est". See also PL 17,700.

[45]Glorieux, Pour revaloriser Migne, p. 14; see Maximi episcopi Tauriensis Sermones, #49.

[46]Ibid., pp. 194-5, section 4, lines 98-103.

[47]Ibid., p. 95, lines 1-3: "Hiero, super Math. ait: 'Symoni, qui credebat in petram Christum, Petri largitus est nomen, ac secundum mataphoram petre recte dicitur ei: "edificabo ecclesiam meam super te."'"

[48]Ibid., p. 11, lines 3-5.

[49]Ibid., p. 4, lines 19-22.

[50]The subtitle is significant: "Secundum hebraicam veritatem et veterum orthodoxorum patrum monumenta summo studio elucubrata, . . ." (Coloniae: Quentel and Calenius, 1560).

[51]Ibid., "Epistola nuncupatoria," f. a 3: "Delegit itaque ex utroque instrumento eos libros, quos suis auditoribus non minori cum utilitate, quam voluptate praelecturum se existimavit. Atque ex veteri quidem testamento Psalmos Davidicos, ex novo autem Euangelium Matthaei,

iuxta orthodoxorum patrum expositionem, et sacrosanctae Ecclesiae de fide ac religione doctrinam, plenioribus commentarijs illustravit."

[52]Ibid., p. 150 wherein Bredenbach cites Erasmus' work with Latin manuscripts dealing with "Quem dicunt homines esse."

[53]Ibid., "Quam ardenti numinis invocatione est opus, quum designandus est antistes Ecclesiae? Designatur quidem Petrus hoc loco Pontifex: . . ."

[54]Ibid.: "scilicet, tanquam Iesu amantissimus, et futurus princeps ordinis Apostolici."

[55]Ibid., p. 151: "Varie hic interprenlatur petram. Augustinus in homilia huius loci per petram intelligit Christum ipsum. Decimo vero tractatu super Iohannis epistolam, petram interpretatur fidem. Nonnulli professionem quam hic facit Petrus, petram dici opponantur. Plurimi asserunt ipsum Petrum hoc loco a Domino vocari petram, super quam aedificaturus sit ecclesiam suam."

[56]PL 38,479: "Quia enim Christus petra, Petrus populus christianus. Petra enim principale nomen est. Ideo Petrus a petra, non petra a Petro: quomodo non a christiano Christus, sed a Christo christianus vocatur. 'Tu es' ergo, inquit, 'Petrus, et super hanc petram' quam confessu es, 'super hanc petram' quam cognovisti, dicens, . . .: id est, Super me ipsum Filium Dei vivi, aedificabo Ecclesiam meam. Super me aedificabo te, non me super te."

[57]Augustine, Commentaire de la Première Épître de S. Jean, ed. P. Agaësse, SC, 75 (Paris: Cerf, 1961), X, 1, p. 410: "Videte quae laudes prosequantur hanc fidem: 'Tu es Petrus, et super hanc petram aedificabo Ecclesiam meam.' Quid est: "Super hanc petram aedificabo Ecclesiam meam'? Super hanc fidem, super id quod dictum

est: 'Tu es Christus Filius Dei vivi.' 'Super hanc petram, inquit, fundabo Ecclesiam meam.' Magna laus. Ergo dicit Petrus: . . .: dicunt et daemones: . . . Hoc Petrus, hoc et daemones: eadem verba, non idem animus. Et unde constat quia hoc Petrus cum dilectione est; daemonis autem sine dilectione."

[58]Bredenbach, . . . commentaria, p. 151: "Harum interpretationum nulla est, quae non habeat graves authores et pium sensum."

[59]Ibid.: "Prima enim, praeterquam quod Augustinum habet, videtur consonare alijs scripturis, quae Christum aperte nominat petram, ut apud Paulum I Corinth. 10. Petra autem erat Christus. Et apud Matthaeum cap. vigesimo primo, dicitur lapis angularis, et I. Cor. 3 dicitur fundamentum: Fundamentum, inquit, aliud nemo potest ponere, praeter id quod positum est, quod est Iesus Christus."

[60]Ibid.: "Chrysost. et Theophylactus secundam et tertiam ita coniungunt, quasi eodem tendant. Chrysostomi verba sunt: Et super hanc petram edificabo ecclesiam meam, id est diem et confessionem. Et post disputationem, quam interponit de aequalitate petris et filij, filio haec tribuit verba: Ego tibi dico, tu es Petrus, et ego super te aedificabo Ecclesiam meam. Similiter Theophylactus, Remunerat, inquit, Petrum Dominus, mercedem illi dans magnam quod super eum aedificavit Ecclesiam. Quia enim confessus erat eum Dei filium Petrus, dixit, quod haec confessio quam confessus est, fundamentum erit futurum credentium, ita ut omnis homo extructurus fidei domum, hoc facturus sit fundamentum."

[61]See chapter one for a discussion of the Theophylact passage.

[62]Ibid.: "Tertia vero, qua Ecclesia super Petrum dicitur aedificari, plurimos habet et

gravissimos authores, adeoque eosdem illos quos
duae illae superiores: . . ."

[63]Ibid.: "ut manifestum fit, nihil hic esse
dissidij inter sanctos illos doctores, sed omnes
has interpretationes pulchre in unum convenire
posse, si pius adsit interpres."

[64]Ibid., pp. 151-152: "Nam et Divus Augustinus multis locis Petrum vocat petram, super
quam Dominus aedificavit Ecclesiam suam, ut in
libro contra epistolam Donati, et alijs multis,
quorum plerosque indicavit Iohannes Roffensis
episcopus contra Luterum de primatu Romani
Pontificis: ubi et multos alios indicat huius
interpretationibus et sententiae authores: . . ."
Having already examined many of the places in
which Augustine speaks of petra=Petrus, we will
hold off further discussion here.

[65]. . .Ioannis Fischerii, Roffensis in
Anglia episcopi, opera . . . (Wirceburgi:
Fleischmannus, 1597), p. 543: ". . . Basilius
libro secundo adversus Eunomium, de signis
quibusdam Petrum exprimentibus verba faciens.
Per hanc vocem, inquit, intelligimus Ionam, qui
fuit ex Bethsaide, Andrea fratrem, qui ex piscatore in apostolatus ministerium vocatus est.
Qui quoniam fide praestabat, Ecclesiae in seipso
aedificationem suscepit."

[66]Bredenbach, . . . commentaria, p. 151:
". . . inter quos sunt Basilius Magnus libro
secundo contra Eunomium, Ambrosius sermone 47 de
fide Petri, D. Cyprianus aliquot locis, qui in
tertia Epistola lib. 1 ubi multis argumentis et
scripturis asserit authoritatem sacerdotibus et
Episcopis, docet hoc semper fuisse haeresum et
schismatum seminarium, quod sacredotibus non sit
praestitia obedientia: nec unus, inquit, in
Ecclesia ad tempus sacerdos, et ad tempus iudex
vice Christi cogitatur."

157

[67]Ibid., p. 152: "Et Cypriano antiquior Tertullianus libro de praescriptionibus haereticorum: Latuit, inquit, aliquid Petrum aedificandae ecclesiae petram dictum, claves regni coelorum consecutum, et solvendi et alligandi in coelis et in terris potestatem?" Cf. Fisher, opera, p. 553 for the earlier citation from Tertullian.

[68]Tertulliani opera, pars I: Opera catholica adversus Marcionem, CCSL I (Turnholti: Brepols, 1954), "De praescr. haer. ," c. 22, p. 203, lines 4ff.

[69]Bredenbach, . . . commentaria, p. 152.

[70]Ibid.: "Et nemo orthodoxorum est, quod equidem sciam, qui ab hac interpretatione abhorruerit."

[71]Ibid.: "Sed quid interim dicemus ad id, quod primo loco dictum, et scripturis comprobatum est, Christum ipsum esse petram, et fundamentum, propter quod nemo potest aliud ponere?"

[72]Ibid.: "Dicemus, non minus consistere posse, Christum esse petram et fundamentum, et Petrum esse petram et fundamentum, quia quod Iohannes Euangelista cap. 1 scribit, Christum esse lucem veram, qui illuminat omnem hominem venientem in hunc mundum, et quod Matt. cap. 5. Dominus Iesus ipse dicit Apostolis, Vos estis lux mundi."

[73]Ibid.: "Unde D. Hierony. in commentarijs in hunc locum, Sicut ipse, inquit, lumen Apostolis donavit, ut lumen mundi appellarentur, ceteraque; ex Domino sortiti sunt vocabula, ita et Simoni, qui credebat in petram Christum, Petri largitus est nomen, et secundum metaphoram petrae recte dicitur ei, Aedificabo ecclesiam meam super te." Bredenbach editorially adds: "Verum quod quaeso miraculi est, si illum admittit in tituli consortium, cui officij dignitatem

communicat, cui potestatem facit remittendi et retinendi peccata, quod est solius Dei."

[74]Ibid.: "Audiamus itaque sanctum illum Pontificem Leonem eius nominis I. luculenter docentem, qua ratione et quo discrimine Christus dicatur petra, et fundamentum, et qua Petrus. Quia tu, inquit, es Petrus, id est quum ego sim inviolabilis petra, ego lapis angularis, qui facio ultraque unum: ego fundamentum, propter quod nemo potest aliud ponere: tunc tu quoque petra es, quia mea virtute solidaris, ut qui mihi potestate sunt propria, sint tibi mecum participatione communia." See PL 54, 150.

[75]Ibid.: "Iam quod Origenes in tractatu in hunc locum, quem Erasmus fecit Latinum, negat super unum Petrum aedificari Ecclesiam, eo pertinet, ut nos omnes adhortetur, ut per imitationem Petri studeamus et nos fieri petrae, hoc est, vivi quidam lapides ex quibus Ecclesia aedificatur. Petra est enim, inquit, quisquis Christi discipulus est, ex quo biberunt de spirtuali consequente eos petra. Non pertinet autem ad abrogandum primatum Petri in Ecclesia."

[76]Ibid., p. 152[b]: "Nam hunc primatum alias illi diserte tribuit, ut homilia decimaseptima in Lucam, ubi ait: Ergo scandalizati sunt universi, intantum, ut Petrus quoque Apostolorum princeps, tertio denegarit. Et sub finem libri quinti, in epistolam Pauli ad Romanos: Et Petro inquit, quum summa rerum de pascendis ovibus traderetur, et super ipsum velut super terram fundaretur Ecclesia, nullius confessio virtutis alterius ab eo nisi charitas exigitur. Item in Exodum homilia quinta: Magno illi Ecclesiae fundamento, petraeque solidissimae, super quam Christus fundavit Ecclesiam suam, vide quid dicatur: Modicae fidei, quare dubitatsti?"

[77]See Origen, Homélies sur s. Luc, ed. H. Crouzel, F. Fournier, and P. Perichon, SC, 87 (Paris: Cerf, 1962), homily 17, section 6, pages

256, 258.

[78]PG 14, 1053.

[79]Origen, "In Exodum Homilia," PG 12, 329 C-D.

[80]Bredenbach, . . . commentaria, p. 152[b]: "Porro quae in hunc locum scripsit, magis libet pie interpretari, quam damnare: alioqui si quis contentiosus defendat, aliam eius fuisse, mentem, respondebimus, Origenem etiam in alijs, et gravibus quidem esse lapsum. Atque ob id non huius unius in hunc locum iudicium, deberre praeferri caeteris omnibus, tum aliorum, tum ipsius Origenis interpretationibus et sententiis."

[81]Ibid.: "Praeclare itaque scriptum est a Divo Hieronymo libro primo contra Iovinianum: Super Petrum fundatur Ecclesia, licet idipsum in alio loco super Apostolos fiat, et cuncti claves coelorum accipiant, et ex aequo fortitudo Ecclesiae super eos solidetur, tamen propter ea inter duodecim unus eligitur, ut capite constituto, schismatis tollator occasio."

[82]PL 23, 256ff as cited in Quellen zur Geschichte des Papsttums, p. 165: "At dicis, super Petrum fundatur Ecclesia:. . ."

[83]Bredenbach, . . . commentaria, p. 152[b].

[84]Ibid.: "Nobis certum est, ne latum quidem pilum recedere ab ea interpretatione ac sententia, quam nobis tanto consensu tradiderunt tot tam praeclara Ecclesiae Dei lumina, ipsorum etiam Apostolorum discipuli."

[85]Ibid., p. 152[b] - p. 153: "Quam et ipsa verborum dominicorum vis ac series, et rei ipsius de qua agitur, natura flagitat. Tu mihi expende verborum 'dúnamai.' Ego, inquit dico tibi. Ego qui potestatem habeo praestandi efficiendique

160

quae dico: dico tibi, non cuius ex circumstanti-
bus, sed tibi: Quid dico? quod tu es Petrus.
Non solum diceris, verum etiam es Petrus. Et
super hanc petram, nimirum, quam ego hisce meis
efficacibus vergis firmo, solidamque et immobilem
facio, ut sit inviolabile fundamentum, hoc est,
super te, aedificabo Ecclesiam meam."

[86]Ibid., p. 153[a]: "Porro ne quis cavil-
letur, non eundem posse esse Petrum et petram,
quod Petrus a petra denominari videatur, ut
iustus a iusticia: . . ."

[87]Ibid.: sciendum, Petrum hic nihil aliud
significare quam petram, quod manifestum est ex
ca. 1 Euangelij Iohannis, ubi dicitur ei, Tu
vocaberis Cephas, quod teste Euangelista idem
est quod petrus; . . ."

[88]Ibid.: "petrus aliud, quam quod Latine
dicitur, saxum, Latine vero et graece petra: . . ."

[89]Ibid.: "quod expresse docet Hieron. in
epistolam ad Galatas, his verbis: Non quod aliud
significet Petrus, aliud Cephas, sed quod quam
nos Latine et Graece petram vocemus, hanc
Hebraei et Syri propter linquae inter se viciniam,
cephan nuncupent." See PL 26, 366 B, especially
note 3 on that column which mentions that some
Palatinate manuscripts have "quem nos Latine et
Graece Petrum vocemus, Hunc Hebraei . . ."

[90]Ibid.: "Haec Hieronymi verba confirmat
Elias ille Levita, nobilis nostra aetate apud
Iudaeos grammaticus, in opera cui titulum fecit
ṬŠBY id est, Thesbites, ubi sic scribit: ḴĒPĀ'
SĪM͑ÔN BĒN KĒPĀ HĀYÂ 'EHḤĀD MĪTTALMÎDYĀW SEHL YĒŠÛ
ḤANÎSṚÎ Wᵉ 'ŌMRÎM B'WWNGYLYON KÎ BĀRÎSÔNĀH HĀYÂ
Šᵉ MÔ SĪM͑ÔN BAR YÔNĀH Wᵉ YĒŠÛ QĀRÂ' Šᵉ MÔ KĒPĀ'
ÛMÎBSAR: TARGÛM ŠEHL SEHLA͑ KĒPĀ ŠEHHÛ Lᵉ ŠÔN
HŌZEHQ Bᵉ KAMMÂ Mᵉ QUŌMŌT RĀMAW LŌ ŠEHHÛ YĪH YEH RŌ'
Š Wᵉ ḤŌZEHQ 'ᵉ MŪNĀTŌ Lᵉ BAD. QeRÂ'O KĒPĀ' Wᵉ
KĒN ÛL 'EHBEHN NĪGAT TARGÛM ÛL KEH PĀ' MATKᵉ LĀ'
Wᵉ KĒN Šᵉ MÔ Kᵉ LĪŠÔN RŌMÎ PĒṬRŌ Wᵉ 'EHBEHN NĪQRÂ'

161

B^eLA'AZ P^eRÊDA'." I wish to acknowledge the
help of Rev. Thomas Caldwell and of Sister Ruth
Graf with the Aramaic translation and the trans-
literation of the Aramaic.

91This is the judgment of Fr. Caldwell.

92Bredenbach, . . . commentaria, p. 153^a:
"Haec Paulus Fagius ita vertit Latine Chephah)
Schymeon filius Chepha, unus fuit ex discipulis
Iesu Nazareni, de quo ferunt in Euangelio, quod
illi primum nomen fuerit Schymeon bar iona,
Iesum vero vocavisse eum Chepha, quod fortitu-
dinem et munitionem significat. Nam Thargum
Hebraicae vocis SEHLA'est KÊPÄ', et pro fortitu-
dine in multis locis usurpatur. Voluit autem
Christus eo innuere, quod futurus esse caput et
robur suae fidei: ob id vocavit eum KÊPÄ'.
Item ubi textus Hebraeus habet, In lapidem
offendiculi: Thargum dicit L^eKÊPÄ' MATK^eLÄ'.
Similiter et in lingua Romana Petrus nominatur.
Necnon et Itali lapidem pereda vocant. Haec
illa Iudaeus, adhuc in suo Iudaismo perdurans."

93Ibid., p. 153^b: "Neque opinor quod
Dominus Iesus illum Graeco vel Latino nomine
vocaverit Petrum, sed, ut scribit Iohannes, Syro
duntaxat KÊPÂ', quod quum petram, hoc est, saxum
seu lapidem significet, Euangelista, vel si quis
Euangelistam ex Hebraea linqua in Graecam trans-
tulit, vertit 'pétros,' potius quam 'pétra,' non
quod aliud significet, sed quod viro aptius esse
videretur in forma masculina: Caeteri quoque
tum apostoli, tum Euangelistae, nunc Syro nomine
KÊPÂ', nunc Graeco Petrum nominant."

94Ibid., "Quin etiam in Euangelio Matthaei
quod habemus Hebraicum, utrobique idem per omnia
nomen est KÊPÂ'. Sic enim scriptum est: WA
'ÄNI 'ÖMER L^eKÄ KÎ 'ATÄH KÊPA' W^e 'AL KÊPÄ' HAZÖ'
T 'EHBNEH 'EHT MAQHÊLÎ. Quod ad verbum dixeris
latine, Et ego dico tibi, quod tu es petra, et
super hanc petram aedificabo Ecclesiam meam.
Vides itaque palam ex genuina ipsius vocabuli

significatione convinci, Petrum esse ipsam petram, super quam Dominus dicit se aedificaturum esse Ecclesiam suam."

[95]Ibid.: "Iam quod ad verborum seriem, et ad rem de qua agitur, attinet: Quum Dominus Iesus hoc loco beatum praedicet Petrum, eiusque sui de illo tam eximij elogij causas velit indicare, et rationes reddere, quarum prima est revelatio quae illi facta est a patre caelesti: postrema vero, quod ipse daturus sit illi claves regni coelorum: quid quaeso ineptius fuerit, absurdiusque, quam hunc tam compendiosum sermonem interrumpere alio, quo referat quid super semetipsum sit aedificaturus? Quid enim hoc ad Petrum magis, quam ad caeteros? Quum autem petram accipimus ipsum Petrum, omnia cohaerent aptissime, pulcherrimoque procedunt ordine."

[96]Ibid., pp. 153[b]-154a: "Porro quod necesse sit unum in Ecclesia hac militante adhuc in terra, esse primarium Episcopum, supra verbis Divi Hieronymi dictum est, et omnes semper orthodoxi patres docuerunt, ipsaque rei necessitas palam loquitur, quo conservetur unitas et concordia, qua nihil magis in suis probat Christus. De qua re copiose ac erudite scripsit nostra aetate Albertus Pigius in Hierarchia Ecclesiastica. Fuisse etiam in vetere lege talem in sacerdotio principatum, manifestum est: de quo Deuteronomij decimosceptimo inter caetera sic praecipitur: Qui autem superbierit, nolens obedire sacerdotis imperio, qui eo tempore ministrat Domino Deo tuo, ex decreto iudicis morietur homo ille, et auferes malum de Israel: cunctusque populus audiens timebit, ut nullus deinceps intumescat superbia." The rest of this section (p. 154[a]) deals with the continuing necessity of this primatial office after the departures(!) of Christ and Peter, Anacletus' testimony about the primacy of the Roman church over all the other churches, the castigation of certain (unnamed) persons who would deny that Christ established such a primatial order within

163

the church, and an evaluation of the meaning of
evil popes.

[97]Q-E, II, 206.

[98]Ibid.

[99]John W. Montgomery, "Sixtus of Siena and
Roman Catholic Biblical Scholarship in the
Reformation Period," <u>ARG</u> 54 (1963), 223.

[100]The edition to be used here is that
published at Lyons by Pesnot in 1575.

[101]Sisto da Siena, "De annotationibus et
censuris in interpretes et expositores divinorum
novi Testamenti voluminum," <u>Bibliotheca sancta</u>,
2 vols. (Lugdunum: Pesnot, 1575), vol. II,
liber sextus, p. 139^{a}C-D.

[102]Ibid., p. 139^{a}D: "Idem quoque habet
tractatu in Ioannem centesimo vigesimo quarto in
haec verba: Super hanc, inquit, petram aedificabo
ecclesiam meam. petra enim erat Christus, super
quod fundamentum etiam ipse aedificatus est
Petrus. fundamentum quippe aliud nemo potest
ponere praeter id, quod positum est Christus
Iesus."

[103]Ibid., p. 139^{a}D-E: "Haeretici nostrorum
temporum irrident nos, quod exponentes propositam
Christi sententiam, Tu es Petrus, dicamus Petrum
esse petram, super quam fundata sit ecclesia,
contra Augustini explanationem, et Pauli vocem,
nullum ponentis fundamentum praeter Christum."

[104]Ibid., p. 139^{a}E-139^{b}A: "Quibus respon-
demus, nos praesentem Augustini expositionem
toto pectore amplecti, et nostram quoque interpretationem, ut ab eodem Augustino acceptam,
firmiter retinere, is enim in primo Retractionum,
capite vigesimo primo utranque approbans, nec
alteram alteri praeferens, his verbis utitur:. . ."

[105]Ibid., p. 139[b]A-B: ". . . cui Augustine
sicuti non contradicimus, ita nec aliud ponimus
fundamentum primarium praeter Christum. credimus
enim, et certa fide fatemur, Christum esse
primum ac potissimum totius ecclesiastici aedifi-
cij fundamentum; sed super hoc etiam fundamentum;
sed super hoc etiam fundamentum afferimus alias
petras superimpositas, nempe Petrum, et caeteros
Apostolos, quod Ioannes in Apocalypsi nominat
duodecim fundamenta coelestis Hierusalem.
quibus reliquas ecclesiasticae structurae partes
superaeficatas esse non dubitamus."

[106]Ibid., p. 139[b]B-p. 140[a]A.

[107]Ibid., p. 139[b]C: "Et in Matthaeum capite
decimo sexto, Christus de veritate dicebat
Petro, Tu es Christus filij Dei vivi: in quo et
beatificatus est, et per promissionem fieri
meruit ecclesiae fundamentum."

[108]Ibid., p. 139[b]D: "Hilarius canone in
Matthaeum decimo sexto haec verba ad eundem
modum exponit: quanquam huius verba Erasmus
contendat pertrahere in alium sensum, adiiciens
in margine scholium huiusmodi, Ecclesiae fundamentum est fides. quibus verbis interpretari
voluit Hilarium, quasi sentiret fidem esse
fundamentum, et petram, non autem Petrum.
Hilarius tamen apertissime de Petro loquitur, ut
legenti eius verba manifestum est." Further
discussion of the actual words of Hilary will
be found in the treatment of Cornelius Jansen
who finally does cite the actual text of Hilary.

[109]Ibid., p. 139[b]D - p. 140[a]A: "Sed, ut
etiam Erasmus donemus Hilarij mentem hoc loco
non facile deprehendi, quid ad ea dicturus est,
quae idem hac de re in expositione psalmi 103.
his verbis, meridiana luce clarioribus, scribit?
Cum Iesus quaedam de passione sua locutus ad
discipulos fuisset, et Petrus tanquam indignum
hoc de filio detestatus esset, Petrus, cui
superius claves coelorum dederat, super quem

165

ecclesiam aedificaturus erat, adversus quem
portae inferi nihil valerent, quique in terris
vel soluisset, vel ligasset, ea in coelis vel
soluta persisterent, vel ligata. hunc itaque,
tali conuicio detestantem hoc sacramentum
passionis, tali responso excepit: Vade post me
Satana; scandalum mihi es, tanta enim ei religio
fuit pro humani generis salute patiendi, ut
Petrum, primum filij Dei confessorem, ecclesiae
fundamentum, coelestis regni ianitorem, et in
terreno iudicio iudicem coeli, Satanae conuicio
nuncuparet. . . ." Sisto's numbering of this
Psalm as 103 differs from that of other sixteenth century exegetes such as Maldonado who
number it as 131. Cf. PL 9, 730.

[110]Ibid., p. 140[a]B-C: "Ioannes Bonderius
in Concertationibus aduersus huius saeculi
haereses titulo trigesimo primo, articulo quarto
refert hunc locum inter eos, quos Lutherani
inducunt contra primatum Petri, dicentes ecclesiam non esse in primis fundatam super Petrum,
sed super singulos quodque fideles."

[111]Ibid., p. 140[a]C: "Et ad haec addit,
expositionem Origenis typicam esse, et secundum
allegoriam, quae ad confirmanda dogmata afferi
non solet, idque ex eo liquere, quod Origenes
portas inferi peccata, claves regni coelorum
virtutes interpretetur."

[112]Jansen, . . . commentariorum in suam
concordiam, ac totam historiam euangelicam
partes IV (Moguntiae: Wulfraht, 1624), p.
418[a]: "Circa quae verba videndum quid per
petram hanc, super quam Dominus dicit se aedificaturum suam Ecclesiam, sit potissimum intelligendum, maxime ob contentiosos quosdam nostrae
tempestatis homines. Cum enim communiter etiam
ab antiquissimis et omnibus catholicis scriptori-
bus per petram hanc Petrus ipse intelligatur, ac
inde colligatur Petri in omnes Apostolos prima-
tus, quem in tota Ecclesia eius in sede Romana
successores haereditario iure obtineant, quidam

hunc primatum in Petro aut successoribus eius
tollere cupientes, omnibus nervis hunc non esse
necessarium, nec genuinum huius loci sensum
ostendere conantur."

[113]Ibid.: "Et imprimis Augustinum proferunt,
qui doceat per petram hanc Christum ipsum intelligendum esse, scribens sic super Ioannem tractatu ultimo: Ecclesia fundata est super petram,
unde et Petrus nomen accepit. Non enim a Petro,
petra: sed Petrus a petra: sicut non Christus
a Christiano, sed Christianus a Christo vocatur.
Ideo quippe ait Dominus: 'Super hanc petram
aedificabo Ecclesiam meam,' quia dixerat Petrus:
'Tu es Christus filius Dei vivi.' Super hanc
ergo, inquit, petram, quam confessus es aedificabo Ecclesiam meam. Petra erat Christus, super
quod fundamentum etiam ipse aedificatus est
Petrus. Fundamentum quippe aliud nemo potest
ponere, praeter id quod positum est, quod est
Christus Iesus. Unde idem Augustinus cum in
libr. quodam contra epist. Donati interpretatus
fuisset Petrum esse petram, in qua fundata sit
Christi Ecclesia, locum illum sic retractat in
libro Retractionum priore, capite vigesimo
primo. . . . Quae Augustini loca novatores
huius temporis diligenter annotaverunt, ac
subinde ea proferunt, approbantes quidem Augustini sententiam, eatanus quatenus significat se
malle per petram non intelligere Petrum: sed
tamen fere non sequentes eum, in eo quod per
petram vult intelligendum esse Christum, quod
durior et coactior videatur interpretatio,
subintelligere super hanc petram, quam confessus
ets, et ob id per petram, fidem ipsam in Christum
quam professus fuit Petrus intelligere malentes
super quam aedificata ecclesia, firma persistit
contra omnes adversarias potestates."

[114]Ibid., 418[a-b]: "Et huius suae inter-
pretationis auctores proferunt quosdam antiquorum
patrum. Et imprimis Hilarium, qui libr. 6. de
Trinitate loco superius citato sic habet. Super
hanc igitur confessionis petram, ecclesiae

aedificatio est. Et post pauca loquens de fide
Petri, quam hic confessus est. Haec (inquit)
fides ecclesiae fundamentum est, per hanc fidem
infirmae adversus eam sunt portae inferorum.
Haec fides regni coelestis habet claves. Haec
fides quae in terris solverit aut ligaverit, et
ligata sunt in coelis, et soluta. Sic ille.
Afferunt et Cyrillum libr. 4 de Trinitate sic
scribentem Petram opinor per agnominationem,
aliud nihil quam inconcussam et firmissimam
discipuli fidem vocavit, in qua Ecclesia Christi
ita fundata et firmata esset ut non laberetur,
et esset in expugnabilis inferorum portis imperpetuum manens. His addunt et Chrysostomum et
Theophylactum: quorum ille in hunc locum scribens,
Petram interpretatur fidem et confessionem:
iste vero sic habet. Quia confessus erat eum
Dei filium Petrus, dixit quod haec confessio
quam confessus est, fundamentum erit futurum
credentium, ita ut omnis homo extructurus fidei
domum, hoc iacturus sit fundamentum. Probant
autem etiam rationibus. Petrum non posse intelligi petram super quam aedificata est Ecclesia,
nempe eis quae monerunt Augustinum, ut magis in
aliam inclinaretur sententiam, qua per Petram
Christus intelligeretur, nimirum quia Paulus
dixit: 'Fundamentum aliud nemo potest ponere,'
et caetera: 'Petra erat Christus,' et quia non
est dictum Simoni: Tu es Petra sed tu es Petrus,
unde volunt nomen, 'Petrus,' sic esse derivatum
a petra, ut Petrus sit quasi petreius, ac si
quis a lapide lapidonem diceret, aut a saxo
saxeum. Et magis adhuc confirmant debere aliud
intelligi per Petrum et per petram, quia dixit
Dominus, 'έπὶ taútē tē pétrạ'id est, super hanc
petram, non'έπὶ taútọ pétrō,' id est, super hunc
Petrum, cum tamen saxum Graecis aeque dicatur
'pétros' atque 'ē pétra.'" See PL 10, 186-187
regarding Hilary's position.

[115]Ibid.: "Verum contra hos per petram
hanc debere intelligi ipsum Petrum, primum
quidem planus literae contextus demonstrat. Cum
enim pronomen, 'hanc,' demonstret aliquam petram

de qua fuit semo, nec de alia petra habitus est sermo quam ea qui dictus est Petrus, satis liquet aliam petram non monstrari per pronomen, 'hanc.'"

[116]Ibid.: "Nam Hebraice petra dicitur Ceph, Syriace vero Cepha, quod nomen in Bibliis Chaldaicis fere positum est, ubi in Hebraicis est SL⁽ Selagh, ut Psal. 39. 'Et statuit super petram pedes meos,' et aliis locis, etiam his quibus mystice per petram Christus significatur, ut Numer. 20 ubi dicitur Deus dedisse Hebraeis aquam de petra, quam Paulus interpretatur significasse Christum."

[117]Ibid.: "Si ergo cogitemus Christum dixisse pro Petrus et hanc petram, Tu es Cepha et super hanc Cepha aedificabo Ecclesiam meam, quomodo certum satis est eum dixisse, ut iam patet ex Syriaco Euangelico, nemo non mox certissimum esse videbit, aliud non esse intelligendum per id super quod dicitur aedificanda Ecclesia, quam eum cui dictum est, Tu es Cepha. Sicut si apud nos diceretur, Tu es saxum, et super hoc saxum aedificabo, aliud nemo intelligeret significari per saxum and per hoc saxum."

[118]Ibid.: "Istud si perpendisset D. Augustinus non iudicasset esse dubitandum quid per petram debeat intelligi, sed certissimum habuisset, per petram debere intelligi Petrum. Sic enim dicit: Non enim dictum est ei, Tu es petra, sed, 'tu es Petrus,' significans se non dubitaturum, si dictum fuisset ei, tu es petra, quomodo dictum esse Simoni in ea lingua qua Dominus utebatur, ex dictis est luce clarius."

[119]Ibid., pp. 418[b]-419[a]: "Cepha enim petra interpretatur et saxum, quamvis Graeci maluerunt commutando nomen Syriacum in Graecum dicere Petrus quam petra, quod masculinum 'ὁ pétros,' magis viro conveniat quam feminum 'ἐ pétra,' cum alioqui utrumque nomen illis idem significet. Quod autem interpres Matthaei Graecus, quisquis

is fuit, mutavit genus, hinc videtur facturum,
quod sicut pro nomine proprio viri magis convenit masculinum, 'Petrus,': ita dum appella-
tive saxum significandum est, magis apud eos
receptum est dicere 'e pétra' quam 'o pétros.'"

[120]Ibid., p. 419[a]: "Porro hanc loci istius
intelligentiam, quam primum contextus literae
indicat, ac deinde certissimam facit idioma quo
Christus est usus, postremo confirmat etiam
concors omnium patrum interpretatio, quorum
omnium sententias quoniam prolixum esset afferre,
et alii, inter quos maxime Pighius libr. 3. de
Ecclesiastica Hierarch. eas prolixe citant,
aliquot tantum in medium producemus."

[121]Ibid.: "Itaque Tertullianus Apostolorum
temporibus vicinis, lib. de praescriptione
haereticorum sic habet: Latuit aliquid Petrum
aedificandae Ecclesiae petram dictum, claves
regni coelorum consecutum et caetera. Origenes
in Matthaeum de Canone novi testamenti: 'Petrus,'
inquit, super quem Christus fundavit Ecclesiam,
duas tantummodo epistulas scripsit. Iterum hom.
5 super Exodum: Magno illi Ecclesiae fundamento,
petraeque solidissimae, super quam Christus
fundavit Ecclesiam suam, vide quid dicatur,
'Modicae fidei quare dubitasti?' Sic et Cyprianus
in variis locis super Petrum dicit fundatam
Ecclesiam. In epistola ad Iubaianum: Manifestum
ast [sic], inquit, ubi et per quos remissio
peccatorum dari possit. Nam Dominus primum
Petro, super quem aedificavit Ecclesiam suam, et
unde unitatis origionem instituit et ostendit,
potestatem istam dedit. Et infra in eadem
Christus Ecclesiam suam, quae una est, fundavit
super unum. Iterum ad Cornelium, Petrus, super
quem aedificata ab eodem Domino fuerat Ecclesia,
unus pro omnibus loquens, et Ecclesiae voce
respondens ait: 'Domine ad quem ibimus?' et
caetera. Basilius libr. 2 adversus Eunomium:
Per hanc, inquit, vocem intelligimus Ionae
filium qui fuit ex Bethsaida, Andreae fratrem,
qui ex piscatore in Apostolatus ministerium

170

vocatus est. Qui quoniam fide praestabat, Ecclesiae in se aedificationem susceptit. Ambrosius in sermone ad commissam sibi Ecclesiam de natali Petri et Pauli: Diximus, inquit, frequenter ipsum Petrum a Domino Petram nuncupatam, sicut ait: 'Tu es Petrus et super hanc petram aedificabo Ecclesiam meam.' Longum nimis esset et supervacaneum caeteros adducere, cum ex his Graecis et Latinis patribus satis pateat queae fuerit ab initio Ecclesiae semper in his verbis intelligentia."

[122]S. Thasci Caecili Cypriani opera omnia, ed. G. Hartel, CSEL 3:II (Vindobonae: C. Geroldi filium, 1868), ep. LXXIII, pp. 783-784.

[123]Ibid., p. 786: ". . . an ad ecclesiam quae una est et super unum qui et claves eius accepit Domini voce fundata est?"

[124]PG 29, 578-579.

[125]Maximus Episcopi Taurinensis Sermones, ed. A. Mutzenbecher, CCSL, XXIII (Turnholti: Brepols, 1962), Sermo IX, 1, p. 31, line 23 - p. 32, line 31: "Diximus frequenter ipsum Petrum petra(m) a domino nuncupatum, sicut ait: 'Tu es Petrus, et super hanc petram aedificabo ecclesiam meam.' Si ergo Petrus petra est, super quam aedificatur ecclesia, recte primum pedes sanat ut sicut in ecclesia fidei fundamenta continet, ita et in homine membrorum fundamenta confirmet. Recte, inquam, primum in christiano pedes curat, ut iam non trepidus nec imbecillis sed robustus et fortis possit super petram ecclesiae incedere." Erasmus edited this sermon as one of Augustine's.

[126]Ibid., p. 32, lines 33-40.

[127]Ibid., p. 419[a]: "Quod autem adversarii imprimis quidem, D. Augustinum, eiusque rationes pro se adferunt, dicendum, Augustinum quidem nusquam asserere, non posse intelligi Petrum esse Petram supra quam aedificanda sit Ecclesia,

sed expendum relinquit; utrum sensum ex duob. quos ponit quis amplecti debeat, liberum studioso faciens utrum amplecti malit."

[128]Ibid.: "Rationes autem quae movent eum ut significet malle per petram intelligere Christum, parum sint efficaces. Nam quod movet eum quia non est dictum: Tu es petra, sed Petrus, prius solutum est. Quod autem affert ex Paulo de fundamento, nihil etiam urget, cum Paulus de primo loquatur fundamento cui omnes innituntur, cui et Petrus innitebatur. Alioqui enim et Apoc. 21. duodecim fundamenta civitatis novae Hierusalem dicunter esse duodecim Apostoli, et Paulus ipse Ephesios aedificatos dicit super fundamentum Apostolorum et Prophetarum."

[129]Ibid.: "Caeterum authoritates quas afferunt adversarii ex Hilario, Cyrillo, Chrysostomo, et Theophylacto, nec illis patrocinantur, nec communi intelligentiae quicquam obsunt, sed eandem omnino confirmant. Nam praeterquam quod in aliis scriptorum locis aperte dicunt super Petrum fundatam Ecclesiam, etiam in illis locis hoc dicunt, in quibus interpretantur petram, fidem et confessonem Petri. Et fidem quam intelligunt esse petram, quae sit fundamentum Ecclesiae, non intelligunt quemadmodum adversarii, fidem cuiusvis hominis, aut fidem in genere acceptam, sed singulariter fidem ipsius Petri, quam quandoque dicunt petram et fundamentum Ecclesiae: aliquando ipsum Petrum, eo quod haec duo in idem coincidant, propterea quod Petrus petra sit dictus et fundamentum, ratione suae fidei solidae."

[130]Ibid., p. 419[b]: "Et mox subiicit, Alium deinde honorem ei praebet, cum dicit, 'et ego dabo tibi claves regni coelorum.' Intellexit ergo illis verbis: 'et super hanc petram,' et caetera quendam honorem illi delatum, quod non erit, si intelligas significari super fidem in genere fundatam Ecclesiam." He does continue the claim that Chrysostom used the words "super

te" in paraphrasing "super hanc petram."

[131]Ibid.: "Idem observare licet in locis
citatis ex Hilario et Cyrillo, quorum ille in
Matthaeun super hoc loco scribens aperte interpretatur per petram Petrum, eumque fundamentum
vocat quamvis aliquis parum syncerus annotaverit
in margine in libris a Frobenio excusis, Ecclesiae fundamentum fides: cum tamen sic scribat:
Dignus iudicatus (de Petro loquitur) qui quod in
Christo Dei esset, primus cognosceret. O in
nuncupatione novi nominis felix Ecclesiae
fundamentum, dignaque aedificatione illius petra
quae infernas leges, et tartari portas, et omnia
mortis claustra dissolveret. O beatus coeli
ianitor, cuius arbitrio claves aeterni aditus
traduntur? et catera. Quomodo quaeso his
verbis significatur, quemadmodum notatur in
margine, Ecclesiae fundamentum esse fidem, et
non potius ipsum Petrum?" Cf. PL 9, 1009-1010.

[132]Ludwig, Die Primatworte, pp. 59-60.

[133]PL 9, 1009-1010: "Et dignum plane
confessio Petri praemium consecuta est, quia Dei
filium in homine vidisset."

[134]Ibid., p. 418[a-b]: "Et imprimis Hilarium,
qui libr. 6 de Trinitate loco superius citato
sic habet. Super hanc igitur confessionis
petram, ecclesiae aedificatio est. Et post
pauca loquens de fide Petri, quam hic confessus
est: Haec (inquit) fides ecclesiae fundamentum
est, per hanc fidem infirmae adversus eam sunt
portae inferorum. Haec fides regni coelestis
habet claves. Haec fides quae in terris solverit
aut ligaverit, et ligata sunt in coelis, et
soluta. Sic ille." Cf. PL 10, 186-187.

[135]Ibid., p. 418[b]: "Asserunt et Cyrillum
libr. 4 de Trinitate sic scribentem: Petram
opinor per agnominationem, aliud nihil quam
inconcussam et firmissimam discipuli fidem
vocavit, in qua Ecclesia Christi ita fundata et

firmata esset ut non laberetur, et esset inexpugnabilis inferorum portis imperpetuum manens." Cf. PG 75, 866 where the subject concerns that the Son is neither a creature nor a reality about to be made.

[136]Ibid.: "Cyrillus vero etiam apertius sic interpretatur libr. 2. Comment. in Ioannem circa illa verba, Tu vocaberis Cephas, sic scribens: Nec Simon fore iam nomen sibi, sed Petrus praedicit, vocabulo ipso commode significans, quod in eo, tanquam in petra lapideque firmissimo, suam esset aedificaturus Ecclesiam. Haec ille." Cf. PG 73, 219.

[137]Ibid.: ". . . ita Simon per suam fidem factus est Petrus, hoc est saxum, . . . Ex quibus et satis consequi videtur, non sic quid dicitur de aedificanda Ecclesia super Petrum, pertinere ad successores ipsius Petri sede Romana, sicut ad ipsum Petrum."

[138]Ibid.: "Successores n. sicut capita sunt Ecclesiae Christianae totius quae illis in episcopatu existentibus est in terris: ita etiam sunt fundamenta et primi lapides, super quos Ecclesia in terris existens fundatur. Petrus vero non solum fundamentum fidelium qui cum ipso fuerunt in terris, sed totius omnino Ecclesiae fidelium, qui post eum vel crediderunt, vel credituri sunt in Christo."

[139]Ibid.: "Unde quanquam quae sequuntur Petro promissa, 'Et tibi dabo claves regni coelorum,' et caetera aeque pertineant ad Petri successores, atque ad ipsum Petrum, ut post dicetur, haec tamen promissio, aedificabo Ecclesiam meam super te, proprie ad ipsum Petrum pertinere videtur, sicut illi proprium est nomen Petrus, et non commune cum successoribus cuius nominis ratio explicat his verbis, 'et super hanc petram aedificabo Ecclesiam meam.'"

[140]"The Preface to the Reader," The New Testament of Jesus Christ . . . (Rhemes: Fogny, 1582), b ii^v.

[141]Ibid., p. 44 [marginal note].

[142]Ibid., p. 46.

[143]Ibid.

[144]Ibid., p. 46.

[145]CSEL, vol. XXXIX, "In Psalmum LXIX Ennaratio," verse four, p. 934, lines 33-36. For Sermo 29 see PL 39, 2123 (sermo CCIII). I have been unable to locate Sermo 49 on John and Sermo 15 (de sanctis).

[146]PL 34, 825ff.

[147]CCSL XIV, VI, 97, p. 209, lines 1044ff.

[148]PL 24, 43-44 with regard to Isaiah 2:2.

[149]Epiphanius, Ancoratus und Panarion, ed. K. Holl, GCS 25 (Leipzig: Hinrich, 1915), p. 16, lines 4ff, especially lines 21-22. Cf. PG 43, 31-34.

[150]PL 54, 1031ff. I was unable to locate the references to Gregory.

[151]PG 83, 551.

[152]The New Testament of Jesus Christ . . ., p. 46.

[153]For the Augustine reference see PL 43, 30: Peter's see is the rock.

[154]DTC 9:2, 1774.

[155]Juan de Maldonado, "In s. Matthaeum commentaria," in Scripturae sacrae cursus completus . . ., ed. J. P. Migne, vol. 21 (Parisiis:

Apud editores, 1841), col. 809: "Sunt inter
veteres auctores, qui interpretentur, 'super
hanc petram,' id est, super hanc fidem, aut
super hanc fidei confessionem, qua me Filium Dei
vivi esse dixisti, ut . . . et Gregorius Nyssenus
in lib. contra Judaeos, et Chrysost. . . . orat.
2 adversus Judaeos, . . . auctor Commentariorum
in Epistolas D. Pauli, qui Ambrosio tribuuntur,
in c. 4 Epistolae ad Galat. Longius etiam a
sensu recedens D. August. interpretatur, tract.
in Joan. 27 . . . Quas interpretationes aliter,
quam prae se ferunt, intelligendas Calvinistae
multo avidius quam veritatem amplexi sunt: . .
." Gregory's authorship of Contra Iudaeos
(Testimonia adversus Iudaeos) is spurious; PG
46, 193-233 contains no references to Mt. 16:18.
Chrysostom's second oratio contains no references
to Mt. 16:18; see PG 48, 857-862. Regarding
pseudo-Ambrose: PL 17, 379-385 contains no
references to Mt. 16:18; perhaps chapter four is
a misprint for chapter two of this commentary.
Regarding Augustine: Tractatus 27 on John's
gospel contains no references to Mt. 16:18.

[156]Ibid.: "Nunc nihil magis a sensu Christi
alienum cogitari potuit, quam ut dicere voluerit
super seipsum, aut super aliam rem quam super
Petrum fundaturum Ecclesiam."

[157]Ibid., cols. 810-811: "Primum, quis non
videt pronomen demonstrativum 'hanc' positum
esse loco relativi, perinde ac si dixisset: Tu
es petra, super quam aedificabo Ecclesiam meam?
Petrus enim, et petra idem sunt. Nam quod
Calvinus dicit non sine causa evangelistam
orationem variasse, . . . Nec enim Matth. Graeca,
sed Hebraica, aut Chaldaica, et Syriaca lingua,
ut in praefatione probavimus, Evangelium
scripsit. . . . Secundo autem loco, ubi de
aedificii fundamento agebatur, non Petrum, sed
petram dixit, quamvis idem utrumque nomen signi-
ficaret, quia in ejusmodi aedificiis nomen
petrae feminum magis est usitatum."

[158]Ibid., col. 811: "Quaeret aliquis, cur ergo Christus non aperte, et uno verbo dixit 'super te' aedificabo Ecclesiam meam? Responsio est facilis, ne locutionis gratia et energia periret, quae in eo consistebat, ut cum de Ecclesia Christus, tanquam de aedificio aliquo ageret, accomodate ad aedificium loqueretur: non fuisset, autem accomodate locutus, si dixisset, super te aedificabo Eccleisam meam, quia aedificia non super homines, sed super petras fundari solent: . . ." I am unable to make sense of the statement immediately following which appears simply to be begging the question on Maldonado's part: "Praeterea, sin sensus esset 'super hanc petram' id est, super hanc fidem, aut super meipsum 'aedificabo Ecclesiam meam,' maxime propter adversariorum rationem, qui existimant Petrum non pro se tantum, sed pro omnibus apostolis respondisse: 'Tu es Christus filius Dei vivi, . . . '"

[159]Ibid., col. 812: "Ad haec conveniebat utique, ut quemadmodum Christus apostolos duo-decim ad duodecim patriarcharum similitudinem elegeret; ita unum veluti Abrahamum eligeret, qui propter majorem fidem omnium caput, et ut Abrahamum veteris, ita ille evangelicae Eccle-siae fundamentum esset: paria enim in utroque sunt omnia; fide Abrahamus excelluit, et Petrus: nomen Abrahamo, quia pater multarum gentium futurus erat mutatum est, Genesis 17,5, et Petro, quia omnium Christianorum futurus erat pater et caput."

[160]Ibid., cols. 812-813: "Denique super ipsum Petrum Ecclesiam aedificatam fuisse omnes prorsus, praeter haereticos, veteres auctores docuerunt. Quorum sententias etsi alii dili-genter investigatas recitaverunt, tamen quia res est hoc tempore maximi momenti, non praeteribo, locos solum indicabo, verba ipsa si quis desider-abit, apud auctores leget . . . . ita Hippolytus in libro de Consummatione mundi; . . . ita

177

Tertull. . . ., et in libro de Pudicitia; . . .
ita Gregorius Nazianz. in orat. de Moderatione
in disputationibus servanda; ita Basilius in
hom. de Poenitentia, . . .; ita auctor Commen-
tarior. in epist. D. Pauli, qui vulgo Ambrosio
tribuuntur, ad Galat. 2; ita Leo, serm. 2 de
Petro et Paulo, et in epist. ad episcopum Vien-
nensem, et in epist. ad Geminianum; ita totum
Calcedonense concilium; ita Juvencus; ita Psellus
apud Theodoretum, lib. 3 in Cantica; . . ."

161PG 10, 914.

162See Tertullian's "De Pudicitia," ed. E.
Dekkers, in Tertulliani opera, pars II: Opera
Montanistica, CCSL II (Turnholti: Brepols,
1954), XXI, 9-10, p. 1327: "De tua nunc sententia
quaero, unde hoc ius ecclesiae usurpes. Si quia
dixerit Petro Dominus: 'Super hanc petram
aedificabo ecclesiam meam, tibi dedi claves
regni caelestis,' vel: 'quaecumque alligaveris
vel solveris in terra, erunt alligata vel soluta
in caelis,' idcirco praesumis et ad te derivasse
solvendi et alligandi potestatem, id est ad
omnem ecclesiam Petri propinquam? Qualis es,
evertens atque commutans manifestam Domini
intentionem personaliter hoc Petro conferentem?
'Super te,' inquit, 'aedificabo ecclesiam meam,'
et: 'dabo tibi claves,' non ecclesiae, et:
"quaecumque solveris vel alligaveris,' non quae
solverint vel alligaverint."

163See PG 36, 194: "Vides quemadmodum ex
Christi discipulis, magnis utique omnibus et
excelsis, atque electione dignis, hic Petra
vocetur, atque Ecclesiae fundamenta ic fidem
suam accipiat, . . ."

164See PG 31, 1483-1484: ". . . cumque
audisset: 'Petra es,' praeconio nobilitatus
est. Quanquam autem petra est, non ut Christus
petra, sed ut Petrus petra: Christus enim vere
petra est inconcussa: Petrus vero propter
petram. . . . Petra est, petram facit, et

servis dat sua."

165See PL 17, 368: "Petrum solum nominat, et sibi comparat, quia primatum ipse acceperat ad fundandam Ecclesiam: se quoque pari modo electum, ut primatum habeat in fundandis gentium Ecclesiis:. . ."

166See PL 54, 145-146 and 629 (Epistola 10).

167See Conciliorum oecumenicorum decreta, ed. J. Alberigo et al (Basil: Herder, 1962), p. 61: "Quibus etiam epistulam maximae et senioris urbis Romae praesulis beatissimi et sanctissimi archiepiscopi Leonis quae scripta est ad . . . archiepiscopum Flavianum . . ., consequentissime coaptavit utpote et magni illius Petri confessioni congruentem et communem quamdam columnam nobis adversum prava dogmata existentem, ad confirmationem rectorum dogmatum."

168PL 19, 238: "Tu nomen Petri digna virtute tueris. Hae in mole mihi, saxique in robere ponam/Semper mansuras aeternis moenibus aedes."

169PG 122, 537-686.

170Ibid., col. 813: ". . . et Chrysost., homil. 2 in psal. 50." I have been unable to locate this.

171Ibid., col. 813: "Ex quo apparet hos auctores, qui 'super hanc petram,' id est, super hanc fidem exponendum esse dixerunt, aliter quam haeretici intelligunt, interpretandos esse. Commodissima autem interpretatio mihi videtur, si dicamus eos dicere voluisse super fidem, et confessionem Petri Ecclesiam aedificatam, id est, super Petrum propter fidem et confessionem quemadmodum et omnes alii senserunt auctores."

172Ibid.: "Certe ex ipsorum verbis manifes-

179

tum est eos, quod nunc haeretici negant negare
noluisse Petrum esse fundamentum Ecclesiae."

[173]Ibid., col. 814: "Dicet aliquis, si
omnes alii non solum apostoli, sed etiam prophetae,
ut ait D. Paulus, fundamentum Ecclesiae sunt,
quid his verbis singulariter Petro concessum
est: 'Tu es Petrus . . .'"

[174]Ibid.: "Resp. hoc illi concessum esse,
ut inter omnes prophetas et apostolos primum
post Christum Ecclesiae fundamentum sit, et
locum illius absentis teneat. Nam his verbis
aliquid uni Petro singulare concessum esse satis
a nobis supra probatum est. Cum autem alii
etiam fundamentum sint, nihil aliud concedi
potuit, quam ut secundus post Christum fundamenti
lapis esset, et eo modo, quo Christus, id est,
ita ut in eo non una tantum pars, sed tota
Ecclesia niteretur."

[175]Ibid.: "Hoc interest, quod Christus sua,
Petrus Christi virtute fundamentum est; et
Christus nullo alio, Petrus vero alio, id est,
Christo nititur fundamento."

[176]Sebastian Barradas, Tomus II commentariorum in concordiam et historiam quatuorum
euangelistarum (Moguntiae: Lippius, 1605), p.
686ªD: "De promissione summi Pontificatus facta
Petro." The first volume of this work was
published at Coimbra in 1599; the Mainz edition
appeared during 1601-1612.

[177]Ibid., p. 687ªD-E: "Quid nomine petrae
hoc loco sit intelligendum ambigitur. . . . D.
Ambrosius ad Ephes. 2. Super hanc petram, hoc
est, in hac Catholicae fidei confessione statuo
fideles ad vitam, et caetera. D. item Greg.
Nyss. in fine libri contra Iudaeos: . . . D.
Greg. in Psal. 7. poenit. Christus (ait) est
petra, a qua Petrus nomen accepit: et super
quam se aedificaturum ecclesiam dixit, et
caetera." The reference to Ambrose is actually

pseudo-Ambrose who is commenting on Ephesians
2:20; see PL 17, 402. The Gregory of Nyssa
reference I have been unable to locate.

[178]Ibid., pp. 687^{a}E-687^{b}A: "Germanus
perspicuusque sensus est, quo petra Petrum
significat."

[179]Ibid., p. 687^{b}A: "Id quod manifestissime
ipsa verborum flagitat structio."

[180]Ibid., p. 687^{b}B-C.

[181]Ibid., p. 687^{b}A-B: "Reddit enim Dominus
rationem nominis 'Petri,' quod Apostolo imposu-
erat. Quasi dicat: Tu es Petrus a me appellatus.
Etenim super te, tanquam super petram, aedificabo
ecclesiam meam. Sic angelus nominis Iesu rationem reddit Matth. 1 'Vocabis nomen eius Iesum:
ipse enim salvum faciret populum suum a peccatis
eorum.' Sic nominis Abraham causa indicatur Gen.
17. 'Appellaberis Abraham, quia patrem multarum
gentium constitui te.' Eundem in modum hoc loco.
Tu es Petrus. i. nomen tuum est petra, sive
significans petram. et ego super hanc petram, id
est, super te, ecclesiam meam aedificabo. Haec
est tui nominis ratio. Ideo te petram voco, quia
super te ecclesiam extruam."

[182]Ibid., p. 687^{b}C: "Equidem et si Christus
nomine Petri non fuisset usus, sed nomine Simonis,
quod petram non significat: tamen verba illa de
Simone dicta esse, verborum constructio ipsa
clamaret. Si sic dixisset: 'Tu es Simon, et
super hanc petram aedificabo ecclesiam meam.'
Sensus sane esset: Tu es Simon, et super te
tanquam petram aedificabo ecclesiam meam."

[183]Ibid., p. 687^{b}C-D: "At dicent imperiti
homines, Christus est ecclesiae fundamentum,
iuxta illud 1. Cor. 10 'Fundamentum aliud nemo
potest ponere, praeter id quod positum est, quod
est Christus Iesus, et c.' ergo Petrus petra, et
fundamentum ecclesiae dici non potest."

181

134Ibid., p. 687bD-E: "Discant hi ex aedificiis non unum tantum esse fundamentum lapidem,
sed multos. Quemadmodum ergo in aedificiis sic
in ecclesia, lapis maximum praecipuumque fundamentum Christus est. Super Christum fundatur
ecclesia primo. illi Petrus tanquam petra fundamenti secunda innititur. Hinc illud Pauli ad
Ephes. 2. 'superaedificati super fundamentum
Apostolorum et Prophetarum, ipso summo angulari
lapide Christo Iesu, et c.' et Apoc. 21. 'Murus
civitatis habens fundamenta duodecim. et in ipsis
duodecim nomina Apostolorum Agni, et c.' Quam-
obrem Augustinus Christum fundamentum fundamentorum esse ait. Ps. 86. Ut noverimus, inquit,
quia fundamentum Christus, et primum, et maximum
fundamentum, inquit Apostolus, nemo potest
ponere, praeter id, quod positum est, quod est
Christus Iesus. Quomodo ergo fundamenta Prophetae, et Apostoli, et quomodo fundamentum
Christus Iesus, quo ulterius nihil est? Quomodo
putamus, nisi quemadmodum aperte dicitur sanctus
sanctorum: sic figurate fundamentum fundamentorum. Si ergo sacramenta cogites, Christus
sanctus sanctorum, si gregem subditum cogites,
Christus pastor pastorum, si fabricam cogites,
Christus fundamentum fundamentorum, . . ."

135Ibid., p. 688aA: "Hilarius lib. 6. de
Trinitate, sic scribit: Post sacramenti confessionem beatus Simon aedificatione ecclesiae
subiacens: et claves regni coelestis accipiens,
. . ." Cf. PL 10, 172.

136Ibid., p. 688aA-B: "Chrysost. hom. 4 de
verbis Isaiae, Petrus (ait) basis ecclesiae, . . .
hom. 3 in c. 1 Matth. Petrus factus est ecclesiae fundamentum, . . . hom. 55. in Matth. Petrum,
inquit Chrysostomus, universo terrarum orbi
Christus praeposuit, . . ."

137Ibid., p. 688aE: "lege tract. 7 in Ioan.
ad illa verba: 'Respondit Nathanael, etc.'"

138Ibid., p. 688bA: "et Isai. 2. Petrum,

182

inquit, Christus Petram appellavit, super quam petram promisit aedificare ecclesiam suam, . . ."

189Ibid.: "et haeresi 59. Sanctus ille Petrus summus Apostolus, qui vere nobis factus est firma Petra, fundans fidem Domini, super quam aedificata est ecclesia per omnes modos, et c."

190Ibid., p. 688^b: "D. Cyp. de simplicitate praelatorum: Loquitur Dominus ad Petrum: 'Tu es Petrus, et super hanc petram, et c.' super unum aedificat Ecclesiam, et illi pascendas oves mandat, et c. et in tract. de habitu Virginum: Super Petrum posuit Dominus, et fundavit ecclesiam et c."

191Ibid., p. 688^{b}C: "et lib. 1. adversus Pelagianos, super Petrum ecclesia Domibi stabili mole fundata est, et c."

192PG 56, 123. I have been unable to locate his third Homilia on Mt. 1 and the quoted section from his fifty-fifth Homilia on Mt.

193CCSL XXXVI, tractatus VII, section 20, p. 79.

194PG 30, 234: Basil is commenting on Isaiah 2:2.

195PG 41, 1030: "Qui (Petrus) quidem solidae petrae instar nobis exstitit, cui velut fundamento Domini fides innititur, supra quam Ecclesia modis omnibus extructa est. In primis quidem, quod Christum Dei vivi Filium esse confessus est, idque vicissim audiit: 'Supra hanc,' solidae fidei 'petram aedificabo Ecclesiam meam.'"

196PL 4, 461. I have been unable to locate his "De simplicitate praelatorum."

197PL 23, 529: "C. Haec argumentatio tortuosa est, ecclesiasticam simplicitatem inter

philosophorum spineta concludens. Quid Aris-
toteli et Paulo? Quid Platoni et Petro? Ut ille
enim princeps philosophorum, ita hic apostolorum
fuit, super quam Ecclesia Domini stabili mole
fundata est . . ."

[198]Ibid., p. 688[b]C-D: "Cum enim Christus in
terris manere noluerit (sic enim oportebat fieri)
vicarium aliquem relinquere opus fuit, et ecclesiae universae unum moderatorem, unumque caput:
ut schismatis, et haereseon tollere occasio. . . .
Una ecclesia, unum pastorem, unum in terris post
Christum fundamentum, unum postulat moderatorem."

[199]Ibid., p. 688[b]D: "Hic Petrus fuit.
fuitque post Petrum quilibet Petri successor in
Romana Cathedra. Est vero hodie S.D.N. Clemens
VIII. Pontif. Max."

[200]Ibid., p. 688[b]D: "Illud adverte Petram
non significare hoc loco lapidem quemvis, sed
Rupem. Quemadmodum Isaiae. 2. . . . c.7
. . . c.51 . . ."

[201]Ibid., p. 688[b]E: "Propterea enim Petrae
sive Rupis tibi nomen indidi, ut ipso etiam
nomine ecclesiae meae fundamentum pastorem, caput
principemque te esse, demonstrarem."

[202]Ibid. ". . . Unam ecclesiam in una petra
extruam, uni corpori unum caput dabo. Voluit
enim Christus ecclesiae principatum esse optimum,
nempe monarchicum."

CHAPTER IV

"PETRA VARIA"

Previous chapters have shown that the patristic and medieval understanding of the "petra" of Mt. 16:18 was polysemous and this diversity could exist in the same author. Such coexistence of different meanings continues in the sixteenth century in the commentaries of Tacitus Nicolaus Zegers, René Benoist, and Manuel de Sa.

Zegers' "Scholion in omnes novi testamenti libros" (1553)

Tacitus Nicolaus Zegers was born in the latter half of the fifteenth century; his birthplace is either Diest or Brussels in Brabant, The Netherlands.[1] After becoming a Franciscan he studied under Titelmans.[2] Because of his rapid progress in Greek and Latin literature (note the assumed name Tacitus) he succeeded Titelmans in the chair of Sacred Scripture at the Franciscan college in Louvain in 1536 and remained there through 1548. He died in 1559.

His Epanorthotes sive castigationes in Novum Testamentum, published at Cologne by the sons of Arnold Birckman in 1555, contains no references to Mt. 16:18. His Scholion in omnes novi testamenti libros . . . was published again at Cologne by the descendants of Birckman in 1553 and were republished there in 1558. Zegers' opening letter to the pious reader, most likely to "candidates for sacred theosophy,"[3] makes clear the intent of Zegers in authoring such a

text. First he distinguishes scholia from commentaries and places his work in the former
category.[4] These scholia will concern not every
verse but rather those passages which need exposition because of their obscure meaning or ambiguous reading.[5] He says that he will stress what
he understands to be "the primary sense" and
where a verse seems to admit of many meanings he
will note the more probable meanings.[6] At the
end of this letter he lists his sources or
authorities: Augustine, Guillaume Budé, Cajetan,
Erasmus, the Glossa ordinaria, Jean de Gagny,
Chiari, Sebastian Münster, Nicolaus of Lyra,
Lefèvre, Stunica, Thomas Aquinas, and Valla.[7]

His note to Mt. 16:18 like all of his
notes is very brief: "That is, upon this firm
confession of faith, or as Augustine interpreted,
upon this rock which you have confessed and which
you have recognized in saying, 'Thou art the
Christ the son of the living God,' that is, upon
me, Christ the son of the living God."[8] Zegers
thus interprets "petra" in terms of both Peter's
confession of faith and Jesus himself. He also
relies on one of Augustine's sermons (on Mt.
14:24-33) which has been frequently referred to.[9]
Finally, Zegers makes no reference to the controversies over this passage, an approach in keeping
with his original intention in writing these
brief notes. He wished to extricate himself
from "all questions, arguments, entanglements,
assertions, heresies, and difficulties."[10]

René Benoist's "Locorum praecipuorum sacrae scripturae . . . conquisitio . . . et expositio" (1566)

René Benoist was born in 1521 at Charon-
nières in the parish of Savennières, near Angers.
He became a diocesan priest in 1553 and was so
popular that in his own time he earned the name
"Pope of the marketplace." Much of his career
was spent in controversies with Calvin and the
Hugenots. In order to combat the influence of

Reformed translations of the Bible in France he
produced a translation of his own (1566) although
he lacked sufficient expertise in both Hebrew and
Greek. Because of its "Genevan" quality, his
translation was condemned by the Sorbonne in
1567, 1569, and 1572 and by Pope Gregory XIII in
1575. Benoist died in 1608.

His exegetical works include: Nouveau
Testament de N. S. Jesus-Christ, latin et
francois . . . Avec annotations et expositions
des lieux les plus difficiles (Paris, 1566),
Locorum praecipuorum Sacrae Scripturae . . .
(Paris, 1566); Stromata in universum organum
biblicum . . . (Paris, 1564). The very title
page of Benoist's commentary indicates both
context and audience. He will attend to those
passages which the Calvinists of his day "abuse,"
thus flying in the face of Catholic faith and
evangelical truth.[11] Benoist is writing self-
consciously for students of scripture, preachers,
and controversialists.[12]

He begins his discussion of Mt. 16:18f by
adverting to the position of French Calvinists
who argued against relating this verse to the
pope since Christ the Rock said the church would
be founded on himself.[13] Benoist responds by
combining the older patristic idea of reward with
the more recent juridical understanding of this
verse: "For it is manifest from the text itself
that Christ himself promised blessed Peter
privilege and office excelling in Christ's
church, in compensation for the confession that
Peter had uttered about Christ's divinity united
personally and inseparately to his humanity."[14]
Though he has rejected the Calvinist identification of "petra" with Jesus, he goes on to admit
that Christ is truly the head and foundation of
the church, but adds that since Christ is no
longer visible in his ministry, it is necessary
that there be a visible minister and such was
Peter in a way that went beyond the otherwise
democratic structure of the early church.[15]

Benoist concludes from this analysis of Mt.
16:18f that in this most ordered church by the
very ordering of Christ himself there is "a
primary and principal minister and vicar; he who
does not recognize this person . . . does not
correctly recognize Christ."[16] The original
concern with the Protestant charges against the
papacy continues though, for Benoist is concerned
to meet the charge that the "tibi" of Mt. 16:19
does not apply to Peter's successors. By now it
seems that Benoist is chiefly concerned with
showing that Mt. 16:18-19 is compatible with the
claims of sixteenth century Roman Catholicism regarding the office and power of the papacy.

Abruptly, however, Benoist returns to Mt.
16:18 itself and says:

> By these words we are taught that as a
> reward --since blessed Peter first made
> that confession of divinity and humanity
> of Christ, in which confession the Chris-
> tian religion and the Church is founded --
> Peter received from Christ this power and
> dignity, because his situation is first
> among those who preached this confession
> in order to found the church. Therefore
> he is called Peter and upon such a rock
> [confession of faith] the church was
> founded by Christ ("ab ipso"); so that
> clearly Peter was the principal and first
> promulgator of this confession, which was
> first revealed to him by God.[17]

Having thus argued that Mt. 16:18 is
compatible with the idea that the pope is the
head and foundation of the church and also that
the rock is Peter's confession of faith, Benoist
adds another idea, one he explicitly singles out
as his own: there is a significant difference
between the power of administering the church and
the apostolate itself. The pope has succeeded
Peter in the first but in no way can he be called
"apostle," thus setting up a certain distance

between Peter and any individual pope. The importance of this is that the latter office (apostolate) is concerned with the establishing of the church ("ad fundandam sine restrictione Ecclesiam").[18] Benoist's last comment is interesting in that he adds another opinion of his, that is, that he would not have sided with those who affirmed that bishops are immediately sent by and depend upon Christ alone and not the pope. His reason is the need for one minister in the Church upon whom all others depend and obey.[19]

Manoel Sa's "Scholia in Quatuor Evangelia" (1596)

Manoel Sa was born in Villa de Code, diocese of Braga, in Portugal around 1530. At the early age of fifteen he entered the Society of Jesus at Coimbra. He later taught exegesis at the Roman College. During this time he served on the papal commission concerned with revising the Vulgate. His last ten years were spent preaching in northern Italy. His major exegetical works include Scholia in quatuor evangelia (Antwerp, 1596; later editions in 1602, 1619, 1620) and Notationes in totam scripturam sacram (Antwerp, 1598; later editions in 1601, 1609, 1610, 1620, 1624-1625, and 1651). He died in 1596 near Milan.

Sa's commentary clearly differentiates between the tradition of patristic commenting, which he divides according to the literal and mystical senses,[20] and his own comments which follow immediately after the patristic positions. In his discussion of the literal sense of Mt. 16:18 he begins first with "Petrus": just as the apostles received the name "light of the world" from Jesus the light itself, so Simon who believed in the rock, Christ, received the name "Petrus" -- this is a position of Jerome which has already been cited.[21] Peter is "Petrus" because of the strength of his faith and the constancy of his confession -- this is the po-

sition of the <u>Glossa ordinaria</u>.[22] This material
displays a certain diversity regarding "petra":
the rock is in a certain sense, according to
Jerome, Christ, and in another (indirect) sense,
according to the <u>Glossa ordinaria</u>, Peter's faith.
This diversity continues in the literal sense of
"petra": "The <u>Glossa interlinearis</u> renders it
'Christ in whom you are believing' (Chrysostom).
Jerome interprets it in the sense 'I will build
my church upon you.' Augustine in book one of
the <u>Retractiones</u>, chapter 21, says 'Once I rendered "the church built on Peter," 'often truly I
rendered "upon the rock, that is Christ." Which
of the two opinions is more correct I leave to
the reader to choose.'"[23] What is new here is a
certain "scientific" interest on Sa's part. That
is, he identifies as Chrysostom's what the <u>Glossa
interlinearis</u> left unidentified. This reflects
Sa's larger concern to identify for himself and
the reader such unidentified positions in the
<u>Glossa</u>.[24] It is also interesting to note that
here Sa cites a range of different positions
coming from patristic commenting; no mention is
made of "petra" as faith, however.

Sa indicates no mystical sense to Mt.
16:18 and then proceeds to add his own position:
"petra" refers back to "Petrus." He offers the
by now standard argument that in Greek "pétros"
and "pétra" mean the same, and that Jesus' own
usage ("Cepha") means rock or stone in Syriac.[25]
This remark is even more significant because Sa
does not add additional comments on every verse
but only on those passages which "require more
light."[26]

Conclusion

A willingness to accept a diversity of
meanings for "petra" is present in the commentaries of Zegers (1553), Benoist (1566), and Sa
(1596). Thus, the "petra" is respectively understood in terms of the confession of faith and

Jesus, the confession of faith and Peter, Christ and Peter. This diversity continues the diversity manifested in the great Glossae and earlier in the famous statement by Augustine in his Retractiones. What is new here, even amidst the diversity, is an awareness in Benoist and Sa of the polemical and institutional questions raised about Mt. 16:18. Hence the need for a visible minister in the church and the position of the Calvinists prompts Benoist to discuss "petra" in reference to papal claims.

NOTES FOR CHAPTER FOUR

[1] Servais Dirks, Histoire littéraire et bibliographique des Frères Mineurs de l'Observance de St-Francois en Belgique et dans les Pays-Bas. (Antwerp: Os-De Wolf, n.d.), p. 81.

[2] His Scholion of 1553 on the New Testament though does not list Titelmans as a resource person.

[3] Tacitus Nicolaus Zegers, Scholion in omnes novi testamenti libros, . . . (Coloniae Agrippinae: Apud haeredes Arnoldi Birckmanni, 1553), p. 6.

[4] Ibid., p. 3^v: "Primum itaque (ne forte hic ut improbus conviva pro merenda coenam efflagites) intelligas oportet, non commentarios, sed scholia nos scribere, . . ."

[5] Ibid.: ". . . easque in salebrosos seu impeditos duntaxat locos: qui videlicet, vel propter sensuum verborumve obscuritatem, vel propter lectionis ambiguitatem seu etiam depravationem negocium facessere poterant studiosis."

[6] Ibid., p. 4: "Eum itaque sensum indicasse qui ipsius autoris primarius censebatur, easque salebras ad quas simplex lector aut etiam mediocriter eruditus restitare posset submovisse contenti, reliqua omnia ab aliis petenda praeterivimus: nisi quod plerisque in locis plures sensus eosque probabiliores adscripserimus, prout videbamus probatos autores variare."

[7] Ibid., p. 7^{r-v}.

[8] Ibid., p. 31: "'Et super hanc petram.' Id est, super firmam hanc fidei confessionem. Vel ut interpratatur Aug. super hanc petram quam confessus es, et cognovisti dicens, tu es Ch. fi. D. viv. id est, super me Christum filium Dei vivi."

193

[9]PL 38, 479.

[10]Ibid., p. 3[v]: "Omnium porro omnibus quaes-
tionibus, cavilationibus, nodis, assertionibus,
haeresibus, ac difficultatibus occurrere ac
satisfacere, praeterquam quod id immensum esset
opus postulaturum, longe etiam quod ingenue
fatemur ingenii nostri limites transcenderet."

[11]René Benoist, Locorum praecipuorum sacrae
scripturae, . . . quibus corruptis inscite et
prave detortis abutuntur huius tempestatis
haeretici contra fidem Catholicam, et veritatem Euangelicam conquisitio, et Catholica expositio: quae Christianorum adversus omnes nunc
vigenteis haereses, Panoplia merito dici potest.

[12]Ibid.: "Opus cum omnibus Scripturae sacrae
studiosis tum maxime concionatoribus Catholicis,
et Ecclesiasticis quibus libet perutile: atque
potissimum iis quibus cum haereticis frequens est
disputatio necessarium."

[13]Ibid., p. 46[r]: "Quo loco male intellecto,
abutuntur, qui ex illo colligunt Papam, id est
primum Ecclesiae ministrum male dici caput seu
fundamentum Ecclesiae, quia videlicet (aiunt
illi) Christus dixit suam Ecclesiam fundandam
supra sese, qui est Petra."

[14]Ibid.: "Nam manifestum est ex litera ipsa,
Christum promisit se beato Petro privilegium et
officium excellens in sua Ecclesia, in compensationem confessionis quam fecit de eius Divini-
tate, humanitati personaliter et inseparabiliter
coniuncta." He adds that otherwise Jesus would
not have promised Peter the keys: "Quorsum enim
speciatim adiunxisset, se ipsi daturum claves
regni caelorum?"

[15]Ibid.: "Et si igitur solus Christus vere
et proprie est Ecclesiae caput et fundamentum,
qui eam suo sanguine lavat et purificat, quique
ipsius unicus est sponsus, et eandem suo spiritu

194

fovet, et omnipotenti virtute sua sustinet et
firmat: tamen cum in caelos conscenderit, nec
visibiliter in ea nunc aliquid ministret, operae
pretium et necessarium est in ipsa esse aliquem
ministrum visibilem, qui eius vices suppleat, et
hominibus corporatis corporaliter et sensibiliter
Divina et sacra, per corporata et sensibilia
ministret. Talis fuit primus beatus Petrus, cui,
et ii reliqui Apostoli in Apostolatus vocatione,
et verbi Dei praedicatione pares erant, ipso
tamen in regenda Ecclesia inferiores fuerunt."
As evidence for Peter's unique position in the
church, Benoist goes on to cite the sermons of
Acts where Peter speaks first, Luke 22:32 ("but I
have prayed for you that your faith may not fail;
and when you have turned again, strengthen your
brethren"), and John 21 ("Feed my lambs . . .
feed my sheep").

[16]Ibid., p. 47: "In Ecclesia igitur ex
ordinatione Christi, quae est ordinatissima, est
quidam primus et praecipuus minister eius vicar-
ius, quem qui non agnoscunt, Christum, qui hanc
ipsi delegavit potestatem, recte agnoscere non
possunt."

[17]Ibid., p. 47[v]: "Sunt igitur diligenter
expenenda verba illa Christi: Tu es Petrus et
super hanc petram aedificabo Ecclesiam meam.
Quibus docemur quod in compensationem, quia
beatus Petrus primus fecit illam confessionem
Divinitatis et humanitatis Christi, in qua confessione fundatur religio Christiana et Ecclesia,
is accepit eam a Christo potestatem atque dignitatem, quod primus inter eos est habitus, qui eam
confessionem ad fundandam Ecclesiam praedicaverunt.
Ideo enim dicitur Petrus: et super talem petram,
Ecclesia ab ipso fundata est: ut videlicet
praecipuus et primus esset promulgator eius
confessionis, quae ei primo a Deo revelata est."

[18]Ibid.: "Notatu tamen interim dignum est
(meo quidem iudicio) quod etsi summus Pontifex
hodiernus, successit beato Petro in potestate

administrandae Ecclesiae, non tamen in aposto-
latu, qui in eo consistit, quod ad fundandam sine
restrictione Ecclesiam, a Christo ipso missi sunt
duodecim, qui idcirco Apostoli sunt vocati. Hoc
autem quia etiam beato Paulo concessum fuit, ideo
Apostolus merito dicitur. Certum est igitur nec
summum Pontificem, nec alios episcopos dici posse
Apostolos."

[19]Ibid., p. 48: "Nec sane illis calculum
meum addiderim, qui affirmarent episcopos nostros, non a Papa, sed a solo Christo immediate
mitti et pendere: etenim si unus non sit in
Ecclesia minister cui omnes obediant Christiani,
et a quo reliqui Christiani mittantur et depen-
deant, non satis sane video qua ratione Ecclesia
Catholica una possit dici."

[20]Sa says here he is adopting "the universal
interpretation," although he is aware that the
distinction between the two senses is somewhat
arbitrary with regard to what gets placed where;
see his "Notationes ad scholiorum intelligentiam"
in Scholia in quatuor evangelia, ex selectis
Doctorum sacrorum sententiis collecta . . .
addita et quedam . . . (Lugduni: Cordon, 1610),
[*4]: "Distinximus, quo tota res esset facilior,
universam interpretationem in sensum Litteralem
et Mysticum, quamquam non ignoramus, quaedam
posita in Litterali quae ad Mysticum, nonnulla
etiam in Mystico quae ad Litteralem potius quibusdam forte pertinere videbuntur, noluimus in re
hac nimia uti religione, contenti viam aperuisse
quam doctiores possint facili negotio explanare."

[21]Ibid., p. 95: "Hier. sicut ipse lumen
Apostolis donavit, ut lumen mundi appellentur,
ita Simoni credenti in petram Christum Petri
nomen dedit. . . ." Cf. chapter one.

[22]Ibid.: "Glo. est Petrus ob fidei fortitu-
dinem, et confessionis constantiam." Cf. PL 114,
142.

[23]Ibid.: "Int. id est, Christum in quem credis. Chry. [followed by special siglum indicating a new position will follow] Hier. id est, aedificabo Ecclesiam super te. Aug. I lib. retract. ca. 21. aliquando exposui in Petro aedificatam Ecclesiam, saepe vero super petram, id est, Christum, quarum sententiarum, quae sit probabilior lector eligat."

[24]Ibid., *3^V: "Ne quis forte miretur in Interlineari, quae sic notatur. Inter. aliquando auctoris alicuius nomen praeponi, aliquando vero postponi: sciendum est, cum in principio ponitur post signum. Inter. esse partem ipsius Inter-linearis, quae sic interdum solet citare auc-tores: quando vero in fine adijcitur, illud nostrum est, qui plerisque in locis indicare voluimus, unde illa Interlinearis accepta sit."

[25]Ibid.: "de qua proxime dixerat, Tu es Petrus. Graece enim idem 'pétros' et 'pétra,' et quidem Cephas, seu Cepha, qua voce Christus usus, Syriace lapis, seu saxum. Heb. Ceph."

[26]Ibid., [*4]: "Adiunximus tandem aliunde collecta quaedam, in eos praesertim locos qui lucem maiorem requirere videbantur; eaque seorsim sub Additionis titulo: noluimus enim caeteris immiscere, quod non essent tant auctoritatis; quamquam multa meo quidem iudicio non sunt, quod ad veritatem attinet, inferiora: . . ."

CONCLUSION

The investigation of twenty-eight commentaries on Matthew by twenty-one sixteenth century
exegetes results in the following conclusions:

1. Sixteenth century Roman Catholic
"petra" commenting is certainly not monolithic.
Four interpretations exist: faith, Christ,
Peter, and combinations of two of these positions.

2. With the year 1560, however, one
discerns a shift toward a monolithic view. From
that date onward almost all Roman Catholic
exegetes understand the "petra" of Mt. 16:18 to
be Peter and sometimes also his successors the
popes; Arias is the exception (1575). Anti-
Luther feelings and a concern to protect Peter's
governance of the church were operative in this
shift.

3. The petra=fides line stresses an
inclusive understanding of faith: every Christian can utter Peter's confession of faith and
thus what is said to Peter on account of this
confession may be attributed to any Christian.
The early writers Origen and Chrysostom were
especially relied upon as authorities for this
view. The medieval notion of a confession of
faith separate from the person of Peter continues
in the sixteenth century position.

4. The petra=Christus line holds that
the firmness and solidity of "petra" can point
only to Christ and certainly not to the very
fluctuating and unstable Peter. This understanding is very medieval as is its stress on Mt.
7:24 and I Cor. 3:11. The sixteenth century
omits the Eph. 2:20 connection and brings in

199

I Cor. 10:4. Prominent forerunners of this view include Augustine, the two great _Glossae_ and Pierre d'Ailly.

5. The _petra=Petrus_ line consciously reflects opposition to Protestant "petra" positions. This line stresses that there is a need for an institutional "petra" (the papal office) in the light of Christ's departure and absence. This line alone, especially in Bredenbach, employs the supposed Aramaic background of Mt. 16:18. While seeking to appropriate all other patristic interpretations in terms of Peter and sometimes Rome, this line rarely establishes the contextual character of the various patristic remarks. Not all of these exegetes included Peter's successors: Jansen in fact excludes the popes from consideration as "petra."

6. The final line admits of diverse understandings of "petra." This diversity continues that manifested in Augustine's _Retractiones_ statement and in the two great _Glossae_. The polemical and institutional concerns also surface here.

Erasmus' Note on Mt. 16:18 in his Various Editions of the NT

'Quia tu es.' ὅτι quod, non   1516
quia, id est, dico te esse Petrum.
Petrus autem Graecis saxum significat, pétros: quemadmodum et Cephas
Syro sermone, // ut testis est   1519
Hieronymus, // non Hebraico, soli-   1516
ditatem sonat. Saxum enim illum
appellat, quod solidus sit in confessione fidei, et non vulgarium
opinionum levitate huc et illuc
vacillet: et super istam petram, hoc
est, solidam istam fidei professionem,
extruam Ecclesiam meam, in quo fundamento si constiterit, nec inferi
quicquam adversus illam poterunt,
// nedum homines. // // In eam senten-   1519, 1527
tiam Theophylactus et Chrysostomus,
quem citat Catena aurea. // Etiamsi   1516
divus Augustinus in Homilia hujus
loci haec verba, super hanc petram,
ipsi accomodat Christo, non Petro: Tu
es, inquit, Petrus et super hanc
petram, quam confessus es, super hanc
petram, quam cognovisti, dicens, Tu
es Christus Filius Dei vivi, aedificabo Ecclesiam meam, id est, super
meipsum Filium, Dei vivi aedificabo
Ecclesiam meam. Super me aedificabo
te, non me super te. Nam volentes
homines aedificari super homines,
dicebant, Ego quidem sum Pauli, ego
autem Apollo, ego vero Cephae, ipse
est Petrus. Et alii qui nolebant

aedificari super Petrum, sed super
petram, Ego autem sum Christi.
// Idem libro Retractationum I. cap.   1527
XXI recenset utramque sententiam, propensior tamen in hanc, ut Petrus profitens Christum Filium Dei vivi typum
gerat Ecclesiae, cui traditae sint
claves. Caeterum Lectori liberum
facit eligere, utram voluerit. //
Proinde miror esse, qui locum hunc   1516
detorqueant ad Romanum Pontificem //,
in quem haud dubie compteunt in   1519
primis velut in Christianae fidei
principem. At non in hunc unum, sed
in omnes Christianos, quod elegantur
indicat Origenes Homilia prima harum
quas habemus. // Verum sunt quibus   1516
nihil satis est, nisi quod sit immodicum. Ita quidam ad invidiam usque
Franciscum prodigiosis efferunt
laudibus, quem exprimere magis oportebat, quam in immensum attollere. Nam
Deiparae Virgini, et Christo fortasse
non potest adscribi nimium. Quanquam
hic quoque optarim omnes tam ad
imitandi studium inflammatos, quam
quosdam videmus sedulos in exaggerandis laudibus. // Divus Cyprianus in   1519
Epistola primi libri tertia videtur
accipere super Petrum esse fundatam
Ecclesiam, Petrus tamen, inquiens,
super quem ab eodem Domino fundata
fuerat Ecclesia. Nisi forte sic   ○
excusandus est Cyprianus, quod Petrum
hic non pro homine illo, sed pro typo
accepit, quod propemodum indicant
quae sequuntur: unus pro omnibus
loquens, et Ecclesiae voce respondens, ait, Domine quo ibimus? //
// Similiter excusari possunt loca, in   1527
quibus S. Hieronymus in Epistolis
videtur dicere super Petrum fundatam
Ecclesiam Christi. // Itaque Petrus   1519
saxeus solidam Ecclesia fidem reprae-

sentat. // Caeterum nostra interpre-   1516
tatio verbis duntaxat diffidet ab
Augustiniani, quam ideo induximus,
quod illius videretur coactior, ad
quam tamen maluit deflectere, quam in
alterum incurrere scopulum, videlicet,
ut in homine poneret Ecclesiae fundamentum.

        // Non praevalebunt adversus   1519
eam.) Notavit hujus sermonis amphibologiam Origenes, quod pronomen eam,
vel petram referre potest, vel Ecclesiam. Verum id ad sententiam perparvi refert. //

LIST OF ABBREVIATIONS

ARG   Archiv für Reformationsgeschichte
(Leipzig and Gutersloh, 1903ff)

CC   Corpus Catholicorum (Münster i. W.,
1919ff)

CCSL   Corpus Christianorum "Series Latina"
(Turnhout, 1954ff)

CIC   Corpus iuris canonici, ed. E. Friedberg,
2 vols. Leipzig, 1879-1881)

DTC   Dictionnaire de theologie catholique
(Paris, 1930-1950)

EE   Opus epistularum Des. Erasmi . . ., ed.
P. S. Allen (Oxford, 1906-1958)

GCS   Die griechischen christlichen Schriftsteller der ersten drei Jahrhunderte
(Leipzig, 1897ff)

Glorieux   Palémon Glorieux, Pour revaloriser
Migne: table rectificatives, Cahier
supplémentaire aux Mélanges de
Science religieuse 9 (1952) (Lille,
1952)

Holborn   . . . Ausgewählte werke, . . ., ed. H.
Holborn (Munich, 1933)

LB   . . . Erasmi . . . Opera omnia, 10
vols. (Leiden, 1703-1706)

Mansi   Sacrorum conciliorum nova et amplis-
sima collectio (Florence, 1759ff)

PG   Patrologiae cursus completus . . .
              Series graeca, ed. J. P. Migne, 161
              vols. (Paris, 1857-1866)

PL   Patrologiae cursus completus . . .
              Series latina, ed. J. P. Migne, 221
              vols. (Paris, 1844-1904)

Quellen   Quellen zur Geschichte des Papsttums
              und des römischen Katholizismus, 6th
              ed., edited by C. Mirbt and K. Aland
              (Tübingen, 1967).

Q-E   Scriptores Ordinis Praedicatorum, ed.
              J. Quetif and J. Echard (Paris,
              1910-1934)

SC   Sources chrétiennes (Paris, 1941ff)

ZKG   Zeitschrift für Kirchengeschichte
              (Stuttgart, 1877ff)

BIBLIOGRAPHY

Primary Sources

The Acts of the Parliaments of Scotland. Edin-
    burgh: Record Commission, 1814-1844.

Ailly, Pierre d'. Questiones . . . super primum,
    tertium et quartum sententiarum . . . Theolo-
    giae laudes una cum principio in cursum
    bibliae. Questiones in vesperiis . . . N.p.:
    [J. Petit], n.d.

Ambrose. Aeterne rerum conditor. PL 16. Paris,
    1880. Col. 1473.

_____. "In epistolam beati b. Pauli ad
    Ephesios." PL 17. Paris, 1879. Cols. 393-
    426.

_____. "In epistolam beati Pauli ad Galatas."
    PL 17. Paris, 1879. Cols. 258-394.

_____. Expositio evangelii secundum Lucam . . .
    Edited by M. Adriaen. CCSL, 14. Turnholti:
    Brepols, 1957.

Arbres, Jean d'. Commentarii . . . in quatuor
    domini evangelistas. Parisiis: J. de
    Roigny, 1529.

_____. . . . theosophiae . . . complectens
    sanam et luculentam difficillimorum locorum
    cum veteris tum novi testamenti exposi-
    tionem, . . . 2 vols. Parisiis: S. Colin-
    aeus, 1540.

Augustine. Prima - [undecima] pars librorum
    . . . Augustini . . . [Basileae: Frobenius
    et al., 1506].

207

_____. Opera omnia. Edited by D. Erasmus. 10 vols. Basileae: Frobenius, 1528-1529.

_____. Annotationum in Job. PL 34. Paris, 1887. Cols. 825-886.

_____. Commentaire de la Première Épître de S. Jean. Edited by P. Agaësse. SC, 75. Paris: Cerf, 1961.

_____. Ennarationes in Psalmos. Edited by D. E. Dekkers and J. Fraipont. CCSL, 39. Turnholti: Brepols, 1956.

_____. In Johannis evangelium tractatus CXXIV. Edited by D. R. Willems. CCSL, 36. Turnholti: Brepols, 1954.

_____. Psalmus contra partem Donati. PL 43. Paris, 1865. Cols. 23-32.

_____. Retractionum libri duo. PL 32. Paris, 1887. Cols. 583-636.

_____. Sermones. PL 38-39. Paris, 1865.

Augustinus Nebiensis. . . . in universa quatuor evangelia Octaplum . . . N.p.: n.p., n.d.

Avendano, Alfonso de. Commentaria in evangelium divi Matthaei, . . . 2 vols. Matriti: P. Madrigal, 1593.

Baronio, Cesare. . . . Annales ecclesiastici . . . 37 vols. Barri-Ducis: J. Guerin, 1864-1887.

Barradas, Sebastian. . . . Commentariorum in concordiam, et historiam evangelicam. Conimbricae: A. de Maris, 1599.

_____. . . . Commentaria in concordiam et historiam evangelicam. 2 vols. Moguntiae: B. Lippius, 1601-1605.

Basil the Great. Adversus Eunomium. PG 29. Paris, n.d. Cols. 497-768.

_____. Enarratio in prophetam Isaiam. PG 30. Paris, 1888. Cols. 117-668.

Beda, Noël. Annotationum . . . in Jacobum Fabrum Stapulen sem libri duo . . . [Coloniae: Quentel, 1526].

Beaux-Amis, Thomas. Commentariorum in evangelicam harmoniam, sive concordiam . . . 4 vols. Parisiis: G. Chaudiere, 1583.

Bellarmino, Roberto. Disputationes . . . de controversiis. 3 vols. Ingolstadius: D. Sartorius, 1586.

Benoist, René. Stromata in universum organum biblicum . . . Lutetiae: J. Macaeus, 1564.

_____. Locorum praecipuorum sacrae scripturae . . . Parisiis: N. Chesneau, 1566.

_____. Le Nouveau Testament de N. S. Jesus-Christ, latin et francais . . . avec annotations et expositions des lieux les plus difficiles. Parisiis: Nyvelle, 1566.

Benoit, Jean. Biblia sacra . . . cum quibusdam annotationibus . . . Parisiis: S. Colinaeus, 1541.

_____. Novum Testamentum, haud poenitendis sacrorum doctorum scholiis, . . . Parisiis: S. Colaeus, 1543.

_____. Biblia sacra . . . 2nd edition. Parisiis: S. Colinaeus, 1552.

_____. Clarissima et facillima in quatuor sacra Iesu Christi evangelia, necnon in Actus Apostolicos scholia . . . I. Benedicti ura emendata. N.p.: n.p., 1552.

_____. Novum testamentum. 2nd edition.
Parisiis: Apud Carolam Guillard, 1554.

Biblia cum glossa ordinaria, Nicolai de Lyra
postilla, moralitatibus eiusdem, Pauli
Burgensis additionibus, Matthiae Thoring
replicis. 6 vols. Basileae: J Frobenius,
1498-1502, 1506-1508.

Birrietus, Anton. Commentaria in quatuor evangelia. Parisiis: n.p., 1581.

Bredenbach, Matthias. . . . in sanctum Iesu
Christi evangelium secundum Matthaeum . . .
commentaria. Coloniae: P. Quentel and
Calenius, 1560.

Briçonnet, Guillaume and Marguerite d'Angoulême.
Correspondance (1521-1524). Vol. 1: Années
1521-1522. Edited by C. Martineau and M.
Veissière. Travaux d'Humanisme et Renaissance, 141. Genève: Droz, 1975.

Broickwy, Anton. . . . in quatuor evangelia
ennarationum . . . Coloniae: P. Quentell,
1539.

_____. Concordantiae breviores omnium ferme
materiarum ex sacris bibliorum libris . . .
Parisiis: n.p., 1551.

Brucioli, Antonio. Nuovo commento . . . ne
divini et celesti libri evangelici . . .   In
Vinetia: [F. Brucioli], 1542.

Bullioud, Pierre de. Expositiones et remarques
sur les evangiles . . . Lugduni: Pille-
hotte, 1596.

Bunderen, Johannes van den. Compendium concertationis . . . Venetiis: n.p., 1548.

Capitone, Feliciano. Explicationes catholicae
locorum Veteris ac Novi Testamenti. Edited
by G. Floridus. Venetiis: Guerraei, 1579.

210

Castro, Alphonse de. <u>Adversus haereses.</u> Lugduni:
n.p., 1555

Chiari, Isidoro. <u>Novi Testamenti vulgata quidem</u>
<u>aeditio, . . .</u> 2 vols. Venetiis: P.
Schoeffer, 1541.

_____. <u>Vulgata aeditio Veteris ac Novi Testa-</u>
<u>menti . . .</u> 3 vols. Venetiis: P. Schoef-
fer, 1542.

Chrysostom, John. <u>. . . opera.</u> Basileae: in
officiana Frobenia, 1530.

_____. <u>Adversus Iudaeos orationes 1-8.</u> PG
48. Paris, 1863. Cols. 843-942.

_____. <u>Expositiones in psalmos 43-49.</u> PG 55.
Paris, 1862. Cols. 167-258.

_____. <u>In illud: "Vidi dominum" (Is. 6:1),</u>
<u>homiliae 1-6.</u> PG 56. Paris, 1859. Cols.
97-142.

_____. <u>In Matthaeum homilae 1-90.</u> PG 57, 13-
58, 794. Paris, 1862.

_____. <u>In pentecosten sermo 1.</u> PG 52.
Paris, 1859. Cols. 803-808.

_____. <u>In psalmum 50.</u> PG 55. Paris, 1862.
Cols. 527-532.

_____. <u>In psalmum 50 homilia 1.</u> PG 55.
Paris, 1862. Cols. 565-575.

<u>Conciliorum oecumenicorum decreta.</u> Edited by J.
Alberigo <u>et al.</u> Basil: Herder, 1962.

<u>Concilium Tridentinum: Diariorum, actorum, epis-</u>
<u>tolarum, tractatuorum nova collectio.</u>
Edited by Görres Gesellschaft. Freiburg:
Herder, 1901ff.

<u>Correspondance des réformateurs dans le pays de</u>

211

langue française . . . Vol. 1:1512-1526.
Edited by A.-L. Herminjard. Genève: Georg,
1866.

Critici sacri . . . Edited by John Pearson
et al. 8 vols. Amstelaedumi Ultrajecti:
van de Water, 1698.

Cyprian. Opera . . . Basileae: Frobenius,
1520.

_____. De habitu virginum. PL 4. Paris,
1891. Cols. 451-478.

_____. "De ecclesiae catholicae unitate,"
. . . opera. Edited by M. Benvenot. CCSL,
3. Turnholti: Brepols, 1972. Pp. 249-268.

_____. "Ad Fortunatum," . . . opera. Edited
by R. Weber. CCSL, 3. Turnholti: Brepols,
1972. Pp. 181-216.

_____. "Ad Iubaianum," Epistulae. Edited by
G. Hartel. CSEL, 3, 2. Vindobonae: C.
Geroldi filium, 1868.

_____. De singularitate clericorum tractatus.
PL 4. Paris, 1891. Cols. 911-948.

Cyril of Alexandria. Expositio . . . in Joannis
evangelium. PG 73. Paris, 1864.

_____. De sancta et consubstantiali Trinitate.
PG 75. Paris, 1863. Cols. 657-1124.

Dionysius the Carthusian. . . . in quatuor evangelistas ennarationes . . . Parisiis: J.
de Roigny, 1539.

Epiphanius. Ancoratus und Panarion. Edited by
K. Holl. GCS, 25. Leipzig: Hinrich, 1915.

Erasmus, Desiderius. Erasmi opuscula: A Supplement to the Opera omnia. Edited by W. K.
Ferguson. The Hague: M. Nijhoff, 1933.

_____. Novum instrumentum omne, . . . una cum
annotationibus. Basileae: Frobenius, 1516.

_____. Novum testamentum omne, multo quam
antehac dilengtius . . . recognitum . . .
Basileae: Frobenius, 1519.

_____. Novum testamentum omne, tertio iam ac
dilengtius . . . recognitum. Basileae:
Frobenius, 1522.

_____. . . . Paraphrasis in evangelium
Matthaei, . . . N.p.: n.p. [1522].

_____. Novum testamentum iam quartum accura-
tissima cura recognitum . . . Basileae:
Frobenius, 1527.

_____. Novum testamentum iam quintum accura-
tissima cura recognitum . . . Basileae:
Frobenius, 1535.

Eusebius Emesenus. Homilia de poenitentia. PG
31. Paris, 1885. Cols. 1476-1488.

Fisher, John. . . . opera . . . Wirceburgi:
Fleischmannus, 1597.

Foxe, John. Actes and Monuments . . . London:
Day, [1563]; reprint ed., 8 vols., New York:
AMS Press, 1965.

Gagny, Jean. Clarissima . . . in quatuor sacra
Jesus Christi evangelia, . . . scholia . . .
Parisiis: G. Perier, 1552.

Gasparo, F. a Melo. Commentaria in sacrosanctum
Mathaei evangelium . . . Valladolid: D.
Fernanadez á Cordoba, 1584.

Ghlislandis, Anton de. Opus aureum super evangeliis. [Lugduni]: n.p., 1532.

Glossa ordinaria. PL 114. Paris, 1879. Cols.
9-752.

Gregory Nazianzen. Orationes xlv. PG 35-36, 12-664. Paris, 1886.

Gregory of Nyssa. Testimonia adversus Iudaeos. PG 46. Paris, 1863. Cols. 193-233.

Guillaud, Claude. In evangelium secundum Matthaeum commentarii. Parisiis: J. de Roigny, 1562.

Herborn, Nikolaus. Ennarationes in quatuor evangelistas. Coloniae: n.p., 1546.

Hessels, Joannes. In . . . evangelium secundum Matthaeum commentarius. Louvanii: n.p., 1572.

Hilarion, monachus Januensis. Animadversionum in sacrosancta evangelia IIII evangelia. Brixiae: D. Turlinus, 1567.

_____. Commentariorum in sacrosancta IIII evangelia . . . 2 vols. Brixiae: n.p., 1578.

Hilary. In evangelium secundum Matthaeum commentarius. PL 9. Paris, 1844. Cols. 917-1078.

_____. Tractatus super psalmos. PL 9. Paris, 1844. Cols. 231-890.

_____. De trinitate. PL 10. Paris, 1845. Cols. 25-472.

Hippolytus. In Matthaeum. PG 10. Paris, 1857. Cols. 699-700.

_____. De consummatione mundi. PG 10. Paris, 1857. Cols. 903-952.

Hugo de Sancto Charo. Biblia latina. Basileae: Amerbachius, 1498-1502.

Hus, Jan. . . . opera omnia. Vol. 22: . . . Polemica. Edited by J. Ersil. Prague:

Aacademia H. E., 1966.

Jansen, Cornelius. Commentariorum in suam concordiam, ac totam historiam evangelicam,
partes IV. Moguntiae: Wulfraht, 1624.

Jerome. . . . commentariorum in Isaiam prophetam.
PL 24. Paris, 1845. Cols. 17-678.

_____. Commentariorum in Matthaeum libri iv.
CCSL, 77. Turnholti: Brepols, 1969.

_____. . . . commentariorum in epistolam ad
Galatas . . . PL 26. Paris, 1884. Cols.
331-468.

_____. Adversus Iovinianum. PL 23. Paris,
1883. Cols. 221-352.

_____. Dialogus adversus Pelagianos. PL 23.
Paris, 1883. Cols. 517-618.

_____. Lettres. Vols. 1-2. Edited and
translated by J. Labourt. Paris: Les
Belles Lettres, 1949.

Juvencus. Evangelicae historiae. PL 19. Paris,
1846. Col. 53.

The Prefatory Epistles of Jacques Lefèvre d'Etaples
and Related Texts. Edited by E. F. Rice.
New York: Columbia University Press, 1972.

Lefèvre, Jacques d'Etaples. Commentarii initiatorii in quatuor evangelia. In evangelium secundum Matthaeum. [Meldis: Colinaeus, 1522].

Leo the Great. Epistula x. PL 54. Paris, 1881.
Cols. 628-636.

_____. Epistula cxiv. PL 54. Paris, 1881.
Cols. 1027-1032.

_____. Sermo iii. PL 54. Paris, 1881.
Cols. 144-148.

_____. Sermo iv. PL 54. Paris, 1881. Cols. 148-152.

Letters and Papers Foreign and Domestic of the Reign of Henry VIII . . . 21 vols. Edited by J. Gairdner. London: Her Majesty's Stationery Office, 1880; reprint ed., Vadux: Kraus, 1965.

Lloret, Jeroni. Silvan allegoriarum totius s. scripturae mysticos eius sensus et magna ex parte literales complectentem. Venetiis: n.p., 1575.

Luc de Bruges, Francois. Notationes in sacra biblia . . . Antwerpiae, 1580.

Luther, Martin. . . . Werke. Vol. 2. Weimar: Böhlaus, 1884.

Maes, André. Ad quaedam loca evangelistarum notae. N.p.: n.p., n.d.

Major, John. Quartus Sententiarum . . . Parisiis: Ponchetus, 1509.

_____. In Matthaeum ad literam expositio, . . . [Paris]: J. Granion, 1518.

_____. In primum Sententiarum. Parisiis: [Ascensius], 1519.

_____. In quartum Sententiarum. Parisiis: Badius, 1519.

_____. Historia maioris Britanniae, tam Angliae quam Scotiae . . . N.p.: Ascensius, 1520.

_____. A History of Greater Britain as Well England as Scotland . . . Translated and edited with notes by A. Constable. Publications of the Scottish History Society, x. Edinburgh: Edinburgh University Press, 1892.

_____. In secundum Sententiarum disputationes denuo recognitae et repurgatae. Parisiis: Parvus and Badius, 1528.

_____. . . . In quatuor evangelia expositiones luculente et disquisitiones et disputationes contra hereticos plurime . . . Parisiis: J. Badius, 1529.

_____. . . . in Primum magistri Sententiarum disputationes et decisiones nuper repositae. Parisiis: Parvus and Badius, 1530.

Maldonado, Juan de. Commentarii in iv evangelia. Pont-à-Mousson, 1596-1597; reprint ed., Parisiis: J. P. Migne, 1841.

Maximus of Turin. . . . Sermones. Edited by A. Mutzenbecher, CCSL, 23. Turnholti: Brepols, 1962.

Miletius, Ambrose. Commentaria in evangelium s. Matthaei et in epistulas sancti Pauli. N.p.: n.p., n.d.

Menot, Michel. Opus aureum evangeliorum. Paris: Chevallon, 1519.

Montano, Arias Benito. Liber Iospeh . . . Antwerpiae: Plantinus, 1572.

_____. . . . Elucidationes in quatuor evangelia . . . Antwerpiae, 1575.

_____. . . . Elucidationes in quatuor evangelia . . . Antwerp, 1588.

The New Testament of Jesus Christ . . . Rhemes: J. Fogny, 1582.

Origen. Opera. 3 vols. Parisiis: J. Parvus and J. B. Ascensius, 1512.

_____. . . . Werke. Vol. 3: Jeremiahomilien
. . . Edited by E. Klostermann. GCS, 6.
Leipzig: Hinrich, 1901.

_____. In Exodum homilia. PG 12. Paris,
1862. Cols. 297-396.

_____. Homélies sur Josué. Edited by A.
Jaubert. SC, 71. Paris: Cerf, 1960.

_____. Homélies sur s. Luc. Edited by H.
Crouzel, F. Fournier, P. Perichon. SC, 87.
Paris: Cerf, 1962.

_____. . . . Werke. Vol. 10: Origenes
Matthäuserklärung: Die griechisch erhaltenen
Tomoi. Edited by E. Klostermann. GCS, 40.
Leipzig: Hinrich, 1935.

_____. Commentariorum in evangelium Joannis
tomus ii. PG 14. Paris, 1862. Cols. 103-
196.

_____. Commentariorum in epistolam beati
Pauli ad Romanos . . . PG 14. Paris, 1862.
Cols. 837-1292.

Palacios, Paul de Salazar. In sacrosanctum Iesu
Christi evangelium secundum Matthaeum ennarationes. Conimbricae: Barrerias, 1564.

Pelayo, Alvaro. [De planctu ecclesiae]. [Ulm:
Zainer], 1474.

Pigges, Albert. Hierarchiae ecclesiasticae
assertio. Coloniae: I. Novesianus, 1551.

Preau, Gabriel du. De vitiis, sectis, et dogmatibus omnium haereticorum, . . . Coloniae: Calendius and Quentel, 1569.

Psellus, Michael. Expositio cantici canticorum.
PG 122. Paris, 1889. Cols. 537-686.

_____. Encomium . . . PG 114. Paris, 1903.
Cols. 183-200.

Rocaberti, Juan Tomas de. Bibliotheca maxima
pontifica . . . 21 vols. Romae: I. F.
Buagni, 1698-1699.

Sa, Manoel. Scholia in quatuor evangelia, ex
selectis doctorum sacrorum sententiis collecta. Antwerpiae, 1596; Lugduni, 1610.

Salmeron, Alphonsus. Commentarii in evangelicam
historiam . . . Matriti, 1598-1602; 8 vols.
Coloniae: Hierat, 1602-1604; Coloniae,
1612-1615.

Santotis, Cristóbal. Expositio in evangelium
secundum Matthaeum. Burgis: ex officina P.
Iuntae, 1598.

Sisto da Siena. Bibliotheca sancta. 2 vols.
Venetiis, 1566; Lugduni: Pesnot, 1575.

Suarez, Johannes. Commentaria in evangelium . . .
secundum Matthaeum. Conimbricae, 1562.

Tertullian. "De pudicitia," . . . opera.
Edited by E. Dekkers. CCSL, 2. Turnholti:
Brepols, 1954. Pp. 1279-1330.

_____. "De praescriptione haereticorum,"
. . . opera. Edited by R. F. Refoulé.
CCSL, 1. Turnholti: Brepols, 1954. Pp.
185-224.

Theodoret, Explanatio in Canticum Canticorum.
PG 81. Paris, 1864. Cols. 27-214.

_____. Haereticarum fabularum compendium. PG
83. Paris, 1864. Cols. 335-556.

Theophylact. . . . in quatuor evangelia ennarationes . . . Translated by J. Oecolampad.
Basileae: Craiander, 1527.

Thomas Aquinas. [Catena aurea]. Edited by J.
  Andreae. Romae: Suueynheyn, Pannartz,
  1470.

_____. Opera omnia. Vol. 16: Catena aurea
  in Matthaei evangelium . . . Edited by S. E.
  Frette. Parisiis: Vivès, 1876.

Tomitano. Bernardin. Espositione letterale del
  testo di Matthaeo evangelista . . . In
  Venetia: G. dal Griffo, 1547.

Trejo, Gutierre de. In quattuor evangelia commentarii . . . Seville: P. de Luxan, 1544.

Valdés, Juan de. El Evangelio según San Mateo
  . . . Edited by E. Boehmer. Madrid:
  Libreriá Nacional y Extranjera, 1880.

Valla, Lorenzo. . . . in latinam Novi testamenti
  interpretationem ex collatione Graecorum
  exemplarium Adnotationes apprime utiles.
  Parrhisiis: [Ascensius], [1505].

Vatable, François. Testamenti veteris et Novi
  Biblia sacra . . . cum adnotationibus
  Francisci Vatabli, prout utranque; Regio
  privilegio ornatam Robertus Syephanus anno
  MDXLV. Lutetiae edidit. . . . Hanoviae:
  C. Marnius and I. Aubrius, 1605.

_____. Biblia sacra, cum universis Franc.
  Vatabli, . . . et variorum interpretum,
  annotationibus. . . . editio postrema multo
  quam antehac emendatior et auctior. 2 vols.
  Parisiis: sumptibus societatis, 1729-1745.

Verratus, Giovanni Maria. Evangelium sancti
  Matthaei . . . Venetiis, 1551.

Vio, Tommaso de. De divina institutione pontificatus Romani pontificis super totam ecclesiam a Christo in Petro. [Romae: Silber,
  1521]; reprint ed. Munster: Aschendorff, 1925.

220

_____. Evangelia cum commentariis Caietani
. . . Venetiis: L. Iuncta, 1530.

_____. Evangelia cum commentariis. . . .
Recens in lucem editi. [Parisiis]: J.
Badius Ascensius, I. Parvus, and I. Roigny,
1532.

_____. Jentacula novi testamenti . . .
[Lugduni, 1537].

_____. Praeclarissima sexagintaquatuor nota-
bilium sententiarum Novi Testamenti
literalis expositio . . . Lugduni, 1538.

_____. In sacrosanctum Iesu Christi evangelium
secundum Matthaeum commentariorum libri
quatuor . . . 2 vols. Moguntiae: F. Behem,
1559.

Zegers, Tacitus Nicolaus. Scholion in omnes
novi testamenti libros, quo loci difficiles,
aut etiam ambigui . . . Coloniae Agrippinae: A. Birkmannus, 1553.

Secondary Sources

Andreas, Valerius. Bibliotheca belgica: Facsi-
mile of the Edition Louvain 1643. Monumenta
humanistica belica, 5. Nieuwkoop: B. de
Graaf, 1973.

Atlas zur Kirchengeschichte: die christlichen
Kirchen in Geschichte und Gegenwart. Edited
by H. Jedin et al. Freiburg im Breisgau:
Herder, 1970.

Bainton, Roland H. "The Paraphrases of Erasmus."
Archiv für Reformationsgeschichte 57 (1966),
67-75.

Becker, Ph.-Aug. "Les idées religieuses de
Guillaume Briçonnet, évêque de Meaux."

221

Revue de Théologie et des Questions religieuses (Montauban), 9 (1900), 318-358 and
377-416.

Bedouelle, Guy. Lefèvre d'Etaples et l'intelligence des Ecritures. Travaux d'Humanisme et
Renaissance, 152. Genève: Droz, 1976.

la Bonnardiere, A. M. "Tu es Petrus: La pericope Matthieu xvi, 13-23 dans l'oeuvre de S.
Augustin." Irénikon 34 (1961), 451-499.

Bulaeus, Caesar. Historia universitatis parisiensis . . . Parisiis: Noel, 1665-1673. 6
vols.

Burgess, Joseph. A History of the Exegesis of
Matthew 16:17-19 from 1781 to 1965. Ann
Arbor, Michigan: Edwards Brothers, 1976.

Burns, James. "New Light on John Major." Innes
Review 5 (1954), 83-100.

Congar, Yves. "Apostolicité de ministère et
apostolicité de doctrine: réaction protes-
tante et Tradition catholique." In Volk
Gottes: Zum Kirchenverstandnis der
katholischen, evangelischen und anglikanischen Theologie. Festgabe für Josef Hofer,
pp. 84-111. Edited by R. Baümer and H.
Dolch. Fribourg-in-Br.: Herder, 1967.

_____. "Du nouveau sur la question de Pierre."
La Vie intellectuelle 24,2 (1953), 17-43.

Cullmann, Oscar. Petrus: Jünger-Apostel-Märtyrer.
2nd ed. Zurich: Zwingli-Verlag, 1960; ET:
Peter, Disciple, Apostle, Martyr: A Historical and Theological Study. 2nd revised and
expanded edition. Translated by F. V.
Filson, Philadelphia: Westminster, 1962.

Dirks, Servais. Histoire littéraire et bibliographique des Frères Mineurs de l'Observance

de St-Francois en Belgique et dans les Pays-Bas. Antwerp: Os-De Wolf, n.d.

Ebeling, Gerhard. Kirchengeschichte als Geschichte der Auslegung der Heiligen Schrift. Tubingen: J.C.B. Mohr, 1947.

Emden, Alfred. A Biographical Register of the University of Cambridge to 1500. Cambridge: University Press, 1963.

Feret, P. La Faculté de théologie de Paris et ses docteurs le plus célèbres. Vol. 1: xvie siècle, phases historiques. Paris: Picard, 1900.

Fraenkel, Pierre. "Quelques observations sur le 'Tu es Petrus' chez Calvin, au Colloque de Worms en 1540 et dans l'Institution de 1543." Bibliothèque d'Humanisme et Renaissance 27 (1965), 607-628.

_____. "John Eck's Enchiridion of 1525 and Luther's Earliest Arguments Against Papal Primacy." Studia Theologica 21 (1967), 110-163.

François, Jean. Bibliothèque générale des écrivains de l'Ordre de Saint Benoit, . . Bouillon: Sociéty typographique, 1777; reprint ed., Louvain-Héverlé: Bibliothèque S. J., 1961.

Fröhlich, Karlfried. Formen der Auslegung von Mt. 16,13-18 im lateinischen Mittelalter. Tübingen: Prazis, 1963.

Ganoczy, Alexandre. "Jean Major, exégète gallican." Recherches de Science religieuse 56 (1968), 457-495.

Gillman, Franz. "Zur scholastischen Auslegung von Mt 16, 18." Archiv für katholisches Kirchenrecht 104 (1924), 41-53.

Grendler, Marcella and Paul. "The Survival of
    Erasmus in Italy." Erasmus in English 8
    (1976), 1ff.

Guggisberg, Kurt. "Matthaeus 16, 18 and 19 in
    der Kirchengeschichte." Zeitschrift für
    Kirchengeschichte 54 (1935), 276-300.

Heinrichs, Richard. "Der Humanist Mathias Breden-
    bach als Exeget." Der Katholik 73 (1893),
    345-357.

Heller, Henry. "Reform and Reformers at Meaux:
    1518-1525." Ph. D. dissertation, Cornell
    University, 1969.

Hurter, Hugo. Nomenclator literarius recentiores
    theologiae catholicae . . . Vol. 4: Theo-
    logia catholica tempore medii aevi. Ab
    anno 1109-1563. Oeniponte: Libraria
    academica wagneriana, 1889.

Index aureliensis. Catalogues librorum sedecimo
    saeculo impressorum. Bibliotheca biblio-
    graphica aureliana, 7. Baden-Baden: Founda-
    tion Index Aurelienesis, 1962ff.

Jarrott, C. A. L. "Erasmus' Biblical Humanism."
    Studies in the Renaissance 17 (1970), 119-
    152.

Laemmer, Hugo. Die vortridentinisch-katolische
    Theologie des Reformations-Zeitalters aus
    den Quellen dargestellt. Berlin, 1858;
    reprint ed., 1966.

Lamb, Matthew L. "Introduction." Commentary on
    Saint Paul's Epistle to the Ephesians by
    Saint Thomas Aquinas. Aquinas Scripture
    Series, 2. Albany, New York: Magi, 1966.

Ludwig, Joseph. Die Primatworte Mt. 16:18-19
    in der altkirchlichen Exegese. Neutesta-
    mentliche Abhandlungen, 19, 4. Munster:
    Aschendorf, 1952.

Montgomery, John W. "Sixtus of Siena and Roman Catholic Biblical Scholarship in the Reformation Period." Archiv für Reformationsgeschichte 54 (1963), 214-234.

Nieto, José C. Juan de Valdés and the Origins of the Spanish and Italian Reformation. Travaux d'Humanisme et Renaissance, 108. Genève: Droz, 1970.

Papal Primacy and the Universal Church. Edited by P. C. Empie and T. A. Murphy. Lutherans and Catholics in Dialogue, 5. Minneapolis: Augsburg, 1974.

Pasquier, Émile. René Benoist. Le pape des Halles (1521-1608). Paris: Picard, 1913.

Pia, Karl. "Matth. 16, 18 (Tu es Petrus, etc.) bei Luther." Dissertation, Freiburg i. Br., 1954.

Polman, Pontien. L'élément historique dans la controverse religieuse du xvie siècle. Gemblouz: J. Duculot, 1932.

Ramm, B. L. "The Exegesis of Mt. 16, 13-20 in the Patristic and Reformation Period." Foundations 5 (1962), 206-216.

Die Religion in Geschichte und Gegenwart, 3rd ed. S.v. "Valdès, 2, Juan de," by R. Konetzke.

Renaudet, Augustin. Préréforme et humanisme à Paris pendant les premières querres d'Italie (1494-1517). 2nd ed. Paris: Librarie d'Argences, 1953.

Rickers, Folkert. "Das Petrusbild Luthers. Ein Beitrag zu seiner Auseinandersetzung mit dem Papsttum." Dissertation, Heidelberg, 1967.

Rodríguez Monino, Antonio R. La biblioteca de Benito Arias Montano. Budajoz: Impr. de la Diputación provincial, 1929.

Simon, Richard. Histoire critique des principaux
    commentateurs du Nouveau Testament . . .
    Rotterdam: Minerva, 1693; reprint ed.,
    Frankfurt: Minerva, 1969.

Stegmüller, Friedrich. Reportorium biblicum
    medii aevi. 7 vols. Matriti, 1950-1961.

Stoudt, John. "John Staupitz on God's Gracious
    Love." The Lutheran Quarterly 8, #3 (August,
    1956), 225ff.

Taheny, Theodore. The History of the Exegesis of
    Matthew 16:18-19 in Commentaries of the Early
    Middle Ages. Woodstock, Maryland: Woodstock
    College, 1960.

Tierney, Brian. Foundations of the Conciliar
    Theory: The Contribution of the Medieval
    Canonists from Gratian to the Great Schism.
    Cambridge: University Press, 1955.

Tracy, James. Erasmus: The Growth of a Mind.
    Travaux d'Humanisme et Renaissance, 126.
    Genève: Droz, 1972.

Turmel, Joseph. Histoire de la théologie positive
    depuis l'origine jusqu'au Concile de Trente.
    3rd ed. Paris: Beauchesne, 1904.

Vooght, Paul de. "L'argument patristique dans
    l'interprétation de Matth. XVI, 18 de Jean
    Huss." Recherches de Science religeuse 45
    (1957), 558-566.

Vorgrimler, Herbert. "Das 'Binden und Losen' in
    der Exegese nach dem Tridentinum bis zu
    Beginn des xx. Jhts." Zeitschrift für
    katholische Theologie 85 (1963), 460-477.

Vosté, I. M. "Thomas de Vio, O.P. Cardinalis
    Caietanus Sacrae Scripturae interpres."
    Angelicum 11 (1934), 445-513.

Wadding, Lucas. Scriptores ordinis minorum . . .
     Romae: F. A. Tanus, 1650.

Walz, Angelus. "Von Cajetans Gedanken über
     Kirche und Papst." In Volk Gottes, pp. 84-
     111. Edited by R. Bäumer and H. Dolch.
     FreiburginBr.: Herder, 1967.

Wilcox, Max. "Peter and the Rock: A Fresh Look
     at Matthew 16, 1719." New Testament Studies
     22 (1975), 7388.

Willaert, Léopold. Après le Concile de Trente:
     la Restauration catholique, 1563-1648. N.p.:
     Bloud and Gay, 1960.

INDEX OF PERSONS

231

"Aeterne rerum condi-
  tor," 114
"Annotatio," 3, 80, 83
Apostles, 5, 6, 9, 25,
  30, 40, 69, 70, 74,
  80, 83, 86, 105, 110,
  116, 119, 120, 123,
  128, 136, 138, 188
Apostolate, 188f
Aramaic, 143, 162, 200

Begrifflichkeit, 9f,
  83
Berne Convocation
  (1528), 4
Bible
  Gen. 17:5--140
  Ex. 14:11-12--26,
    120
  Num. 20:2-13--169
  Dt. 17:8-13--125
  Ps. 39--169
    50--138
    103--127, 166
    118:22-23--11
    131--166
    142--139
  Is. 2:2--141, 175,
    183
    2:10--142
    6:1--141
    7:19--142
    51:1--142
  Mt. 1--141
    1:21--140
    5:14--119
    7--100
    7:24--81, 86,
      100, 199
    7:24-25--9, 21,
      36, 37, 80, 81,
      82, 100

Bible (continued)
  Mt. 7:25--34, 100
    14:24-33--18, 117,
      125, 186
    16--36, 71, 112
    16:1-19--71
    16:13--116
    16:13-18--4
    16:13-19--6, 44,
      134
    16:13-20--6, 11,
      13
    16:16--116
    16:16, 17, 19--12
    16:16-18--18
    16:17-18--108
    16:17,19--12
    16:17-19--4, 8, 11,
      43f
    16:18--passim
    16:18-19--4, 5, 14,
      82, 109, 187f
    16:19--12, 29f, 33,
      70, 73, 76, 82,
      113, 118f, 124,
      127, 132, 134,
      188, 194
    16:20--71
    16:23--107
    18:15-19--6
    21:42--117
    27:51, 60--21
  Mk. 8--36
    15:46--21
  Lk. 2:35--120
    5:2--114f
    6:48--21
    8:6, 13--21
    9--36
    9:20--135
    22:31--110
    22:31f--21

233

Protestant(s), 1, 3, 5, 11, 128, 133, 200

"Ratio nominis," 140
Realism, 72
Revelation, 24, 44, 81, 107, 124, 188
Rhemes NT (1582), 8, 105, 133-135
"Rock," see "Petra"
"Roman Catholic," 3
"Rupes," 142

Sacraments, 140
Satan, 29, 30, 40, 107
"Saxum," 16, 29, 106, 122, 129, 138
Scholasticism, see John Major
"Scholion," 3, 39, 186

Senses of scripture, 19, 105, 106, 110-112, 145f, 186, 189, 190, 196
"Sermo," 3, 12
"Sixteenth century," 2
Syriac, 16, 52, 122-123, 129, 131, 136, 139, 190

"Terminist Scotism," 72
Theology, 71f
Trent, Council of, 39, 42, 128

"Verbum," 80-82, 86
Vulgate, 15, 23, 27, 30f, 35, 37, 39, 42, 60, 74, 80, 83, 85, 86, 107, 116, 122, 189

Wycliffites, 77